On Ordinary Heroes
and American Democracy

ON POLITICS
L. Sandy Maisel, Series Editor

On Politics is a new series of short reflections by major scholars on key subfields within political science. Books in the series are personal and practical as well as informed by years of scholarship and deliberation. General readers who want a considered overview of a field as well as students who need a launching platform for new research will find these books a good place to start. Designed for personal libraries as well as student backpacks, these smart books are small format, easy reading, aesthetically pleasing, and affordable.

Titles in the Series
On Foreign Policy, Alexander L. George
On Thinking Institutionally, Hugh Heclo
On Ordinary Heroes and American Democracy, Gerald M. Pomper

GERALD M. POMPER

ON ORDINARY HEROES
AND AMERICAN DEMOCRACY

Paradigm Publishers
Boulder • London

PHOTO CREDITS: Page 33: Peter Rodino Archives, Law Library, Seton Hall University; Page 61: L. Tom Perry Special Collections, Harold B. Lee Library, Brigham Young University; Page 87: American Memory Collection, Prints and Photographs Division, Library of Congress; Page 111: Courtesy of Judge William Wayne Justice; Page 137; Department of Health and Human Services. New York World-Telegram and Sun Collection, Print and Photographs Division, Library of Congress; Page 161: From a painting by Jared Bradley Flagg (1861), in Frederick G. Harrison, Biographical Sketches of Preeminent Americans (E. W. Walker Co., 1892); Page 185: The Ida M. Tarbell Collection, Lawrence Lee Pelletier Library, Allegheny College; Page 213: U.S. News and World Report Collection, Prints and Photographs Division, Library of Congress.

All rights reserved. No part of the publication may be transmitted or reproduced in any media or form, including electronic, mechanical, photocopy, recording, or informational storage and retrieval systems, without the express written consent of the publisher.

Copyright © 2007 Paradigm Publishers

Published in the United States by Paradigm Publishers, 3360 Mitchell Lane Suite E, Boulder, CO 80305 USA.

Paradigm Publishers is the trade name of Birkenkamp & Company, LLC, Dean Birkenkamp, President and Publisher.

Library of Congress Cataloging-in-Publication Data

Pomper, Gerald M.
  On ordinary heroes and American democracy / Gerald M. Pomper.
   p. cm. — (On politics)
  Originally published under title: Ordinary heroes & American democracy. New Haven : Yale University Press, c2004.
  Includes bibliographical references and index.
  ISBN-13: 978-1-59451-391-6 (hc)
  ISBN-10: 1-59451-391-0 (hc)
   1. Politicians—United States—Biography. 2. Political activists—United States—Biography. 3. Judges—United States—Biography. 4. United States—Officials and employees—Biography. 5. Journalists—United States—Biography. 6. Heroes—United States—Biography. 7. United States—Biography. 8. United States—Politics and government—Anecdotes.
  9. Democracy—United States—History—Anecdotes. I. Pomper, Gerald M. Ordinary heroes & American democracy. II. Title.
  E176.P778 2007
  973.09'9—dc22
  [B]
2006035978

Printed and bound in the United States of America on acid free paper that meets the standards of the American National Standard for Permanence of Paper for Printed Library Materials.

Designed and Typeset in ITC Galliard by Straight Creek Bookmakers.

Contents

Acknowledgments		vii
Introduction: Heroism in the New Century		xi
1	We Call Them Heroes	1
2	Models of American Heroism	12
3	Peter Rodino: A Hero of the House	31
4	Arthur Watkins: A Hero of the Senate	58
5	Harry Truman: A Hero as President	84
6	Wayne Justice: A Hero of the Judiciary	108
7	Frances Kelsey: A Hero of Bureaucracy	134
8	Thurlow Weed: A Hero in Party Politics	159
9	Ida Tarbell: A Hero of the Press	183
10	John Lewis: A Hero of Social Movements	210
11	Ordinary Heroes and American Democracy	236
Notes		257
Index		295
About the Author		303

Acknowledgments

This book praises seemingly ordinary men and women who have advanced heroic causes within the institutions of U.S. politics.

In seeking to understand these persons and their work, I employ diverse methods. As a political scientist, I use the techniques and scholarship of my discipline to study the formal bodies and political influences of U.S. government. I also attempt to employ the techniques of history and literature, although I do not claim to be a professional in either field. The sketches of the individuals included in this book are not full biographies, but I hope they are valid partial portraits, illuminating what Leon Edel has called "the myths behind the individual, the inner myth we all create in order to live, the myth that tells us we have some being, some selfhood, some goal, something to strive for."

This work also reflects my personal experience as both a scholar and a teacher. I intend it to be not only a work of academic research but also a possible instrument of civic education. Whether in classrooms or beyond, I hope that readers will learn about the diverse—and decent—institutions of U.S. politics and the varied—and good—people who serve the nation in those institutions. Neither the United States nor its government meets utopian ideals, but in my view they are worth both praise and the dedication we pay when we seek their improvement.

This book has existed in my thoughts for two decades. I owe its realization to many people, and now can thank them, however inadequately. Gordon Schochet has been especially helpful with his rare combination of caring and intellect. The work has greatly benefited from discussions over the years with Mike Aronoff, Robert Cohen, Fred Greenstein, John Hart, Irving Horowitz, Theodore Lowi, Maureen Moakley, George Schroepfer, Ed and Lynn Sternstein, Judith Temkin, Samuel Temkin, Daniel Tichenor, and Mike and Naomi Wish.

As the book came closer to reality, Dennis Bathory and Nancy Schwartz offered me their helpful comments and the opportunity to publish a preliminary chapter in a book celebrating the life of Wilson Carey McWilliams. Still teaching and learning, Carey died, too young, in 2005. He inspired all of us, and I hope some of his wisdom is reflected in this work.

When the project moved forward, I had the research assistance of talented undergraduates at Rutgers University on individual chapters, specifically Allison Ames (on Truman), Avram Fechter (Weed), Erika Sondahl (Watkins), and Laura Yorke (Kelsey). Rutgers, and especially its Eagleton Institute of Politics, also provided financial support, while Edith Saks and Joanne Pfeiffer proved to be extraordinary secretaries. At Yale University Press, which published the original edition, editors John Covell and John Kulka were encouraging and incisive in their criticisms. Pamela Holway and Heidi Downey provided expert copyediting.

For this new paperback edition, I have benefited greatly from the support, advice, and creativity of Paradigm Publishers, a new and innovative enterprise in the social sciences. I am particularly thankful for the leadership of Sandy Maisel and Jennifer Knerr.

Friends and colleagues who read these chapters provided the greatest intellectual contributions—and much emotional support. They have improved my knowledge, my writing, and my confidence. I am deeply appreciative of this consummate help from

Milton Finegold, Amy Fried, Milton Heumann, Elizabeth Hull, Stanley Kelley, Ruth Mandel, Francesca Polletta, Alan Rosenthal, Patricia Sykes, and Marc Weiner. As readers will soon see, I gained both knowledge and inspiration from interviews with the persons among those portrayed in this book still living during the time of my research: Frances Kelsey, William Wayne Justice, John Lewis, and Peter Rodino. Congressman Rodino did depart from us in 2005; I will always be grateful to have come to know him as a public servant of grace, intellect, and admirable patriotism.

Marlene M. Pomper has done it all—on this book and in our life. She has heard (perhaps too much) about this book from the beginning, has expertly edited multiple drafts and provided the fullest encouragement, even in difficult times. Her insights and research made a particularly valuable contribution to the material in Chapter 2, "Models of American Heroism"; indeed, she deserves the largest share of the credit for that chapter.

These chapters praise the heroism of ordinary people. They were first inspired by the quiet heroism of my parents, Moe and Celia Pomper, my brother Isidor, and my virtual parents, Emanuel and Lillian Michels. No monuments exist to commemorate them, but their unsung deeds enabled me to gain a formal education, to develop an appreciation of diverse lives, and to enjoy the benefits of a nation whose heroes they admired. My own children, Marc, David, and Miles, and my adult daughters, Rayna and Erika, have aided in the creation of this work in manifold ways: in discussions, by reading particular chapters, and by offering recommendations on everything from the title to the subjects of the individual chapters. More generally, as they make their own substantial contributions to the nation, they have provided renewed inspiration. I hope that the stories told in this book will inspire my grandchildren to become democratic heroes of the twenty-first century. With that wish in mind, I dedicate this book to beloved Aidan, Daniel, Jacob, Nora, and Zachary.

Let us now sing the praises of famous men,
the heroes of our nation's history....
Some there are who have a left a name behind them
to be commemorated in story.
There are others who are unremembered,
and it as though they had never existed.

—*Ecclesiasticus,* 44.1, 8–9

How rare is a woman of valor,
Her worth is beyond rubies....
Extol her for the fruit of her hand,
And let her works praise her in the gates.

—*Proverbs,* 31.10, 31

If a man has any greatness in him, it comes to light, not in one flamboyant hour, but in the ledger of his daily work.
—Beryl Markham, *West with the Night*

Introduction: Heroism in the New Century

It's startling, even embarrassing.

"Who are the heroes of our time?" readers may ask. But there are no obvious answers. In the following chapters, we will meet men and women who resisted governmental abuse, fostered the lives of children and immigrants, created political alliances to promote freedom at home and abroad, and successfully resisted racial and economic oppression. Yet, moving ahead in the twenty-first century, we cannot readily name comparable persons among our contemporaries.

President Ronald Reagan might help us. "Those who say that we are in a time when there are no heroes," he declared in his first inaugural address, "just don't know where to look." A year later, he directed praise to the "countless quiet, everyday heroes of American life—parents who sacrifice long and hard so their children will know a better life than they have known; church and civic volunteers who help to feed, clothe, nurse, and teach the needy; millions who have made our nation, and our nation's destiny, so very special—unsung heroes who may not have realized their dreams themselves but who then reinvest those dreams in their children."[1]

These are admirable persons, to be sure, but they are different from the "ordinary heroes" portrayed here. The persons in this book are not heroic by dint of their personal virtues. In contrast to Reagan, who was skeptical of the worth of government, the figures in the following chapters are worthy precisely because of their political roles. They are not notable because of a single "profile in courage," like the persons memorialized by John Kennedy.[2] Their heroism comes from the work they do consistently throughout their careers in government and politics. Rather than viewing them as isolated heroes, we reflect on their institutional heroism.

The paucity of ordinary heroes within contemporary politics is surprising. We would think that heroes would be more likely to emerge in times of crisis. The persons praised in this book came at such times—when the United States faced threats to its Constitution, its civil rights and liberties, its historic foreign allies, its economy and health, even its very existence as a united nation. To meet the needs of their era, ordinary people—journeymen legislators, an accidental president and a scorned judge, a reclusive woman journalist and an obscure black student, a cautious bureaucrat and a forgotten politician—became ordinary heroes within the institutions of the nation.

Crises and threats still face the United States, yet heroes of matching stature are not evident. Their absence is not due to a decline in the personal character of Americans—we are still a nation of enterprising doers. More likely, today's dearth of heroes indicates problems with our institutions, not our people. To pursue an explanation, we might examine three possible sources of contemporary heroism: war, the aftermath of 9/11, and "whistleblowing."

War Heroes of Our Time

War is often the occasion for heroism. But can we readily name a contemporary parallel to the historic icons of military gallantry such as Ethan Allen of the Revolutionary War, Sergeant Alvin York of World War I, or the D-Day invaders of World War II (see page 240)? It may be significant—but dispiriting—that the most recent of our acknowledged war heroes are Senators John Kerry and John McCain, whose celebrated (albeit sometimes controversial) deeds occurred more than three decades ago during the Vietnam War.

In the past fifteen years, the nation has fought three wars; the latest—in Iraq—has become the third longest in U.S. history. But who are their illustrious heroes? We do look for idols in these wars, but their stories often fail to meet the test. One narrative is illustrative—an early report of the Iraq war, which told of the courage of a woman marine, Jessica Lynch. Ambushed in a supply mission, Lynch was reported to have fought alone against her attackers. Further digging by reporters, however, found that the dramatic reports "got much of it wrong in the beginning, erroneously reporting that she fought to her last bullet despite gunshot and stab wounds, when in fact she was likely unconscious and probably did not fire a shot."[3]

The Iraq war has not yet produced men—or women—who have gained public renown. The reason is not the unpopularity of the war itself; even its opponents have praised the soldiers on the ground. More significant is the configuration of the combat, with U.S. troops relying on advanced technology rather than individual courage to gain victories. As military professionals explain, "'We don't charge up hills with machine gun nests anymore.' Moreover, the insurgents' tactics—remotely detonated explosives and suicide bombers—also mean U.S. troops often don't have the opportunity to respond heroically."[4]

In the Iraq war, the decline of traditional military heroism is marked by the absence of its ultimate symbol, the Medal of Honor, awarded to only 3,440 individuals throughout U.S. history. The medal is virtually unknown in this war—only one has been awarded over the entire course of the conflict (compared to 244 in Vietnam).

Rather than such iconic figures, the most publicized Americans in this conflict have been those charged with torture of prisoners. It is not a time for heroes.

The Heroism of 9/11

If we lack heroes, we do not lack occasion for outstanding deeds. On September 11, 2001, the nation entered a persistent crisis created by the direct attacks of terrorist bombers. Heroism was evident that horrific day—and described in the first chapter of this book—but these events have not given us new exemplars beyond the days of the attacks and the rescues of victims. Instead, the stories of 9/11 have provided narratives of hindered heroes—persons whose worthy efforts were blocked by faulty government institutions.

Consider two civil servants whose stories became known after the tragedy. Coleen Rowley was a Federal Bureau of Investigation (FBI) Special Agent in Minneapolis in August of 2001. She became suspicious of Zacarias Moussaoui, a member of the al Qaeda network planning the 9/11 attacks, who was taking flying lessons locally. Rowley asked her superiors for authorization to obtain a warrant to search Moussaoui's computer and personal effects, a prescient effort "to keep someone from taking a plane and crashing into the World Trade Center." FBI headquarters denied further investigation, concluding that "this was not going to happen and that they did not know if Moussaoui was a terrorist." By its timidity, the FBI lost a possible opportunity to publicize, uncover, and abort the 9/11 plot.[5]

Richard Clarke had an even more significant position, as the terrorism expert at the National Security Council. He repeatedly warned of the dangers of al Qaeda, but was repeatedly rebuffed by his superiors. As early as 1996, he sensed the possibility of airplane hijackings and suicide crashes. Limited action during the Clinton presidency was followed by inaction and postponements in the Bush administration. As late as only one week before the 9/11 attacks, Clarke was still waiting for direction, pleading "Are we serious about dealing with the ... threat? Is [al Qaeda] a big deal?" His proposed plan was still on the president's desk when the hijacked airplanes hit their targets.[6]

The frustration experienced by Coleen Rowley and Richard Clarke—and later treatment of them—contrasts sharply with the success of another bureaucrat, Frances Kelsey of the U.S. Food and Drug Administration, described in Chapter 7. All three did their proper jobs as civil servants—locating dangers to the public, warning their superiors, and proposing corrective action. Kelsey had the support of her bosses, and preserved public health against a cruel drug; Rowley's and Clarke's portents of danger were largely ignored. Kelsey was promoted and honored for decades; Rowley and Clarke were soon moved out of their jobs, and their contributions demeaned.[7]

The Hero as Whistleblower

We might find heroes in bureaucracy if we looked for a "whistleblower, an employee who refuses to engage in and/or reports illegal or wrongful activities of his employer or fellow employees."[8] Two people provide recent examples of significant whistleblower efforts in government, one civilian, one military.

Dr. Jonathan Fishbein conducted research on AIDS at the National Institutes of Health. Finding faults in research and administration, he complained to both his superiors and outsiders. For his pains, he was fired, apparently "for raising safety concerns in government AIDS research. NIH said he was fired for poor performance even though he had been recommended for a cash performance bonus just weeks before he was notified of his termination." His story led to press reports of "safety problems with federal AIDS research in the United States and Africa, sexual harassment of female NIH workers, and the use of foster children to test AIDS drugs." Eventually reinstated, he soon changed jobs to avoid unpleasantness at NIH.[9]

A second notable whistleblower came out of the Iraq war. At the U.S. prison of Abu Ghraib in 2003, prisoners were severely abused, including sexual brutality and physical torture. A later investigation found that "numerous incidents of sadistic, blatant, and wanton criminal abuses were inflicted on several detainees. This systemic and illegal abuse of detainees was intentionally perpetrated by several members of the military police guard force."[10]

In January 2004, Sergeant Joseph Darby, a member of the U.S. military police, "alerted the U.S. military command, [providing] a compact disc of photographs and an anonymous note to ... the U.S. Army Criminal Investigation Command, triggering an investigation. The pictures showed prisoners naked, being forced to engage in simulated oral sex and other sex acts; images of a female soldier, grinning and pointing at the genitals of a hooded naked prisoner." First seeking anonymity, Darby "agonized for a month before delivering the pictures, but finally decided to blow the whistle on his colleagues, saying their conduct 'violated everything I personally believed in and all I'd been taught about the rules of war.'"[11] Service members directly involved in these abuses were later tried, convicted, and imprisoned.

Whistleblowers such as Fishbein and Darby are courageous and admirable individuals. They furthered noble goals, the health of AIDS victims and the fair treatment of prisoners. Other whistleblowers have gained recognition and some measure of protection for their public service.[12] But their very achievements are also indicators of failures in the processes of government. They provide contrasts, not parallels, to our "ordinary heroes" of politics. The persons portrayed in this book worked successfully within the institutions of government. When they saw an abuse of power, they met it through impeachment in the House of Representatives (Chapter 3), censure in the Senate (Chapter 4), and judicial review (Chapter 6). The actions of Fishbein and Darby—who are more akin to contemporary "antiheroes"—imply, however, that there are ominous defects in these institutions.

The Decline of the Republic?

Politics is more than politicians. The health of the U.S. republic does not rest primarily on the vigor of its practitioners. Although better leaders will presumably provide better rulership, good government more basically requires appropriate institutions that will endure even the faults of fallible men and women.

The priority of institutions rather than persons was a basic premise to the writers of the Constitution. Warily assuming the self-centered nature of all people, "A properly designed state, the Fathers believed, would check interest with interest, class with class, faction with faction, and one branch of government with another in a harmonious system of mutual frustration."[13]

In our own time, we should recall the fundamental premises of the Constitution and its authors. If we lack heroes, the problem is not simply the individual deficiencies of President George W. Bush—or his predecessors or his Democratic Party opponents. The problem is more general, the decline of the institutions that provide the nurturing soil for the flowering of heroism in the U.S. republic.

The republican system established by the Constitution involves a series of checks and balances both within government and in the relationships among citizens and government. The most important check is elections, "a dependence on the people," which enable popular majorities to "defeat ... sinister views by regular vote." But, as James Madison taught, that check alone is insufficient to achieve good government: "experience has taught mankind the necessity of auxiliary precautions." Understanding the realities of politics, the Founders' guiding principle was that "ambition must be made to counteract ambition." Structuring the inevitable competition among politicians and autonomous institutions would be "the means of keeping each other in their proper places."[14]

Current trends in U.S. politics have undermined the republican structure. Within the national government, there has been an evident decline in the checks and balances among the formal institutions, as the executive branch has aggrandized power. In an earlier time, President Harry Truman, even as he confronted the Soviet Union in the Cold War, could succeed only by persuasion of other political leaders (Chapter 5). But the September 11 attacks on the United States have provided the occasion for swelling presidential power.

A crisis as profound as the "war on terror" undermines institutional autonomy, two political scientists argue:

> War is always bad news for checks and balances. War always means executive authority, and it's even an authority that the Supreme Court tends to look at only retrospectively. So in the post 9/11 climate, there is likely to be a continuation of the expansion of the power of the executive.
>
> It is not only that war enhances executive power, but it is the nature of this war, too. It is an open-ended war, a war that isn't going to end. So indefinitely into the future, you can project there is going to be a need for security, the kind of security that the executive is charged with providing.[15]

Even beyond the specific circumstances arising from 9/11, the Bush administration has employed the "war on terror" to vastly expand executive power. It has asserted the authority to interpret statutes contrary to the specific intent of Congress. Using an innovative procedure of "signing statements" rather than using his constitutional veto, President Bush "has claimed the right to ignore more than 750 laws enacted since he became president." Going further, leaning on the slim reed of the president's title of commander-in-chief, the White House has asserted the right to intercept telephone calls, scour bank records, imprison suspected terrorists for years without trial, threaten reporters with jail for revealing information, and create military commissions to try alleged terrorists, unlimited by statute or the Geneva Convention.[16]

These expansions of presidential power may be partially restricted by the courts and Congress,[17] but they are more than the overreach of a specific president. They create precedents, and temptations, for any future president in any situation of threat—and those occasions are likely to last throughout this young century. At the same time, they weaken the opportunities for effective action by persons in other fields of politics. Madison warned, "It is a melancholy reflection that liberty should be equally exposed to danger whether the government have too much power or too little."[18] The dangers also exist when one part of government is too strong and others are too weak.

In republican government, checks and balances also exist outside of the government itself. There is a deliberate distancing between citizens and public officials. Keeping its distance, government does not control all of the lives of citizens; it leaves them considerable autonomy and large spaces of personal freedom and privacy.

In turn, citizens of the republic do not govern directly. Instead, they control government through political parties (Chapter 8), the press (Chapter 9), and social movements (Chapter 10). Government stands outside the immediate passions of the populace, enabling public officials to use their experience and judgment to advance the nation's lasting goals, subject to the ultimate control of popular elections.

Institutional heroes need space to create heroism. A well-designed republican system, in contrast to direct democracy, Madison hoped, creates such space for "proper guardians of the public weal." The effect of representative elections, he argued, would be "to refine and enlarge the public views, by passing them through the medium of a chosen body of citizens, whose wisdom may best discern the true interest of their country."[19]

In current U.S. politics, the distance between governed and governors has decreased significantly, limiting the institutional space for ordinary heroes. Officials have less ability to take a long-term policy perspective as they face unrelenting investigation and 24/7 media coverage, the fads of referenda campaigns, the narrow claims of internet bloggers and special interest contributors, and the skepticism of a public that has become convinced that "public officials don't care much what people like me think."[20]

In turn, government representatives have invaded the space of citizens. In the most intrusive cases, this invasion affects personal civil liberties. But the deeper threat may be the techniques that politicians have developed to control, rather than respect, public opinion. Through continual polls, focus groups, manipulative advertising, and news management, politicians become no more than participants in a "permanent campaign," leaving them no time or inclination to be public guardians. Instead of leadership and heroism, one critic writes, politicians "have fixed upon the crudest and easiest forms of communication: they've gone negative, they've counseled the robotic repetition of market-tested phrases. They've put democracy in a Styrofoam cage."[21]

It is hardly surprising that politicians will do whatever wins power; that was always the expectation of the constitutional writers. What has changed is that their inherent ambitions now require unceasing attention to every passing popular fancy and now demand unceasing effort to control and manipulate public opinion. Heroism in democratic institutions requires that leaders be deliberate, fair, farsighted, and personally disinterested. Such characteristics, evident at the nation's founding, may be archaic in modern times.[22] They surely cannot be found in officials who try, simultaneously and inelegantly, to keep their ears to the ground, their noses open to the wind, and their bodies bending to sense the shifting forces of current opinion—but close their eyes to storms approaching on the horizon.

Heroes in the New Century

Americans have always sought heroes (as detailed in Chapter 2); we will surely continue the search. Even in the difficult circumstances of our own time, there are individuals who arouse some tentative promise that heroism will again emerge. In recent actions in war, the aftermath of 9/11, and whistleblowing, exemplary individuals have used their institutions to advance the public good.

In Iraq, even the shame of Abu Ghraib has brought a man of honor to the fore. After the mistreatment of prisoners became known, Major General Antonio Taguba conducted a thorough investigation and reached severe judgments. Rather than take the easy course of blaming only those immediately involved, he went up the chain of command, condemning the unit commander's "poor leadership and the refusal of her command to both establish and enforce basic standards and principles among its Soldiers," and recommended disciplinary action against ten particular persons—seven of them officers.[23] General Taguba used the army's own institutional procedures to redeem its honor.

In the aftermath of the terrorist attacks in 2001, two other "guardians of the public weal" came forward: Thomas Kean, former governor of New Jersey, chair of the 9/11 commission, and former Congressmember Lee Hamilton, its vice chair. That commission, Kean believed, was "set up to fail," equally divided among partisan appointees in the midst of a presidential election. These leaders met the obstacles, bridged the partisan divisions, and overcame White House hostility to the investigation and its initial refusal to provide documents and witnesses. They brought the commission to a unanimous set of findings and strong recommendations.[24] Although independent commissions have little authority, Kean and Hamilton were still able to use a weak institution to promote a vital national objective.

Whistleblowers can learn from another figure, special counsel Patrick Fitzgerald. A U.S. attorney, he was appointed to identify and prosecute persons in the Bush administration who criminally leaked the name of a covert CIA operative, allegedly in retaliation for her husband's published criticism of the Iraq war. Fitzgerald proved to be a relentless prosecutor, who also respected the privacy and reputation of possible suspects. After a two-year investigation, Fitzgerald disappointed all partisans. He indicted Lewis Libby, chief of staff for Vice President Dick Cheney, but found insufficient evidence to prosecute Karl Rove, the president's chief political adviser. In the process, Fitzgerald won universal acclaim, providing a model for those who would improve the work of government.

Perhaps the actions of these persons, although limited in scope, portend the emergence of larger heroes. When they arrive, future U.S. leaders may gain the inspiration to protect its institutions by heeding the examples of the persons profiled in this book. Reader, meet them now.

Notes

1. The inaugural address (January 20, 1981) is available at www.yale.edu/lawweb/avalon/presiden/inaug/reagan1.htm. The next quotation is from Reagan's State of the Union speech (January 26, 1982), available at www.nationalcenter.org/ReaganStateofUnion82.html.

2. John F. Kennedy, *Profiles in Courage* (New York: Harper, 1956).

3. Eric Slater, "Another Ambush Hero Enjoys Smaller Spotlight," *Los Angeles Times*, November 2, 2003. Lynch herself modestly demurred.

4. Tom Vanden Brook, "Only One Medal of Honor Given in Iraq, Afghan Wars," *USA Today*, December 12, 2005, available at www.usatoday.com.

5. National Commission on Terrorist Attacks upon the United States, *The 9/11 Report* (New York: St. Martin's, 2004), pp. 392–397.

6. *The 9/11 Report*, p. xliii and pp. 492–98. For his own account, see Richard Clarke, *Against All Enemies* (New York: Free Press, 2004), Chapter 10.

7. Five years after these events, a U.S. Department of Justice report both praised and criticized Rowley. Astonishingly, she was chastised for not seeking a search warrant through a slower process than the expedited effort she unsuccessfully pursued (*New York Times*, June 20, 2006, p. A12).

8. Robert Pack, "Whistleblowers and the Law," *Washington Lawyer* (June 2001).

9. John Solomon, "NIH Reinstates Specialist Who Alleged Misconduct in Federal AIDS Research," Associated Press, December 24, 2005, available at www.whistleblowers.org.

10. These conclusions are from the official U.S. army investigation by Major General Antonio Taguba, "Article 15-6 Investigation of the 800th Military Police Brigade," available at news.findlaw.com/cnn/docs/iraq/tagubarpt.html.

11. WashingtonTimes.com/national/20040806_101703_5440r.htm. For a full report, see Seymour M. Hersh, *Chain of Command* (New York: Harper Collins, 2004).

12. See the Web site of the National Whistleblower Center,

established in 1988: www.whistleblowers.org. However, legal protections were narrowed recently by the Supreme Court in *Garcetti v. Ceballos,* No. 04-473 (2006).

13. Richard Hofstadter, *The American Political Tradition* (New York: Knopf, 1955), pp. 8-9.

14. The quotations are from Madison's most famous writings, *The Federalist Papers* 10 and 51 (New York: Modern Library, 1941), pp. 53-61, 335-340.

15. W. Carey McWilliams and Alan Rosenthal, in Gerald M. Pomper and Marc D. Weiner, eds., *The Future of American Democratic Politics* (New Brunswick, NJ: Rutgers University Press, 2003), p. 219.

16. Elizabeth Drew, "Power Grab," *New York Review* 53 (June 22, 2006): 10-15.

17. Presidential power in regard to judicial treatment of alleged enemy combatants was limited by the Supreme Court in *Hamdan v. Rumsfeld,* No. 05-184 (2006). However, the ruling won by a slim 5-3 majority.

18. James Madison, "The Question of a Bill of Rights," letter to Thomas Jefferson (October 17, 1788), quoted by Roger Dean Golden, "What Price Security?" in D. Howard Russell, et al., eds. *Homeland Security and Terrorism : Readings and Interpretations* (New York: McGraw-Hill, 2006).

19. Madison, *The Federalist Papers* No. 10, p. 59.

20. In 1956, only 26 percent of the nation took this negative attitude; by 1994, the skeptical proportion had risen to 66 percent (*The ANES Guide to Public Opinion and Electoral Behavior,* Table 5B.3), available at www.umich.edu/~nes/nesguide.

21. Joe Klein, *Politics Lost* (New York: Doubleday, 2006), p. 240.

22. See Gordon Wood's discussion of the founding generation, *Revolutionary Characters* (New York: Penguin, 2006), pp. 1-27.

23. "Article 15-6 Investigation of the 800th Military Police Brigade," pp. 44-49.

24. Philip Shenon of the *New York Times, The 9/11 Report,* pp. xxvii-xxx.

Chapter One
We Call Them Heroes

Recall these heroes.

In the ancient world, the demigod Achilles, angered by the loss of his mistress, quits the Greek fight against the Trojans. Relenting only when his dearest friend is slain, the warrior vengefully defeats the enemy leader, Hector, in single combat. As Achilles too prepares to die, he brings the Greeks to the eve of their epic victory and is eternally remembered as the hero of the Trojan War.

Three millennia after Troy falls, a new war begins in a new world.

On the morning of September 11, 2001, international terrorists hijack four U.S. airliners loaded with fuel for cross-continental trips. They crash two of the aircraft into the twin towers of the World Trade Center in New York and a third into the Pentagon in Washington, D.C. When the hijackers meet resistance from the passengers on the fourth plane, apparently headed for the Capitol or the White House, it crashes in rural Pennsylvania. All passengers and crew members die.

Explosions, fires at temperatures of 2000 degrees Fahrenheit, and the collapse of the targeted buildings follow. In New York, within two hours both the World Trade Center towers have fallen, each of their 110 stories caving one after another onto the floors beneath. Five nearby buildings are also wrecked by nightfall. In

Washington, one side of the Pentagon, the world's largest office building, is destroyed. All told, some three thousand people die, most of them incinerated into unrecoverable ashes in monumental buildings transformed into twenty-first-century crematoria. The toll is the greatest one-day loss of lives through violence on American soil since the bloody Civil War battle of Antietam.

These horrific events prompted national recognition of a multitude of heroes.[1] Individuals displayed altruism and bravery in many ways. Doomed airline passengers and office workers sent phone and e-mail messages conveying their love to their families. Tens of thousands evacuated skyscrapers without panic or selfishness. One man perished at the World Trade Center because he would not leave his paraplegic co-worker to die alone. Another group of office workers carried a disabled clerk and her wheelchair down sixty flights of stairs. Executives stayed behind to direct their employees to safety and perished in the engulfing fires.

Volunteers rushed to the disaster areas, digging into the rubble to seek victims even as tons of falling debris threatened their lives. Others offered their homes to displaced local residents, prepared meals for rescue workers, and even played music to hearten them. Across the nation, and throughout the world, millions of people prayed, sent financial contributions that eventually totaled over $1.5 billion, and donated more blood than could be stored in local hospitals.

Among the passengers on board the doomed aircraft, only those on United flight #93 learned, through cell-phone conversations, of the fate that awaited them. Three of these passengers exhibited particularly audacious courage: "If they're going to run this into the ground we're going to have to do something. We're going to rush the hijackers," one of them told his family.[2] In the ensuing struggle the passengers succeeded in diverting the plane, thereby assuring their own deaths but preventing a fourth deliberate crash.

At the crash sites, bravery combined with duty. Policemen and medical professionals attempted to do their accustomed governmental work—providing protection and health care for citizens. Teachers calmly led their pupils to safety amid the din, the terror, and the air thick with ash. As thousands of brokers and clerks fled down hundreds of stairs and survived, firefighters sped past them into the inferno, in an attempt to control the conflagrations and lead survivors to safety. As one journalist observed, "They walked into buildings where they did not work, and restaurants where they could not afford to eat, to save people who might have looked down on them."[3] In New York, 343 firefighters perished, most of their bodies unrecovered and thus never given a formal burial.

Another government worker, New York Mayor Rudolph Giuliani, served as both an effective administrator and a gentle priest during the crisis. Through public statements and personal contacts, the mayor sent messages of consolation, hope, and endurance—in one instance replacing a lost firefighter as best man for a friend's wedding. Although his own life was endangered in the collapse of the city's emergency headquarters, Giuliani organized a comprehensive response that included changing subway and highway routes to maintain a smooth flow of transportation on the dense island of Manhattan, establishing the means to identify and bury thousands of victims, seeking jobs and financial aid for those now without offices, employers, and customers, and winning financial and legislative support from the state and the federal governments.

Prior to September 11, few might have thought the mayor equal to the task. Although he had succeeded in improving life in New York City, particularly by bringing about a dramatic decrease in crime, he had seemed flawed in many ways—overly ambitious, puritanical, and unpleasant to his opponents. Yet in the aftermath of the terrorist attack, even his fiercest critics would praise him ardently. As one commentator summed it up: "Anyone, everyone has a powerful need for reassurance right now, and a desire for protection—

protection from despair and nihilism, from terrorized paralysis, from hate and dark fantasies of doomed revenge. Giuliani has provided that reassurance and protection, and the nation is grateful to him."[4]

Who Are the Heroes?

We learn about heroism from ancient tales, such as that of Achilles, and from brutal modern reality. Both can in particular teach us much about democratic politics, the subject of this book. The contrast between the valor of Achilles and that evident on September 11 illuminates the difference between the fabled exploits of "great men" and the quieter courage of model democrats. Within the structures of a democracy, heroism is based on institutions, not personalities. Our modern exemplars underline the central argument of this book: democratic heroes are ordinary men and women who ably perform their institutional responsibilities in times of crisis.

Achilles exemplifies an altogether different kind of hero. He is the conventional archetype of the hero, an extraordinary individual—the larger-than-life personage for whom the Greeks invented the very word we know as "hero." Just as Agamemnon's soldiers looked to Achilles to defeat their enemy, so we often look for champions to protect us and preserve our society. Typically, our storybooks depict heroes as dramatic figures, while biographies of our traditional heroes generally focus on the unique personal characteristics of their subjects. In contemporary politics as well, we search for the charismatic leader who will easily solve the complex problems of modern life.

This conventional view, however, has serious—and worrisome—implications for democratic politics. Demigods—people like Achilles—are few and far between. Relying on such heroes makes human welfare contingent on the exceptional intervention, often unreliable and always arbitrary, of these unique individuals. The successful resolution of crises then depends essentially on luck—on the chance that extraordinary people will be found to meet a crisis or that some person will undergo an ennobling transformation at the critical moment.

These implications are particularly serious in a democracy. The basic premise of self-government is that the people themselves have enough character and collective wisdom to choose appropriate leaders and resolve their common problems. But this faith hardly fits a populace that depends on heroes such as Achilles. Rather, reliance on such heroes too easily leads to disdain for the staple of democracy, the ordinary citizen. Bertolt Brecht draws this basic distinction in his play *Galileo*. One of Brecht's characters voices the widespread desire for "noble" exemplars: "Unhappy the land that has no heroes." But another character responds skeptically: "Unhappy the land that needs a hero."[5] Human success will require common effort, not extraordinary intervention.

Democracy cannot wait for demigods; it requires "ordinary heroes," apparently undistinguished people, working through the multiple institutions of government, who can do what is necessary in extraordinary moments. These people become heroes not by luck or as the result of miraculous personal metamorphoses. They become heroes by fulfilling their responsibilities as they always have but in a situation in which their qualities are particularly needed. Heroism is potentially widespread but usually latent, unseen until it is evoked by external events.

James Madison recognized the limits of heroism when he argued in *The Federalist* that government must be designed for use by ordinary people: "It is vain to say that enlightened statesmen will be able to adjust these clashing interests, and render them all subservient to the public good. Enlightened statesmen will not always be at the helm."[6] Madison argued that a successful government cannot depend on great men—or, we would add, great women. Instead, for Madison, a democratic republic requires appropriate institutional arrangements that will curb the evils of factions, promote the selection of wise officials, and transform the conflict of personal ambitions into the common good. Appropriate institutions are needed because, in Alexander Hamilton's concurring words, "the passions of men will not conform to the dictates of reason and justice, without constraint."[7]

Madison and Hamilton emphasize institutions, not individuals. But the traditional hero is unconfined by institutions. Indeed, he may be dangerous because he refuses such constraints, as the Greeks themselves recognized in the practice of ostracism, in which persons who had stepped too far out of line were temporarily exiled. Achilles subverts the discipline of the Greek armies, prizing his private anger over the success of his comrades. When he returns to battle, he does so only to settle an individual grudge, not as a leader of Agamemnon's forces. Even as he glorifies Achilles' name, Homer warns of his rage, "murderous, doomed, that cost the Achaeans countless losses, hurling down to the House of Death so many sturdy souls, great fighters' souls, but made their bodies carrion, feasts for the dogs and birds."[8]

The brave men and women who responded to the attacks of September 11 are different; they are people of human dimensions. But their bravery, in many instances, is also notably distinct from the heroes of governmental institutions whom we will consider in this book. Democracy does not depend on any modern Achilles, and it does not demand that men and women show exceptional bravery. What democracy does require is able representatives, administrators, and activists.

Individual actions after September 11, courageous as they were, could not meet the needs of America in this crisis.[9] Rescue, renewal, and ultimate retaliation required collective action on the part of government. The volunteers were soon sent home, despite their earnest commitment, because they were complicating rescue efforts. Charitable contributions, despite their outstanding generosity, proved insufficient; government had to provide the enormous financial resources needed—$55 billion in the first congressional appropriation—to finance military responses, to clear the rubble and rebuild New York, and to maintain the national air transportation system and safeguard airports. The public understood this necessity. After decades in which the citizenry regarded the government with cynicism and even scorn, opinion polls showed a vast increase in confidence in all national institutions, a sentiment still in evidence even a year after the attacks.[10]

The defiant passengers on United flight #93 certainly merit praise and are properly seen as exemplars of personal courage.[11] A secure political life, however, cannot depend either on such individuals or on the improbable chance that they will be available when danger comes along. Businessmen or vacationing families cannot be expected to assure security in the skies. Safe air travel requires governmental action, such as regulations concerning security screening, the provision of air marshals, the identification and control of possible terrorists, or more effective law enforcement on the ground. In keeping with the thesis of this book, public safety and well-being require democratic heroes, people in the government who competently carry out their jobs even at moments of crisis.

Such democratic heroes did exist in the crisis of September 11. They are exemplified by the professional rescuers at the scene. Their bravery was not only an immediate response but also their daily occupation. Mayor Giuliani led these efforts, combining competence and compassion. Soon after, engineers employed in an obscure New York City bureaucracy, the Department of Design and Construction, took on the massive task of recovery and cleared millions of tons of debris from the site rapidly and without a single fatal injury, coming in under budget as well.[12] These are the persons with whom democracy is comfortable, ordinary people who do heroic deeds at a time of crisis simply by carrying out their institutional responsibilities in an exemplary manner. Although often vastly different in social class and background, ordinary heroes use virtually the same words to explain their performance. "I was just doing my job," they usually say, emphasizing their everyday responsibilities rather than their personal qualities. Mayor Giuliani, not known for his modesty, expressed this sentiment as he directed the response to the World Trade Center attack: "These are extremely strong people. And I just reflect them. . . . I just happen to be here. This is my job and I'll do it."[13]

Their "job"—whether a self-designated mission or a paid position—plunges these persons in critical times into situations in which they act heroically, but not self-consciously, out of custom, habit, and the regular practice of their vocations. At the World Trade Center, firefighters died "doing what they were trained to do. They were going to a job, and that was it."[14] This fundamental sense of duty is also illustrated by accountants who uncover corruption and by teachers who inspire their halting students to read. Abroad, countless children were saved from the Nazi Holocaust by nurses and social workers who felt they "had no choice" but to honor the life-affirming tenets of their professions.

It is extremely important to note that heroism, as we use the term in this book, exists only among individuals who are profoundly committed to humanitarian values. The heroism of people who are just doing their jobs is wholly different from petty compliance, or simply "obeying orders," apologies that may be used to excuse passivity or even to condone evil. Such perversion of true duty is exemplified by subordinates who quietly acquiesce in their superiors' brutality or corruption and then claim exoneration on the grounds that they were simply following orders—for "just doing my job." That wicked excuse was used most catastrophically by the Nazi bureaucrats who submissively carried out their murderous assignments. To do a job rightly does not mean following its mechanical routines but meeting its responsibilities. A truly devoted worker will perform his or her duties only to the extent these duties don't conflict with basic ethical principles. There must be more than obedience to superiors; there must also be a commitment to fundamental morality and the higher values of the institution's work, such as honesty, legality, and the protection and well-being of those in their care.

Heroes and Institutions

This book is about eight ordinary heroes in American politics. They are illustrative, rather than unique, figures; readers will surely think of other equally appropriate persons. At a particular time of crisis, these men and women did what they always did, putting the values of their institutions into practice in an exemplary fashion. In the world of politics, they are the equivalent of Pulitzer Prize winners in journalism, deserving honor for doing their ordinary work extraordinarily well. The stories of these eight individuals are inspiring in themselves. We will see them display courage, persistence, and personal virtue (and, yes, occasional bad judgment), and we may take heart from their experience. As Barbara Tuchman points out, "Plutarch, the father of biography, used it for moral examples: to display the reward of duty performed, the traps of ambition, the fall of arrogance." We can learn similar lessons from modern lives.[15]

The events recounted in the following chapters, however, instruct us about more than the virtues of individuals. In reality, these men and women, while decent and even honorable, are not storybook heroes. They are a different kind of hero, important because they did their work in the chambers of Congress, in the offices of the presidency, as judges and bureaucrats, and through political parties, the press, and social movements. These persons and institutions are joined: the institutions are mirrored *in* the persons, as the persons' actions in moments of crisis reflect the traits *of* those institutions. Yet institutions do not achieve their purposes mechanically or inevitably. Political success is uncertain; it depends on real persons who accept the duties and values of their positions. By doing their jobs, the democratic heroes described in this book made the institutions of democracy work.

My concise argument is that these heroes acted not only as virtuous individuals but also as representatives of the specific institutions characteristic of the American political system. Through their examples, they can teach us how those institutions function, how they structure our government, and how they embody the values of our society. In the later sections of each chapter, I will use their stories—supplemented by private interviews and the work of other scholars—to explore the specific institutions within which these individuals played their respective parts. Together, these accounts may provide a general guide to American politics, a journey into the democratic process.

This combined examination of heroes and institutions begins with a review of popular conceptions of heroism. To appreciate the contributions of the men and women described in this book, the concept of democracy's "ordinary hero" must be distinguished from many common and diverse usages. That is the task of the next chapter. The following chapters present the eight political figures. Some names will be familiar, others may be obscure, but all merit attention. Following the order of the Constitution, we will begin with two figures from the legislative branch, Representative Peter Rodino and Senator Arthur Watkins. Heroism in the executive branch is exemplified by President Harry Truman and in the judicial branch by federal district judge William Wayne Justice.

American politics now extends beyond the formal institutions originally established by the Constitution. The bureaucracy has become a fourth branch; its nature will be illustrated by Dr. Frances Kelsey of the Food and Drug Administration. Outside of the halls of government, moreover, political parties, the press, and social movements have long been vital parts of the nation's politics. We will examine these three institutions by means of three portraits, which I have arranged in chronological order: those of Thurlow Weed, a major figure of the nineteenth-century Republican Party, of Ida Tarbell, an investigative reporter during the early twentieth century, and of Representative John Lewis, in his years as a young leader of the civil rights movement. Finally, drawing on the experiences of these eight individuals, I sum up the distinctive qualities of democratic heroism and assess the relative impact of personal characteristics and institutional structures. In concluding, I urge the continuing importance of authentic heroism in our democratic community.

Chapter Two
Models of American Heroism

From childhood on, we sing folk songs and recite poetry, watch films or read stories that evoke heroic images. From Casey Jones, who immortalized our railroad trains, to Casey at the Bat, who immortalized baseball; from Joe Hill, whose ghost reminded us of the fight for organized unions, to Joan Baez, whose songs protested U.S. participation in Vietnam, we learn what our citizens value. As befits our multiracial, multicultural nation, our heroes may be women or men, black like Harriet Tubman, Martin Luther King Jr., or Malcolm X, or white like Abraham Lincoln, Franklin Delano Roosevelt, and Ronald Reagan. They may be Native Americans such as Sacajawea, or Asian Americans such as the senator and decorated veteran Daniel Inouye, or Hispanic Americans such as César Chávez. They may even live beyond our shores, as did Anne Frank and Mother Teresa. They may be as distant as space walkers or as close as our parents.

In American discourse, heroes abound in such numbers and such variety that we may find it difficult to see heroism clearly. The problem becomes even more complicated when we seek to understand the concept within American democratic institutions. To focus

This chapter was written principally by Dr. Marlene Michels Pomper.

our attention, I first examine the diverse ways heroism is defined in American popular culture, generating seven archetypes. I will then narrow the discussion to the particular character of heroism in politics and the ways in which it is shaped by the institutions of American democracy.

The Variety of American Heroes

"Do we still need heroes?" the Heroism Project asks. The project develops curricula and public programs on heroism and American community life. It plans a four-part PBS documentary, *In Search of Heroes: An American Journey,* that will focus on everyday citizens, two from each of four generations, whose actions exemplify such values as "integrity, courage, generosity, tolerance, wisdom and compassion."[1] We do need our heroes, of course, to give meaning to our days. In the words of T. S. Eliot, "human existence" is made up of "undisciplined squads of emotion." To articulate what an essay in *Time* magazine described as our "general mess of imprecision of feelings," we turn to heroes and icons—the nearly sacred models of humanity with which we parse our lives. "Through their triumphs and follies," it is they "who teach us how to live."[2]

We may choose to live vicariously through the deeds of our heroes. While few of us are likely to participate in moon landings or invent a cure for polio or transform the economy, we can enjoy rubbing shoulders with greatness or perching on the shoulders of giants. In *Leaves of Grass,* Walt Whitman taught us to extol the virtue of common citizens, to honor those whose labors built the nation:

> I hear America singing, the varied carols I hear,
> Those of mechanics, each one singing his as it should be
>   blithe and strong,
> The carpenter singing his as he measures his plank or beam,

> The mason singing what belongs to him in his boat, the
> deckhand singing on the steamboat deck,
> The shoemaker singing as he sits on his bench, the hatter
> sitting as he stands,
> The wood-cutter's song, the ploughboy's on his way in
> the morning, or at noon intermission or at sundown,
> The delicious singing of the mother, or of the young wife
> at work, or of the young girl sewing or washing,
> Each singing what belongs to him or her and to none
> else.[3]

Heroes may inspire us to achieve the otherwise unachievable, to go the extra mile. Biographical literature and film make it possible to recapture heroes' journeys and their moments of triumph. Our heroes provide us with diverse and inspirational role models with which to shape our values and guide our career choices. Just as families pass down their tales of triumph and valor from parent to child and grandparent to grandchild, we have been inspired by the heroism of our founding fathers and mothers.

We choose our heroes from among those who exemplify the values that we, as Americans, uphold. They reflect our admiration for both dissenters and traditionalists, for those dedicated to helping others and those who act alone, for traditional role models and for innovators who break the common mold.[4] Our heroes come from the battlefield, the sports arena, the arts, politics, science, and the home. On the one hand, we admire those whose values are consistent with those of our past, such as hard-working Calvinists, defenders of home and hearth, Honest Abes and Florence Nightingales. On the other hand, we admire those who are pioneers or path breakers, advocates of change, whose ships land on uncharted territories or whose space stations orbit the earth.

Today, we still find our heroes, because we still need them. In fact, heroism is ubiquitous in America, to judge by accounts in popular sources. *Newsweek,* for example, has honored "everyday heroes," the term it used for a "diverse bunch—doctors, social workers, a single mother, a basketball great, and energetic high school students [who] each recognized a need, and found an innovative way to meet it."[5] Adopting a different ideological stance, *Mother Jones* gives annual "Heroes" awards to "grass-roots activists," whose actions illustrate "the dailiness of heroism that makes history happen." Among their award winners are a Marine who resisted the Gulf War and an organizer of farm labor.[6]

From still another perspective, the Heinz Family Foundation, proclaiming that "Heroes Walk Among Us," provides annual awards of $25,000 to such persons as the U.S. surgeon general or the chairman of the Chiron Corporation in recognition of their "significant and long-term contributions to the betterment of humanity." Amnesty International bestows the accolade more broadly, offering the title of "Quiet Hero" to those "individuals who in the sanctity and privacy of their own homes will help us save prisoners who are in danger," by displaying an Amnesty International decal, for instance, or endorsing a protest to the prime minister of China, or contributing as little as $15.[7]

Public attitudes toward heroism are not fixed; they vary from one time, and from one culture, to another. Moreover, even the most august political figures have been viewed differently at different times. George Washington, for example, has always been regarded as an American hero, but the reasons have shifted over time. While, as Barry Schwartz has observed, "Washington's early idealization should be understood in the context of a political culture strongly oriented toward republican and Enlightenment ideals," he was later idolized for his defense of order, his sacrifice and disinterestedness, and even his entrepreneurial skills. "Rather than judging Washington in the same way, citizens at different times tended to use disparate criteria of evaluation, which were based in their political culture's core values."[8]

From a long-term perspective, Dixon Wecter finds "visible changes of taste and spirit in our hero-worship as well as in our patriotism." In an earlier "era of oratory," personified by Patrick Henry and Daniel Webster, "our heroes were treated with grandiosity. This was the silver age of our patriotism. Forum and pulpit, Fourth of July and school declamation, poetry and fiction, the art of battle-scenes and equestrian statue and pioneer memorials enshrined them in a vaguely classical and nebulous respect." This period gave way to what Wecter calls "the age of sentiment." "The Lincoln cult, sprouting after the Civil War, drew much sustenance from [such sentiment]. The mothers and the infancy of heroes, their domestic lives and their tender hearts, supplanted the old accent on grandeur. Patriotism, as taught by the McGuffey readers and by children's lives of the great, stressed homely, simple goodness. This idealization marched abreast of the humanitarian spirit in Victorian times: heroes were good to the poor; they cherished children and dumb animals. The great man entered, not to the fanfare and trumpets, but to the still, sad music of humanity."[9]

The heroic ideal also varies over shorter intervals. Leo Lowenthal reports that before World War I popular magazines showed a high degree of interest in political figures and gave almost equal attention to business and professional men, on the one hand, and to entertainers (largely serious artists), on the other. But by the end of World War II, the emphasis had changed considerably. Interest in political figures had dropped by 40 percent, and in business and professional men by 30 percent. But entertainers—now largely popular artists promoted by the mass media—had more than doubled their share of recognition. "We called the heroes of the past 'idols of production,'" Lowenthal concludes, whereas "present-day magazine heroes can be called 'heroes of consumption.'"[10]

Amy Fried offers a scholarly analysis of popular definitions of heroism. Drawing on interviews and employing quantitative methodology, she shows that heroism is defined in widely divergent ways in American culture. Fried locates four distinct perspectives on heroism current among the American public: progressives, who value above all "people who work against injustice and struggle against oppression"; defenders, who particularly praise "military action and the endeavors of the founders of the United States"; nurturers, who adopt a perspective that "turns away from politics" and "orients itself toward the personal and the domestic"; and entrepreneurs, who join "admiration for successful capitalists with a proclivity toward pragmatic action."[11] These models vary from one another, statistically, ideologically, and logically. They vary also in their view of society, from individualistic to communal, and in their attitudes toward politics, from alienation to engagement. As Fried points out, the only shared characteristic is that "the concept of heroism is highly prescriptive and normatively charged," but the variability of understandings "makes it impossible to develop a highly restrictive definition and operationalization."[12]

These heroic models, however, may be short-lived. As cynicism creeps in, it is ever more difficult to immortalize, or even recognize, our heroes. According to psychologist Kenneth Clark, the demise of national heroes results from the fact that "so many things you'd like to see in an all-purpose national hero are controversial." He argues that "the United States is simply too big, too diverse, too contentious a country for us all to agree on one or a few." Moreover, those who place their heroes on a pedestal are likely soon to see them debunked by events and the press. This fate was meted out to Richard

M. Nixon for Watergate, William Clinton for Monica Lewinsky, Charles Lindbergh for his attraction to Nazism, and Paul Robeson for his communist leanings. Celebrity can also destroy heroism for, as Clark says, "we learn too much about everybody."[13]

Even those heroes whose names seem carved in stone may find them expunged and replaced with those deemed more politically correct. Cape Kennedy, originally named for John F. Kennedy, was renamed Cape Canaveral within ten years as a result of complaints by Florida conservatives. To protest slavery and to honor a black physician, a school board in New Orleans decided to rename George Washington Elementary School the Dr. Charles Richard Drew Elementary School.[14] In contrast, heroes who were largely overlooked during their lifetime, such as Harry S. Truman and Robert F. Kennedy, may be resurrected and deified in death.

The war in Vietnam gave rise to much debate over those we emulate as heroes. Some praised the soldiers who served in the military, while others glorified those who chose to avoid the draft by leaving the country or by participating in protest marches. The men and women in each group followed the dictates of their conscience, as heroes are expected to do. Yet the nation overall was bitterly divided in its opinions, a conflict vividly portrayed in the film *The Deer Hunter,* which portrayed both the intensive patriotism and the feelings of betrayal of the characters.

Some heroes remain problematic because the values to which they were, or are, committed are not acceptable to certain people. Thus Angela Davis, Ronald Reagan, Jane Fonda, and Jack Kevorkian are heroes to some and villains to others. We have seen many of our sports heroes fall from grace, including O. J. Simpson and Darryl Strawberry. Disillusioned hero worshippers such as Arianna Huffington say that, for them, there are "no more political heroes, just people who have turned their lives around. They are the role models she wants for her daughters to follow."[15] Political figures who might meet this criterion are President George W. Bush and Kitty Dukakis, for their recoveries from alcoholism and drug addiction.

Some Americans may even find their models in persons that most citizens would despise. The young shooters who killed their teacher and classmates in Littleton, Colorado, and the adult bombers who ended the lives of both toddlers and adults in Oklahoma City, served as negative role models for violent copycats. Search the Internet and one finds groups who praise Nazis, racists, and sadists. The Branch Davidians of Waco, Texas, worshipped their leader, David Koresh, but he led them to their death. Others' heroes are villains, including liberals, feminists, minorities, and the government itself. Such groups function as a mirror image of mainstream society in which the heroes of ordinary folk are transformed into villains.

Indeed, "America has often been indiscriminate about who gets called a hero. The title has been bestowed upon everyone from multimillion-dollar athletes to ordinary men and women who risk their lives to save others. Today, the term is bandied about so loosely, Arnold Schwarzenegger is mentioned in the same breath as Dr. Martin Luther King Jr." But even putative heroes question the easy awarding of the title. When Air Force Captain Scott O'Grady was rescued after a fighter mission in Serbia, he modestly demurred: "Naah, I'm not a hero. All I was was a scared little bunny rabbit, trying to hide, trying to survive." As one commentator appropriately asks: "Are valor and heroism synonymous? Is society debasing the idea of heroism by using it to describe anyone who makes people feel good about themselves?"[16]

Heroic Archetypes

A search of the Internet yielded millions of citations of heroes.[17] Although naturally each of these persons is unique, in these almost numberless American heroes we can identify seven categories, or archetypes. These archetypes differ as to the relative importance placed on individual characteristics and their relative degree of involvement in the general community, particularly its political life. Some heroes are honored principally for their personal character and achievements. They act as admirable individuals, rather than as participants in a political process. Building on the common American focus on individual personalities, these heroes of popular culture typically achieve their honored status in relative isolation. They can be described in terms of three archetypes.

Champions of Adversity. We honor some people because they have overcome enormous personal handicaps. Helen Keller was blind and deaf from childhood, yet she spoke and wrote eloquently.[18] Other champions of adversity include the actors Christopher Reeve and Michael J. Fox, who have used devastating injury and grave illness as opportunities to promote public awareness of, and gain research funding for, spinal cord damage and Parkinson's disease. Even the most renowned political figures may be admired as much for their battles against personal adversity as for their public actions. Franklin Delano Roosevelt was able to lead his country despite being crippled by polio, and former president Ronald Reagan bravely revealed that he was afflicted with Alzheimer's disease, thereby spurring public support for investigations into its causes and treatment.

Trailblazers. Be they explorers, scientists, entrepreneurs, artists, or athletes, trailblazers have the courage, imagination, and talent to accomplish what others have not dared to try. Like Champions of Adversity, they are considered heroes primarily on account of their individual achievements, rather than their direct involvement in the community. Our schoolbooks are filled with tales of their exploits. The explorers who sailed to the New World on Viking, Spanish, and English ships were trailblazers, as were the pioneers who crossed America by horseback, covered wagon, and canoe. Meriwether Lewis and William Clark, with the help of their guide, Sacajawea, opened up the West after the Louisiana Purchase.[19] Their travel journals inspired others to seek adventure and fortune in the newly acquired land.

Trailblazers also are found in more civilized settings. "In the modern world," write two admirers of the entrepreneurial spirit, "the wealth creators—the entrepreneurs—actually travel the heroic path and are every bit as bold and daring as the mythical heroes who fought dragons and overcame evil."[20] These entrepreneurs are risk-taking, creative individuals who strive to turn their dreams into reality. By way of illustration, Andrew Carnegie, in the nineteenth century, and Bill Gates, in the twentieth, have contributed vastly to American industry and technology, thereby fostering economic growth. Americans also value as heroes those who mark new trails in the natural world. Benjamin Franklin and Thomas Edison are honored for their practical inventions, Albert Einstein for working out the theoretical underpinnings of atomic physics and space travel, and Jonas Salk for the development of a vaccine that ended epidemics of polio. Medical researchers who will eventually discover new cures through gene therapy will likely be the heroes of coming decades.

Similarly, American artists and performers put their talent and dedication to use in creating new art forms. From George Gershwin to Isadora Duncan to Bessie Smith, we value our composers, dancers, and singers. In the paintings of Jackson Pollack and Georgia O'Keeffe, we honor our artists. In studios and on stage, they served as trailblazers, intent on breaking away from established styles and expanding artistic horizons. Athletes, too, have captured our imagination because of their record-breaking achievements. Young and old have made heroes of such figures as Babe Ruth, Jackie Robinson, Gertrude Ederle, and Mia Hamm—figures whose heroic appeal is often underscored by their successful efforts to overcome poverty, racism, or sexism.

Nurturers. In contrast to the two preceding archetypes, heroes of this category are not noted for extraordinary personal achievements.

Their heroism instead comes in their service to others, usually in intimate settings. They are individuals who take their personal responsibilities seriously: dutiful parents and spouses, dedicated workers and providers of hope and comfort. Their selflessness and nurturance, in homes, schools, hospitals, churches, and the workplace, enables others to thrive. As one champion of such "anonymous heroism" puts it: "The bravest things we do in our lives are usually known only to ourselves. No one throws ticker tape on the man who chose to be faithful to his wife, on the lawyer who didn't take the drug money, or the daughter who held her tongue again and again."[21]

To many, their greatest heroes are their closest relatives, often their mother and father. In a 1985 study at the University of Wisconsin that asked undergraduates to name their top five heroes and heroines, "the students' own parents were the most frequent first choices."[22] From the time their children are toddlers, parents serve as role models, and youngsters try to walk in their shoes. Often, as they patiently care for autistic children and aging parents, their heroism is all but invisible.

Rescuers. The heroes in this and the following group are relatively more involved in community life and politics, although their heroism is still defined by their individual deeds. Even in a public setting, they achieve recognition by means of personal valor, by acting apart from their fellow citizens. Rescuers act courageously in emergencies and in other dangerous situations. Such individual heroism is often associated with military combat. Its features, both admirable and wretched, were ably captured in the award-winning film *Saving Private Ryan*. As one writer commented, the film "reminds us of the flesh and blood that soldiers are made of [and] shows them ultimately possessing the stomach to see a vital but nasty job through, even at the cost of their lives." It also teaches us "that the men who fought found more ugliness in war than glory, that if they were courageous they were also scared, and that none had to be larger than life to deserve our salute."[23]

Rescuers include volunteers, sometimes anonymous, who suddenly commit themselves to saving threatened lives. One example is Roberto Clemente, a Hall of Fame baseball player. On New Year's Eve of 1972, Clemente was on his way to Nicaragua to aid survivors of an earthquake when his plane crashed.[24] Far more than his athletic skill, the heroic circumstances of his death made him a role model for youth. More broadly, firefighters, police, and emergency medical teams may have saved as many as thirty thousand workers from death by their skilled evacuation of the World Trade Center after the September 11 terrorist attack.

As if to foreshadow that event, heroism was widespread among the hundreds who came to help after one of the worst acts of terrorism in American history. Following the 1995 bombing of a federal office building in Oklahoma City, resulting in 168 deaths, volunteers arrived "from down the street and as far away as New York City—cops, doctors, structural engineers, and firefighters from more than 50 departments. Oklahoma City officials don't even know how many hundreds of emergency workers, and ordinary citizens, rushed to the bombed out Alfred P. Murrah Federal Building on April 19 to help search for survivors and comfort the grieving over the next grueling days that followed. . . . Together, these brave men and women reassured the nation that there is far more heart than hate in the heartland."[25]

Martyrs. These persons go beyond even Rescuers, sacrificing their lives on behalf of others. Combatants killed in military action are the classic example. In remembering them, we increasingly turn to World War II, as is evident in such books as Tom Brokow's *The Greatest Generation,* which extols the self-sacrifice and integrity of that generation of Americans, and in film dramas, such as *Schindler's List* and *Life Is Beautiful,* that focus on individual altruism. In more recent times, American martyrs include leaders who have been assassinated, such as John F. Kennedy and the Reverend Martin Luther King Jr. and the crews of astronauts on the *Challenger* and *Columbia* missions.

Guardians at the Gates. The final pair of archetypes comprise heroes who are more directly involved in public life. Usually standing outside the established processes of politics, these heroes win their accolades by acting independently—as Ralph Nader put it, by "bucking the system and putting themselves on the line because of their ideals."[26] Guardians at the Gates are highly involved in public life, although they may not be active in formal politics. They warn their fellow citizens of dangers, both in the society generally and within government. When Lincoln Steffens wrote his famous muckraking reports, he alerted the public of the dangers of political and business corruption, just as Robert Woodward and Carl Bernstein would later uncover the Watergate scandal.

Within government, this category includes the "whistleblower," who defends the integrity of political institutions by discovering and opposing malfeasance and criminality among public officials. Marie Ragghianti, for example, was chair of the pardons and paroles board of Tennessee. When she discovered that the office of the governor was selling clemencies to convicted criminals, she initiated a federal investigation. Although she was hastily dismissed from her position, she was ultimately vindicated when three persons were convicted and Governor Ray Blanton was ousted from office (and later sent to prison for other crimes). Ragghianti, whose experiences became the subject of a book and a film, won her own reinstatement and later became the administrator, and in 1999 a member, of the U.S. Parole Commission.[27]

Activists, Protesters, and Reformers. Direct political involvement is particularly evident in this final group. From abolitionists to civil libertarians, from suffragettes to women's liberationists, Americans have admired those who have fought for racial and gender equality. Senator Joseph Biden fittingly described political heroes as those with "the courage to seek change when things go stale." They are valued for their "realism, idealism, tenacity, and the ability to sacrifice."[28] History offers us John Brown, Harriet Beecher Stowe, and Susan B. Anthony as examples of courageous individuals who refused to accept the status quo. As compassionate protesters, they not only empathized with the downtrodden, forgotten, or silenced members of society but reached out to help them. Today's activists may lend their support to gay rights or green parties, to a woman's "right to choose" or an embryo's "right to life," or to the control of environmental pollution.

In recent years, women have become prominent social activists, "passionate leaders in fights against toxic waste dumps, against nuclear power, and against nuclear weapons."[29] Karen Silkwood is one well-known example. A chemical technician at Kerr-McGee plutonium fuels production plant in Crescent, Oklahoma, she was the plant's first woman committee member from Local 5-283 of the Oil, Chemical, and Atomic Workers (OCAW) International Union. In 1974, after having her own levels of radioactive contaminants monitored, she blew the whistle on Kerr-McGee's unsafe practices. After she testified about contaminant dangers at a union meeting, her car was involved in a suspicious accident in which she was killed. Books, as well as the movie *Silkwood,* subsequently made her a national hero.[30]

From Heroes to Heroism

"Creating heroes seems as simple as sunlight; it is as difficult to explain."[31] The preceding survey shows us the surfeit of admirable people in America and the gratifying diversity of our values. Heroes are plentiful in American minds and seemingly might include anyone we like a lot. All of us will surely continue to confer the accolade on many worthy people, and none of us has the authority to exclude competing claims. It may even be desirable for society to have multitudes of heroes, which recalls Andy Warhol's sardonic comment that in contemporary society everyone can expect fifteen minutes of fame. But heroism, to be meaningful for politics, must be defined by more than popularity or celebrity or even praiseworthy behavior. We need to draw two conceptual distinctions and to examine their implications for democratic thought.

The first distinction concerns the relative autonomy of individuals. Explanations of heroism typically distinguish between personal characteristics of the heroes and their historical circumstances. In one traditional approach, heroes are "great men" (but typically not great women), who change the world by dint of their extraordinary individual actions. Thomas Carlyle is the classic worshiper of this manner of man: "He is the living light-fountain, which it is good and pleasant to be near. The light which enlightens, which has enlightened the darkness of the world; and this not a kindled lamp only, but rather as a natural luminary shining by the gift of Heaven."[32] Max Weber wrote more analytically of persons invested with "the extraordinary and personal *gift of grace* (charisma), the absolutely personal devotion and personal confidence in revelation, heroism, or other qualities of individual leadership."[33]

Alternatively, a minimalist view of heroes sees them only as the embodiment of impersonal historical forces, passively floating on the ocean waves of events, who "get fame effortlessly because of historical chance."[34] Deterministic theories give little weight to individual initiative, for even "world historic figures" are reduced to mere agents in what Hegel described as the "restless succession of individuals and peoples, which exist for a time and then disappear."[35] In classic Marxist thought, both the victory of capitalism and its defeat by socialism are predetermined, requiring no conscious individual effort. "What the bourgeoisie, therefore, produces above all, are its own grave-diggers. Its fall and the victory of the proletariat are equally inevitable."[36]

We will not delve further into these grand historical theories or attempt to resolve abstract philosophical issues of causality and human autonomy.[37] We will instead accept as a premise that individuals do affect history, at least in some manner. The second conceptual distinction turns on the difference between individual and institutional heroism within the broader governmental process. Many individuals, acting in a multitude of ways, may affect politics, as most of the archetypes discussed above illustrate. Institutional behavior is different. As opposed to individual volition, which is often arbitrary, such behavior follows established rules, practices, and norms, both written and unwritten. The focus in this book is on heroes operating within the institutions of government. James Madison offers an important distinction in this regard. Defending the institutions established by the Constitution and the limits they place on political power, Madison observed: "It may be a reflection on human nature, that such devices should be necessary to control the abuses of government. But what is government itself, but the greatest of all reflections on human nature? If men were angels, no government would be necessary. If angels were to govern men, neither external nor internal controls on government would be necessary. In framing a government which is to be administered by men over men, the great difficulty lies in this: you must first enable the government to control the governed; and in the next place, oblige it to control itself."[38]

In Madison's view, angels — creatures of pure individual virtue — were not likely to be available for American government. Most men and women are not angels, and it would be foolish to await the unknown time of their coming. The appropriate institutions of government, by contrast, not only endure but can enhance our collective life independent of the particular persons holding power. Institutions can develop procedures that will offset the deficiencies of human nature and possibly even encourage people to behave better. That was Lincoln's hope when, in the nation's gravest crisis, he pleaded in his first inaugural address that constitutional institutions could revivify Americans' "mystic chords of memory" and enable them to "swell the chorus of the Union when again touched, as surely they will be, by the better angels of our nature."[39]

Even though in current usage the term *hero* frequently includes people who do not display "superhuman" qualities, the individualist heroes of popular culture are often akin to Madison's "angels." Their description frequently resembles the romantic literary portrait of the rare individual who accomplishes extraordinary things—such as the model hero, Achilles, or the modern savior who, in the words of Joseph Campbell, "dares to heed the call and seek the mansion of that presence with whom it is our whole destiny to be atoned."[40] In contrast, democratic heroes are relatively undistinguished people who nonetheless serve democracy by performing their customary duties in a situation of crisis. To honor democracy, we must do more than speak "in praise of famous men." We need to recognize, with Sidney Hook, that a hero may be "any individual who does his work well and makes a unique contribution to the public good. . . . Daily toil on any level has its own occasions of struggle, victory, and quiet death."[41]

But democratic heroes in politics are more than praiseworthy citizens, and they also differ from great historical figures such as Washington and Lincoln. The political heroes we will consider work in public settings, not as autonomous benefactors. They earn distinction from their work, not their character. Our portrayal of these "ordinary" democratic heroes will accordingly place little emphasis on their personal attributes but will instead stress the institutional context of their actions. These people become heroes by performing their normal jobs, but now at a critical time; they demonstrate not isolated personal virtue but the values enshrined in their political positions. Crisis increases the impact of their duties, but it does not transform such individuals into grander persons. Like other admirable people, democratic heroes often display courage, but it is not the dramatic bravery of medal winners in war. Their courage is revealed in their steady performance of the tasks customary to their political office, no matter what the difficulties. Their distinctive features are visible in the archetype of the Rescuer. In some instances, the Rescuer performs extraordinary deeds that do not form part of his or her everyday life. Roberto Clemente's ordinary work was hitting baseballs, not earthquake relief. When it comes to democratic heroes, however, Rescuers are those who undertake such work as part of their daily routine, as in the case of firefighters. This "courage of constancy" is evident in self-descriptions offered by these ordinary heroes.[42] They repeatedly refer to their "job," their customary duties at work. They accept the common view of heroes as exceptional people; for that reason, they deny their own achievement. In the words of firefighters in San Francisco concerning the rescue of four children from a burning building: "It was the other guys, I just followed them." "I just helped, the others are the real heroes." "It was pretty satisfying. But you should get the story from the rest of the crew. I didn't do much."[43] Such ordinary heroes are exemplified by the archetypes of Guardians at the Gates and Activists, Protesters, and Reformers, who perform service to others. It is their work—customary deeds within established institutions, leading to the resolution of crisis—that this book particularly honors. They are the true democratic heroes.

Democratic heroes are not extraordinary individuals, and they do not require horrific conditions to demonstrate their heroism. We find them among ordinary people doing their customary work, meeting their prescribed responsibilities so as to advance the public interest in situations of political or social crisis. The following chapters recount the democratic heroism of eight Americans, each of whom works within a specific institution of American politics. We will begin with a "workhorse" in the U.S. House of Representatives.[44]

Chapter Three
Peter Rodino

A Hero of the House

At a decisive moment in American history, Richard M. Nixon resigned as president under threat of impeachment. The process leading to Nixon's expulsion began in 1973, when Chairman Peter Rodino initiated an investigation of Nixon by the Judiciary Committee of the House of Representatives. It led the following year to Nixon's indictment by the committee for actions "contrary to his trust as President and subversive of constitutional government, to the great prejudice of the cause of law and justice and to the manifest injury of the people of the United States."[1] Ten days later, Nixon left the White House in disgrace. This critical period provides our first illustration of democratic heroism in American political institutions.

Congressman Rodino was not a "great man," either before or after the Nixon investigation. In a personal interview, he agreed that, without the impeachment crisis, he would be remembered only by "the people who are especially interested, the scholars who write and record."[2] Rodino had patiently climbed the ladder of seniority to become chair of the Judiciary Committee. In twelve terms in the House, he had won the respect of his congressional colleagues, but he had received little public attention. Yet, in a decisive moment, he met the challenge.

Rodino was not typecast to be a hero. Relatively short, with a distinct urban accent, almost too carefully groomed, he would not be mistaken for Jimmy Stewart in *Mr. Smith Goes to Washington*. The product of a decaying urban political machine in Newark, New Jersey, he embodied the declining New Deal Democratic coalition. First elected in 1948 as an advocate of Harry Truman's Fair Deal, he had consistently supported liberal programs, including repeal of the Taft-Hartley labor law, co-authored by his Republican predecessor in Congress.

Proud of his ethnic heritage, he referred to his base constituency as "Italian Americans" or, preferably, as "Americans of Italian descent" and devoted himself to casework, interventions with executive agencies on behalf of his constituents, particularly newer Italian immigrants. One of the first Italian Americans to be elected to Congress, he was extremely sensitive to slurs on his ethnic group. The New Jerseyan led the small Italian American congressional caucus and campaigned to erase the common identification of criminals with the Mafia.

Until the Nixon crisis, Rodino had had little impact on national politics, even after a quarter century in Congress. Most of the legislation he sponsored consisted of private immigration bills on behalf of aliens, typically from Italy, seeking legal admission to the United States. Once admitted and naturalized, these new citizens would presumably vote for their congressional benefactor. Serving a patient apprenticeship, Rodino contributed to the watershed 1960s legislation on civil rights and was the House floor manager for the landmark immigration revision of 1965. Yet no law bore his name, other than the parochial legislation to make Columbus Day a national holiday.

With this limited record of achievement, some of his colleagues and staff dismissed him as a lightweight. Detractors derisively "nicknamed him 'The Leader'—not because of his heroic stands on the issues, but because he loved to lead congressional junkets to foreign

U.S. Representative Peter Rodino

countries."[3] As he quietly accumulated seniority in the House, his New Jersey colleagues sought higher office, as mayor of Newark, as senators, or as governor. Some, like his former roommate in Washington, had gone to jail for bribery and related corrupt actions in office. Rodino stayed in the Capitol, untainted by scandal, although his friendships still led to unsubstantiated suspicions.

Like all politicians, Rodino made re-election his first priority.[4] He won support not as a legislative crusader but through his attention to his individual constituents. His contacts with voters concerned their personal problems with government or their celebrations of births and weddings and mourning at funerals. As African Americans moved into the once solidly Italian neighborhoods in his congressional district, black and white militants threatened his tenure, particularly after a court-ordered redistricting made blacks a majority in his district in 1972. In response, his ethnic sensitivity expanded as he became more active in support of civil rights legislation and added more nonwhites to his staff.

These political concerns affected Rodino even as the impeachment crisis developed. At the same time that Nixon came under attack, unrelated charges of personal corruption led Vice President Spiro Agnew to resign. Under the new twenty-fifth amendment to the Constitution, Nixon nominated Gerald Ford, leader of the House Republicans, to assume the vacant office. The nomination was considered, and approved, by the House Judiciary Committee, with Rodino joining the overwhelming majority. However, Ford came under attack from African American groups for his past opposition to civil rights legislation. Waffling under their pressure, and conscious of the black majority in his district, Rodino ultimately voted against confirmation because of Ford's alleged neglect of "the role of the Federal Government in serving the needs of all our citizens."[5]

Rodino had become head of the Judiciary Committee almost by accident, when the longtime chair, Emanuel Celler, was narrowly defeated in a primary challenge based on his advanced age and astringent personality. Now, as a fledgling committee chairman, Rodino would face the dire possibility of removing an elected president from office for the first time in American history. As we will see, Rodino deftly managed the impeachment inquiry. But how can we explain Rodino's personal accomplishment? What accounts for the ability of a journeyman legislator to master a severe constitutional crisis?

The simple answer is that the congressman "rose to the occasion," that he became on this occasion something of an overachiever, a one-time flash in the pan, destined to revert to obscurity once the crisis was past. But that explanation does Rodino an injustice. More generally, it implies that democracies cannot deal effectively with crises through their existing institutions but must depend on good luck and the rare savior.

Our concept of the democratic hero looks for heroism among ordinary people doing their customary work in moments of crisis. The example of Peter Rodino illustrates this concept. The congressman was effective not because he suddenly acted differently than usual. His accomplishment was based on precisely those same qualities he had shown throughout his legislative career. As he put it himself: "I believe that the very characteristic traits that made it possible for me to be effective in other roles—to be fair, to be decent, without fanfare, without showmanship—were the same in the role that I played as well during the impeachment crisis. That is the role that I've been playing all along. I was just the same Peter Rodino that I've been all the time from the very first day that I came to the Congress, from the very first speech that I made on the floor of the House."

Watergate

Since Watergate took place some time ago, it might be useful to recount the constitutional crisis of 1972–74. The story began with a break-in at the Democratic National Committee's offices in Washington's Watergate complex during the presidential election of 1972. The incident drew only limited attention before Nixon's triumphant re-election, but skilled investigative reporting drew connections between the burglars and the Nixon administration, which in turn led to appointment of a special prosecutor in May 1973 and a televised inquiry by a special Senate committee the following summer. The hearings produced dramatic revelations of apparent crimes in the executive branch and the revelation that a taping system had been set up in the White House that recorded all the president's conversations.[6]

The White House tried a variety of means to thwart the widening probes, including guilty pleas by the original burglars, the resignation of Nixon's top aides, repeated presidential denial of any involvement in the break-in or the subsequent cover-up, and resistance to the release of the White House tapes. In October, as the courts ruled that the president must surrender the tapes, Nixon conducted what became known as the "Saturday Night Massacre," in which he forced the resignations of the attorney general and the deputy attorney general and fired the special prosecutor. When a grand jury indicted his former aides — including the White House's Chief of Staff, domestic policy chief, and Counsel, and the U.S. Attorney-General — for their participation in the cover-up, Nixon was also secretly named as an unindicted co-conspirator.

The dismissals "shocked and frightened the nation. The ominous action raised talk of a coup and prompted comparisons to the Reichstag fire that prepared Germany for the rise of Hitler."[7] Immediately afterward, resolutions to impeach Nixon were introduced in the House and referred to the Judiciary Committee. In the face of public indignity, and under court order, Nixon agreed to release the tapes but delayed compliance until April of 1974, continued to resist full disclosure until a final Supreme Court order in July, and even contemplated a possible evasion of the Court's decision.[8]

As these events unfolded, the House Judiciary Committee conducted its own inquiry behind closed doors, despite continuing resistance from the White House. At the end of July 1974, the committee held thirty-six hours of public hearings over six days, ultimately concluding that Nixon's conduct "warrants impeachment and trial, and removal from office." The committee presented three specific counts of illegal behavior on Nixon's part. The president was accused of obstruction of justice in the investigation of the Watergate crimes, of a series of abuses of power and violations of citizens' constitutional rights, and of subversion of the constitutional separation of powers.

The committee's condemnation came on one-sided and bipartisan votes, severely weakening Nixon's hold on office. Before the House could act on the impeachment, however, the president's position grew desperate. Newly released tapes proved that Nixon had actively participated in the illegal activities and had lied in his previous denials. These revelations guaranteed impeachment in the House and conviction in the Senate. With Republicans leading the refrain, a national chorus of protest convinced the president to leave office voluntarily. He remained resentful, unrepentant, and combative to the end of his life.

Nixon's impeachable conduct involved far more than individual vices. The incumbent president came close to subverting the basic democratic processes of the United States. He and his collaborators spied on their opponents, burglarized offices, employed the IRS, the FBI, the CIA, the Justice Department, and other federal agencies to violate his opponents' constitutional rights, put government appointments and policy up for sale, and engaged in an extensive cover-up of these and other actions.

The president not only attempted to cover up a specific crime, the Watergate burglary, but "the cover-up begat more cover-up, enlarging so as to plant the seeds of its destruction."[9] Nixon also committed a series of other official offenses. Before and after the break-in, Nixon was involved in perjury, the obstruction of justice, bribery, the disruption of protest rallies, and investigations of his opponents' finances and sex lives.[10] Seventy of his collaborators went to jail for these offenses. Overall, concludes an expert reporter, "Watergate was a clandestine domestic operation in which a determined president secretly plotted what amounted to a coup d'état against American constitutional government."[11]

The character of Nixon's offenses is conveyed well by a notorious conversation taped in the White House between the president and the White House counsel, John Dean. In March of 1973, they considered how to continue the cover-up of the original Watergate break-in:

> DEAN: Now, where, where are the soft spots on this? Well, first of all, there's this, there's the problem of the continued blackmail . . . which will not only go on now, it'll go on when the people are in prison, and it will compound the obstruction-of-justice situation. It'll cost money. It's dangerous.
>
> PRESIDENT NIXON: That's right. How much money do you need?
>
> DEAN: I would say these people are going to cost, uh, a million dollars over the next, uh, two years.
>
> PRESIDENT NIXON: We could get that. If you need the money. . . . you could get the money. . . . What I mean is, you could, you could get a million dollars. And we could get it in cash. I know where it could be gotten. . . . I mean it's not easy, but it could be done. But, uh, the question is who the hell would handle it?
>
> DEAN: Well, I would think that would be something that [former Attorney-General John] Mitchell ought to be charged with. . . . And get some, get some pros to help him. . . . Some people are going to have to go to jail. That's the long and the short of it. . . .
>
> PRESIDENT NIXON: The obstruction of justice. . . . I feel, could be cut off at the pass. . . . I wonder if that [the blackmail] doesn't have to be continued? Let me put it this way: let us suppose that you get, you, you get the million bucks, and you get the proper way to handle it, and you could hold that side. It would seem to me that would be worthwhile.[12]

Ultimately, the nation concluded that Nixon must leave the White House. Members of the Judiciary Committee demonstrated that consensus in their final written views. Democrat Charles Rangel, a New York liberal, was "encouraged that the American system permits a black night watchman [at the Watergate headquarters] and the son of an Italian immigrant family sitting as a District Court judge, each through applying the law, to be the instruments of uncovering the most extensive and highly placed corruption in our national history and the bringing to justice of the most powerful men in our society." The Republicans who voted against impeachment before the revelation of the final evidence struck a different and sadder tone, but they still eventually supported Nixon's resignation. In separate views included in the Judiciary Committee report, they observed: "It is striking that such an able, experienced and perceptive man . . . should fail to comprehend the damage that accrued daily to himself, his Administration, and to the Nation, as day after day, month after month, he imprisoned the truth about his role in the Watergate cover-up so long and so tightly within the solitude of his Oval office that it could not be unleashed without destroying his Presidency."[13]

The public supported the committee's judgment. Nixon's approval rating dropped from 68 percent at the beginning of 1974 to 25 percent by the week of his resignation. The hearings had led to an overwhelming popular consensus that Nixon was guilty (82 percent) and that it was better that he resigned rather than stand trial before the Senate (67 percent versus 26 percent). A majority of respondents commended both the committee and Rodino and saw Nixon's removal as "the rebirth of the nation." Even a dozen years later, three out of four respondents endorsed his departure from office.[14]

Nixon's peaceful removal from the presidency sustained American constitutional democracy. In some nations, deposing the head of the government often brings troops into the streets and causes unending political turmoil. Nixon's resignation, by contrast, brought almost universal relief to the nation (and Nixon was ultimately given a state burial). By August of 1974 the nation overwhelmingly wanted Nixon out of office, and the political system responded, calmly. Nixon sent a one-sentence letter of resignation to the secretary of state and boarded his helicopter for his home in California. The nation had a new president—without the need for troops surrounding the Capitol, or mass demonstrations in the streets, or foreign threats, or economic catastrophe.

Rodino in the House of Representatives

This consensual result owed much to Peter Rodino, not as a unique person but as a model member of the House of Representatives. Rodino performed well as an individual. The basis for his success, however, was not his personal virtue but the good fit between his own qualities and the institutional character of the House of Representatives. By guiding the political processes of the Nixon impeachment along accepted institutional patterns, he achieved broad support. His role in the impeachment illustrates our theme, the institutional sources of heroism. Rodino saw himself not as an individually great man but as following what he termed the "Becket principle," referring to the medieval defender of the Catholic Church, Thomas Becket: "the playing of one's role to the fullest."[15] To Tip O'Neill, the Democratic majority leader, this close fit with his role made the chairman "the perfect man for this job."[16]

Rodino was a politician in an institution of politicians; his virtues are the ordinary virtues of his breed. The public and the mass media, however, generally condemn these qualities. Although American citizens are certainly in favor of democracy, they dislike the actual and messy processes of democracy that "in any realistic environment are bound to be slow, to be built on compromise, and to make apparent the absence of clean, certain answers to important questions of the day." Congress is particularly likely to be targeted as a "public enemy." Congress is openly political, whereas Americans seem really to want a "stealth democracy." Voters "dislike compromise and bargaining, they dislike committees and bureaucracy, they dislike political parties and interest groups, they dislike big salaries and big staffs, they dislike slowness and multiple stages, and they dislike debate and publicly hashing things out, referring to such actions as haggling or bickering." Exemplifying these features of open democracy, Congress has become the least esteemed of the branches of government.[17] Even less beloved, "the House has always appeared as confused mélange of inferior men, battling blindly for obscure and even petty causes in parliamentary chaos."[18]

Rodino provides a singular example of how the public benefits from the exercise of ordinary political skills. In the impeachment crisis, he succeeded not by being an extraordinary individual but by using the typical tricks of the political trade. Success in a democratic legislature requires the patient building of support—as is illustrated by the Federal Constitutional Convention of 1787 through to any contemporary city council.[19] Rodino plied his trade. By building a record, he won a place on the congressional agenda. By proceeding cautiously, he gained more attention and support. By pursuing consensus across party lines, he gained broader backing. By compromising on some issues, he won agreement on the central questions. By his evident patriotism, he gained national acceptance of Nixon's condemnation.

The chairman presented a model of cautious leadership. The committee conducted its own investigation, in confidence, and much of the material it gathered remains locked away to this day. Television cameras were present only for the final debate and voting, and Rodino altered the physical structure of the hearings so that the television cameras were unobtrusive.[20] At the climactic moment, the committee's tone was regret over the conduct of the president and dismay over its sad task of judgment. When it was over, an untriumphant Rodino grieved for his country.

The House of Representatives was an ideal arena for the exercise of Rodino's skills. It was originally conceived by the authors of the Constitution as "the grand depository of the democratic principle.... It ought to know & sympathize with every part of the community.... We ought to attend to the rights of every class of the people."[21] It was intended to reflect public opinion more precisely than any of the branches of the national government, with as few as thirty thousand constituents for each representative. When the Constitution was adopted, the representatives were believed to be particularly close to the voters. As Madison wrote, the members of the House "are numerous. They are distributed and dwell among the people at large. Their connections of blood, of friendship, and of acquaintance embrace a great proportion of the most influential part of the society."[22] In modern times, however, members of Congress can no longer maintain these intimate connections to their constituents. By 1974, each represented about half a million people, close to twenty times the number at the adoption of the Constitution. Still, "it is truly representative not only of the people but of the calling of politics.... Politicians all, ... reflecting all the country's ethnic communities, all their prejudices, all their interests."[23]

The House in 1974 reflected its electoral character. Representatives had considerable electoral protection, holding the advantages of name recognition, the perquisites of office, and fundraising contacts over any potential opponents.[24] At the same time, having lost their intimate connections with constituents, the members had to work long and hard to maintain support among voters who were personal strangers. In place of personal ties, they had to cultivate the "trust" of voters by "giving constituents access or the assurance of access, listening to constituent views, explaining their views to their constituents, educating their constituents."[25] If they did gain this trust, members were then freer to take independent policy positions, even on issues as compelling as presidential impeachment.

As the nation has grown, the character of the House has changed. The contemporary nature of the House is greatly affected by its large size, 435 members, and by the large number of constituents in each district. Size is seen by both House members and academic observers as the most significant difference between the House and Senate, influencing a wide range of characteristics, including formal rules, constituency relationships, partisanship, legislative specialization, and even the manners and personal relationships of the members.[26] To operate effectively, the House depends on norms, or standards of behavior. Particularly important are norms of "specialization, reciprocity, legislative work, courtesy, and aspects of apprenticeship."[27]

Within the House, specialization is one major effect of the chamber's large size. There cannot be meaningful debate among hundreds of members. For serious consideration of its business, the House relies on its committees. As Woodrow Wilson explained in his early scholarly work, "the House of Representatives delegates not only its legislative but also its deliberative functions to its Standing Committees. The little public debate that arises under the stringent and urgent rules of the House is formal rather than effective, and it is the discussions which take place in the Committees that give form to legislation."[28]

The Judiciary Committee typified this characteristic of the House. In a chamber focused on lawmaking, it was expected to be particularly skilled in the framing of statutes. It held a defined policy jurisdiction, dealing with such subjects as court organization, civil rights, immigration, and constitutional amendments. By custom, only lawyers were appointed to the group, underlining its expertise; it was the only committee with an occupational qualification.

When the relatively arcane subject of impeachment arose in 1973, the House's natural course of action was to turn to its presumptive specialists on the Constitution, the lawyers of the Judiciary Committee. That course was also appropriate because at the time the committee was relatively moderate in its conduct of business. It was broadly representative of the whole House, with members from all factions of both parties. Partisanship existed within the committee, but it was relatively subdued because attitudes on civil rights, its most volatile issue, did not then divide strictly along party lines. Moreover, the Judiciary Committee was among the more prestigious committees in the House.[29] Even though membership on it could do little to advance their basic interest in re-election, representatives found the committee appealing. To them, it was almost as attractive as the top committees such as Appropriations, which dealt with general issues, and far more desirable than narrower policy or burdensome duty committees such as Education and Labor or House Administration.[30]

Specialization applies to individual members of Congress as well as to committees. Each representative is a specialist, an expert about the politics of his own area and in the particular subject of his or her committee work. Thus, when representatives must make decisions in regard to other subjects, they necessarily depend on the expertise of their colleagues. Providing reliable information to these disassociated experts requires the ability to do careful research, one of the traits valued in Congress. Becoming an expert is hard work, and the House prides itself on its dedicated effort. A former Republican leader, Charles Halleck, emphasized that "the Senate had the show horses, the House had the workhorses. . . . The average Congressman can tell about all he knows on any given subject in five minutes. But over in the Senate they have unlimited debate and it takes them that long to prove that they know as much as we do."[31] A "true House man," in the opinion of the representatives, "is primarily a worker, a specialist, and a craftsman—someone who will concentrate his energies in a particular field and gain prestige and influence in that."[32]

The Nixon Investigation

Rodino, in this legislative slang, was a "workhorse" and a "true House man"—and he bore the labels proudly. His arduous and expert work created the first tangible object needed for the investigation, a voluminous reference book on the arcane subject. The tedious research changed the political climate. "There was now a book on impeachment. It wasn't an undefinable topic any more. . . . Nobody read a line of the book, but everybody held it and looked at the last page to see that it was 718 pages long."[33]

The large size of the House also engenders complex rules, which are necessary to achieve action in a body of 435 talented and usually immodest politicians. Those who master the rules gain additional power as well as additional respect for their expertise. Through his long years in the House and his experience as floor manager for major legislation, Rodino had become a master of the rules, and he would make clever use of that knowledge in guiding the Judiciary Committee in the impeachment decision. For example, he avoided sharp partisan debate in the committee's open hearings by skipping general opening statements and immediately turning the discussion to the specific articles of impeachment.[34]

Caution was another of Rodino's traits that was valued in Congress. Although initially inclined toward impeachment, he made no public judgments—in contrast to other liberal Democrats. He insisted on formal House authorization and funding of the inquiry, to give it greater legitimacy. To preserve his impartial stance, he even disguised his reading materials when traveling and vetoed the appointment of a staff member who had signed a pro-impeachment telegram.[35] When the White House tapes disclosed an anti-Italian ethnic slur made by the president, Rodino insisted that the statement be kept from the public so that his inquiry would not be tainted as a revenge for Nixon's bias.

Democratic Majority Leader Tip O'Neill valued Rodino's caution and used it to convince other House members that Rodino's committee should direct the impeachment inquiry. Yet Rodino's slow pace exasperated zealous Democrats and members of the staff, who privately voiced the derisive complaint that "our chairman is chicken."[36] Even O'Neill grew impatient, pressing Rodino to begin the investigation quickly. These pressures did affect Rodino, leading him at one point to seek psychiatric support at Walter Reed Hospital. But he held to the credo that he laid out at the beginning of the process: "Let us now proceed, with such care and decency and thoroughness and honor that the vast majority of the American people, and their children after them will say, 'That was the right course. There was no other way.'"[37] Looking back recently, he invoked an unknown source: "Those who would enjoy the privileges of liberty must, like men, undergo fatigue in supporting it."

Throughout the proceedings, Rodino maintained his own reputation for fairness and nonpartisanship, and, with few exceptions, neither his colleagues nor the media commented negatively about his performance. The impeachment outcome also boosted the reputation of Rodino's beloved institution, the House of Representatives.[38] In Rodino's view, the ultimate acceptance of the committee's decision justifies his caution. "They wanted me to push," the New Jersey congressman remembered. "I told O'Neill in no uncertain words that I was going to do it my way. I don't mind being called cautious, because I believe that when one is responsible for making decisions that are going to affect the future of the country, one doesn't treat those issues by making snap judgments. Maybe we ought to have a little more of that."

American politicians are seekers of consensus. Although partisanship existed during the impeachment proceedings, it was muted. In seeking consensus, Rodino deliberately courted House Republicans. He appointed Republican John Doar as special counsel for the investigation and Albert Jenner, another Republican, as special counsel for the minority, and he also separated their assistants from the normal partisan staff. In his charge to Doar, Rodino insisted on objectivity: "I said to him, if I find it important enough to veto any of your appointments, if anyone ever indicates they are going to be for or against, if you come to any conclusion before we examine the evidence, or make any reference or recommendation, I said it just this way: 'I am firing you.'"

Overruling his own staff, he allowed the president's personal counsel access to the Committee, thereby gaining Republican support for subpoenaing White House documents and tapes that would ultimately undo the president.[39] The ranking minority member was included in all aspects of the inquiry and given an early opportunity to hear the White House tapes. He encouraged junior Republicans to take independent positions, and the final impeachment resolutions were drafted by Republicans on the House Judiciary Committee and its Republican minority counsel. Even during the committee's public deliberations, he found ways to give more time to those drafting the consensual charges.

His caution and his search for broad and bipartisan support led Rodino to consult frequently with Republicans and Democrats from the South. He insisted on secrecy in the Judiciary Committee deliberations, an uncommon practice for voluble politicians. "Secrecy was necessary so that his committee would not be split prematurely on party lines," explains Theodore White. Rodino had to "buy time for Doar and his staff to assemble the evidence that would erase party lines. To buy time, he would yield to the Republicans on his committee on every procedural point; he would soothe his left-wing Democrats by every guile and flattery he could conceive. He would use his authority only when he must, from time to time, and then he would act as the autocrat of conciliation, compromise, delay."[40]

In the end, the bipartisan approach worked. In the critical vote, seven of the committee's seventeen minority members voted to remove their party's leader from the White House. When Nixon's resignation became inevitable, his fate was relayed to him by a group of prominent Republicans, led by the founder of modern party conservatism, Senator Barry Goldwater, and the national party chairman (and later president), George H. W. Bush.[41]

Compromise, the politician's particular art, was vital in winning this consensus.[42] Originally, five counts were lodged against Nixon. Rodino opposed the most political of these charges, which condemned Nixon for the secret bombing of Cambodia during the Vietnam War, concluding that the bombing, even if unwise, was within Nixon's legitimate authority as commander-in-chief. Over his limited objections, the committee also passed over the president's questionable tax returns (although Rodino now regrets that action, seeing it in hindsight as too forgiving of Nixon).[43] By thus focusing on three central questions of constitutional illegality, Rodino assembled a strong majority.

Like most congressmen, Rodino is also an old-fashioned patriot. A decorated combat veteran and officer in World War II, his office was decorated with an American flag and other national symbols. The walls of his inner office featured autographed portraits of all recent presidents but Nixon. In later years, Rodino became a part-time professor at Seton Hall University's law school. Despite the corruption he had seen and uncovered, his recurrent lesson was the majesty of the Constitution and the American system of government.

A decade after accomplishing the only removal of a president from office in American history, Rodino still conveyed a youthful patriotism: "I do feel a sense of awe and I do have great respect for all that we stand for in this country which, despite its flaws, is the finest nation. And its system is the finest. And naturally, when one thinks about the presidency one has to look upon it with a sense of reverence—a sense of respect—a sense of love." That same patriotism is evident in the chairman's memory of his reaction to the impeachment vote. Normally one would expect the victor in a political battle to feel exaltation at his triumph. But Rodino's response was quite different: "I went inside to a little cubby-office that I had and there was John Doar, and I looked at him, and there was nothing I could say, and I know we all looked solemn. Then I asked them to excuse me and went into the other room. I picked up the telephone and called my wife, and I said to her, 'Well, I guess you know. And I pray to God we did the right thing.' And then I broke down and cried."[44]

With the release of the final, incriminating tapes, the impeachment resolutions never came to a floor vote. The House did accept the report of the Judiciary Committee, recommending Nixon's removal, by a vote of 410 to 3. With a certain wistfulness, Rodino recalled his preparations for a formal House debate: "My proposal was to take those tapes and actually make an audio for use in the House. What a shocker that would have been!"

Rodino continued as chair of the committee for another fourteen years, celebrated for his action but limited in ambition. Despite his new fame, he withdrew his name from consideration as a vice-presidential nominee in 1976 because "I wanted to stay on and do the job I was doing. I didn't want my credibility questioned, that I was going to use it as a launching pad." Returning to his previous role, his legislative record remained sparse, as other representatives took the lead on such issues as immigration reform and civil rights. By 1988 he was forced to face new electoral realities. Blacks were demanding his seat for an African American. Under pressure from a well-financed challenger, he reluctantly retired after twenty House terms.

Rodino happened to be in a particular position at a particular time when he could affect the course of American history. The successful outcome of the impeachment investigation is a tribute to him personally, but it is also significant as a tribute to traits and abilities that are widespread in the nation. As the congressman acknowledged: "We've had many people who had humble beginnings and may not have been extraordinary until the time came that something happened and they were there. There are so many others that have so much to give and who do have a sense of responsibility and a great sense of duty."

A Contrast: The Clinton Impeachment

From the perspective of more than a quarter of a century, the Nixon inquiry and resignation remain remarkable. These actions are even more striking when compared to the later impeachment of another president, William Jefferson Clinton, arising from his sexual entanglements.

The story is well known. Paula Jones, an Arkansas state employee, sued Clinton for alleged sexual advances while Clinton was governor. The lawsuit continued after Clinton became president, amid unrelated investigations into Clinton's presidential actions by Kenneth Starr, appointed as independent counsel under a post-Watergate statute. After Clinton became president, he had an affair with a young White House intern, Monica Lewinsky, prompting Starr to extend his investigation still further. After trying for months to evade the truth, Clinton and Lewinsky ultimately admitted their liaison when audiotapes and other conclusive evidence came to light.

In the fall of 1998, Starr presented a detailed account of the affair and the president's conduct to the House Judiciary Committee and recommended impeachment. The committee held three weeks of public hearings after the 1998 congressional elections and then approved four indictments along straight party lines. As the year ended, the full House quickly voted formal impeachment on two of these grounds—perjury and obstruction of justice—again on cohesive partisan ballots. The Senate conducted a month-long trial on the charges in early 1999 and failed to convict on either of the two counts.

The Nixon and Clinton stories reveal sharp differences, particularly in the performance of the institutions of government. The differences begin with the substantive charges. The grounds for impeachment had been set long ago by Alexander Hamilton: "offenses which proceed from the misconduct of public men, or, in other words, from the abuse or violation of some public trust. They . . . relate chiefly to injuries done immediately to the society itself."[45] Nixon easily met this requirement.

Clinton's conduct was certainly offensive, but the actions that led to his impeachment and trial were trivial in comparison to Nixon's. Clinton's misconduct was essentially private. He had an immoral, crass, even inexplicable—but legal—extramarital affair, then lied about it in an effort to conceal it. In contrast to Nixon's impeachment, there were no substantial charges against Clinton of abusing the formal powers of the president. While Nixon used the FBI in his attempted cover-up, Clinton's affair was documented by the FBI laboratory. Nixon fired the prosecutor investigating his actions; Clinton endured his harassment to the end.

A second difference is simply the pacing of events. Nixon's removal was a slow, deliberative process. More than two years passed from the original Watergate break-in to the House committee action, with investigations pursued by the Justice Department, two special counsels, the courts, and both the Senate and the House. The general public eventually supported Nixon's removal, but it came to that conclusion gradually, and only after the full presentation of his crimes.

The Clinton impeachment and trial were also peaceful, but that is almost the only similarity to the Nixon judgment. Instead of a stately process of deliberation, the Jones/Lewinsky scandal brought heated press attention and frenetic jumping to conclusions. In place of careful examination of charges by the elected members of the House and Senate, the media and the independent counsel played the leading roles. Only the public stayed calm; unwaveringly, it wanted Clinton to remain in office, even while it disapproved his personal conduct. The voters concluded that "the case was never anything more than it appeared to be—that of a humiliated middle-aged husband who lied when he was caught having an affair with a young woman from the office."[46]

The changed character of impeachment cannot be explained simply by the different personalities or circumstances. A larger part of the explanation lies in the changed institutional character of the House of Representatives. Since the time of Rodino, the House had become more hierarchical, more partisan, and simply less pleasant. These changes had begun in the 1980s, during the long period of Democratic dominance.[47] In regard to the Clinton impeachment, however, the most important development was the stunning Republican victory in the 1994 congressional elections, resulting in the party's first House majority in forty-two years. To effect their conservative "Contract with America," Republicans changed House rules to transfer power from the committees to the leadership and insisted on programmatic adherence by committee chairs. One significant result of this focus on ideological purity was the choice, contrary to seniority norms, of Henry Hyde as chair of the Judiciary Committee.[48]

As the parties in the House became more coherently ideological, partisanship became more evident. The proportion of House roll calls which divided the parties rose from 42 percent in 1973 to 73 percent in 1995, and the party loyalty of the average Republican representative rose from 68 percent to 91 percent.[49] With Republicans holding control of the House in 1996, even as Clinton again won the presidency, intense partisanship persisted on Capitol Hill.

This partisanship undermined Republicans' attempts to invoke the prestige that the Judiciary Committee had gained in the Nixon impeachment proceedings. Rodino's picture was prominently displayed, Republican members privately consulted him on procedural issues (and privately praised him), and the Clinton hearings began with references to the earlier deliberations. Rodino himself, however, rejected the comparisons, concluding that "the House chose instead to taint the process from the start with a destructive partisanship while allowing a far-from-independent counsel to intrude upon the sole power of the House to impeach."[50]

The Judiciary Committee, too, had become a far more partisan —and far less attractive—arena in the intervening quarter of a century. At the time of Watergate, it had ranked seventh in appeal among twenty House committees. By 1981, it had fallen to thirteenth place— almost as lowly regarded as the District of Columbia committee. The Nixon impeachment itself had made membership precarious, with some Republican members losing reelection bids in the light of their defense of the president.[51] With the decline of the committee's prestige, "it became increasingly difficult for the leadership to fill vacancies on the panel. Eventually its size had to be reduced and the requirement that all of its members had to be lawyers was dropped."[52]

Reelection goals, always predominant among House Members, subordinated the committee's former policy attractions.[53] The Judiciary Committee became "a body on which few members chose to sit," as they sought to avoid "such hot political issues as gun control, busing and abortion." Appointments to the committee—previously relatively moderate in its membership—became subject to explicit ideological tests, restricted to Democrats who firmly supported the "right to choice" on abortion and tighter gun controls, and to Republicans who were equally adamant on the "right to life" and the "right to bear arms."[54] Any disposition to compromise had been eliminated.

By 1998, the electoral process itself had changed—not in formal terms but in reality. House Members had come to seem virtually invulnerable, as over 90 percent regularly won reelection. But this overall record of success masked uncertainty for individual representatives. No longer could they count on the support of a strong party organization, as Rodino had. The large costs of election, running close to half a million dollars per district, both required constant fundraising and raised the specter of defeat by a well-financed challenger. Special interest groups might target a representative if he or she took the "wrong" position. Even if they seemed likely to win in the general election, representatives still feared defeat in primary nomination contests, where the influence of money or a small ideological group might be decisive. The combined effect of these factors was to induce "a perpetual wariness, a constant search for those issues that might become troublesome in the next campaign."[55] The safer course was to hold rigidly to party loyalty and ideological purity.

Heightened partisanship and ideological commitment have also contributed to deterioration in the House environment, undermining the personal relationships and the institutional norms that can smooth the path of legislative accommodation. In place of institutional loyalty, "the rise of single-interest groups has made posturing almost as important as delivering. . . . The technology of the 'new' politics, moreover, encourages posturing, particularly to targeted audiences." Similarly, there has been a marked decline in the norm of reciprocity, the acceptance of compromise as an honorable and normal practice.[56] These changes to the House since the Nixon years made the Clinton impeachment a more bitter process, and the participants in it more caustic.

Nixon's removal provided precedents for the impeachment of Clinton, but the process was far different. The committee undertook no investigation on its own but instead published the Starr report, unread, on the Internet and then relied totally on its accusatory findings. Partisanship was rife. Possible compromises, such as a resolution of condemnation, were rejected by the party leadership, which insisted on a vote by the lame-duck House. After intensive pressures and divisive arguments, every Republican on the Judiciary Committee and all but five in the House voted for impeachment; their vote was precisely mirrored by the Democratic opposition. In contrast to Peter Rodino, Judiciary Committee Chair Henry Hyde, while courteous in manner, was bitter and ineffective in his efforts to persuade Democrats, the Senate, or the nation. At the end, he was "reduced to the role of Polonius, a partisan moralist, somewhat baffled and pathetic."[57] From his longer perspective, Rodino draws a critical distinction: "Hyde was appalled by the scandalousness of what had been inflicted on the public, by a president who had undoubtedly lied and shook his finger, etc. That is enough to make anyone who is red-blooded say, 'God, what am I dealing with?' But one has to be able to separate that from the command of the Constitution. And one has to remember that we are a nation of laws, not of a man. As soon as we begin to break down [that distinction], the institution of government as we know it cannot exist."

These two impeachments have changed the institutions of the United States. Rodino gave new meaning to the constitutional process of impeachment. With Nixon's unintended help, he revived an antique defense against oppressive government. In 1974, impeachment was the last, yet dreadful, defense of the Constitution. Nixon's forced resignation conveyed the same solemnity as a presidential funeral, conducted more in sorrow than in anger. Incoming president Gerald Ford spoke reassuringly of the end of "our long national nightmare."

In the case of Clinton, the Senate—an institution we will consider in the next chapter—again reflected the solemnity of a constitutional crisis. Insistent on its unique role, and attentive to the public's steady support of Clinton, the upper chamber restrained its members, restrained the media, and restrained partisanship. In deliberate deference to constitutional history, it met in the nineteenth-century Senate chamber, used nineteenth-century rules, and imposed eighteenth-century secrecy on its deliberations. It provided the only dignity evident in the sorry story. The House, in contrast, diminished the nation's political institutions. It conducted Clinton's impeachment as a mixture of bedroom farce and government run by the Marx Brothers. After Clinton's indictment and trial, impeachment could become a partisan habit, potentially as normal as the routine confrontations of budgets, press releases, and campaign debates. The long-term effect of repeated attempts at impeachment could be the decline of the dignity, autonomy, and effectiveness of the House itself.

These two tales demonstrate the impact of individuals and institutional practices. The House worked well in 1974; it bungled in 1998. Good outcomes are not inevitable, nor can successful popular government depend on great men and great women alone. It requires "democratic heroes," apparently unremarkable people who can make institutions work at extraordinary moments. In the Nixon impeachment crisis, Peter Rodino did what he would do at other times, but on a larger stage. This workhorse politician embodied the democratic heroism of a man "just doing his job."

In retirement, Peter Rodino sometimes muses on living a different life, one in which he would have pursued his love of literature, particularly poetry. He is fond of Thomas Gray's praise of ordinary but faithful workers:

> Along the cool sequester'd vale of life
> They kept the noiseless tenor of their way.

The steady chair of the House Judiciary Committee might best be remembered by other lines from the same poem that celebrate

> Some village Hampden that with dauntless breast
> The little tyrant of his fields withstood.[58]

Chapter Four
Arthur Watkins

A Hero of the Senate

In the middle of the twentieth century, American institutions and freedoms were threatened by a reckless United States senator, Joseph McCarthy, Republican of Wisconsin. For nearly five years, in the guise of a crusader against communism, he violated the civil liberties of citizens and the traditions of the Senate. A plain man—Senator Arthur Watkins, Republican of Utah—directed McCarthy's political demise. Serving as chair of the committee that brought McCarthy's censure by the Senate, Watkins is our second ordinary hero.

The Utah senator gained no lasting fame for his effort, even losing his next election in his conservative state. Few histories record his achievement; for example, in his voluminous account of the period, *The Fifties,* David Halberstam fails to mention Watkins even once. His enemies belittled him as "unremarkable . . . mild-mannered. . . . A man with a deeply conventional mind."[1] He himself shunned drama, but he played a crucial role in ending an American political tragedy. This ordinary hero was "in profession a profoundly correct lawyer, in politics a 'regular' Republican loyal to the Eisenhower Administration that McCarthy was endangering, and in moral life an almost painfully ethical Mormon. Thin, gray, sternly upright, shy, and ascetic, looking out upon his fellows from glittering rimless glasses, he had . . . a record for a kind of glacial fairness and cold objectivity, and a matchless general respectability. . . . And under the parsonical manner there was steel."[2]

Watkins had an undistinguished career before his rendezvous with McCarthy. A lawyer, farmer, and newspaper publisher, he had previously won but a single election, for district judge, and devoted most of his efforts to his Mormon church as president of a regional organization within Utah. Surprisingly, with campaign contributions of only $8,000, he was elected as U.S. Senator from a state that leaned toward the Democrats at the time. In the Senate, he concentrated on matters of direct interest to Utah, water and land reclamation, as well as immigration.

Aside from the McCarthy controversy, the Utah senator would be remembered, if at all, for another, but poor, legislative judgment. Watkins was the chief proponent of "Termination" of federal treaty obligations to American Indian tribes. Attacking the historic Indian reservations as "socialism," he "set out to dismantle the reservation system, the programs and services that supported it, and the federal bureaucracy that administered it," leaving Native Americans "without federal tax protection, education, health services, and agricultural assistance." For many tribes, said the National Congress of American Indians, the policy of termination was "the greatest threat to Indian survival since the military campaigns of the 1800s." Within twenty years, the policy was reversed, and tribal rights and property were restored. Watkins lived on, but ingloriously, in Indian memory.[3]

In his general behavior, Watkins seemed out of place in politics, particularly in the Senate, the institution that is the capstone of most American politicians' ambitions. "Mr. Watkins . . . has an air of rectitude that is all but terrifying and a man absolutely without cant," wrote William S. White of the *New York Times*. "The effect is that of a glacially cold and disinterested judge. . . . Senator Watkins, in a magnified way, has many of the traits commonly assigned to introverts. He is rather lonely, wholly abstemious, spare, dry, slightly nervous in manner and a man who could not be imagined in the act of slapping another's back."[4] Watkins' cool, deliberative manner, however, was exactly appropriate for sitting in judgment on his passionate and destructive Senate colleague. There, he brought his judicial experience and, as a committed Mormon, his ethical sensitivity to the task.

Of critical importance for this job, Watkins was dedicated to the Senate as an institution. He had dreamt that he might be tapped for the censure committee, but when this actually happened, his reaction was fear, not hope. Family members urged him to reject the appointment. "Reluctant as I was to accept the assignment," he later recalled, "I felt compelled to do so. Service in the U.S. Senate is one of the highest honors which can come to any citizen, and it has corresponding responsibilities and obligations." He met the criteria for the assignment: "Having been an 'old man' since my mid-thirties (as I used to say, because I had acquired a shock of white hair) and with conservative Republican principles and traditional Mormon ideas about hard work and integrity, I was considered serious and not at all a headline getter. I pursued my assignments in the Senate without fanfare, and liked to consider myself something of an authority on Indian matters and reclamation."[5]

Politically, Watkins shared an electoral history with McCarthy, and they even began to develop a friendship. Both were first elected in the Republican sweep of 1946: Watkins, aged sixty, narrowly, and McCarthy, only thirty-eight, overwhelmingly. Both were reelected in 1952 with a comfortable 54 percent of their states' votes, each running considerably behind Dwight Eisenhower at the top of the Republican ticket. Watkins, however, had increased his share of the vote during his first term, while McCarthy had lost support at home. In 1958, Watkins lost his seat, gaining only 35 percent of the vote, in the face of a national Democratic tide and an independent right-wing opponent. The Wisconsin Senate seat also turned over after

ARTHUR WATKINS: A HERO OF THE SENATE 61

U.S. Senator Arthur Watkins

McCarthy's death in 1957, with the Republican vote dropping to 43 percent.[6]

McCarthyism

The short but dangerous impact of Senator McCarthy began with a speech by the then-obscure senator during the party's 1950 Lincoln Day celebrations in Wheeling, West Virginia. Holding a paper in his hand, McCarthy claimed to have a list of 205 communists and other subversives currently holding positions in the State Department. By the time the story was on the news wires, McCarthy had flown to Salt Lake City, where he now claimed the list comprised

57 suspects. The number would change with the retelling, reaching 81 persons by the time McCarthy went on record in a Senate speech two weeks later.

The perceived threat from these persons would also change, as McCarthy variously described them as "members of the Communist party and members of a spy ring" or "individuals who would appear to be either card-carrying members or certainly loyal to the Communist Party" or simply "loyalty risks." Later investigations would show that his lists were outdated, containing the names of individuals who no longer worked for the government. Many of the charges were ludicrous, including such "offenses" as "entertains Negroes," "a bit Leftist," "a heavy drinker and promiscuous," and "[seen] playing bridge with members of the Soviet Embassy." But McCarthy's basic accusation would persist: the United States government had been infiltrated by agents of its number-one enemy, the Soviet Union.[7]

McCarthy's evidence was weak, derivative, and distorted—yet he drew an immense supportive response, as well as immediate attack. In June 1950, five out of six poll respondents had heard his charges; by a 61-to-31 margin, they were inclined to support his efforts.[8] One source of this support was the anxiety contemporary Americans felt about communism, both foreign and domestic. Abroad, the Soviet Union had dropped the "iron curtain," repressing democracy in central and eastern Europe, and had ended the U.S. atomic monopoly by detonating its own nuclear weapons. China, the largest nation on earth, had been conquered by the communist forces of Mao Zedong. Soon after McCarthy made his charges, U.S. ally South Korea was invaded by communist forces from North Korea. Sent to the rescue, American troops, at first audaciously triumphant, were almost driven from the peninsula in the winter by new attacks from Chinese communist troops.

Domestically, too, there were real communist threats. Spies within the national government had been uncovered, indicted, and convicted, most spectacularly Alger Hiss at the State Department and Julius and Ethel Rosenberg, who worked on the atomic bomb. With national self-confidence shaken, many Americans were receptive to McCarthy's charge that the United States was losing the cold war "not because the enemy has sent men to invade our shores, but rather because of the traitorous actions of those who have had all the benefits that the wealthiest nation on earth has had to offer."[9]

The anticommunist crusade began before McCarthy's speech, and extended further than his own efforts. The concern for "loyalty" affected persons who had no political power, "a Seattle fireman, local public housing officials, janitors, even men's room attendants," as well as teachers. "Lawyers, other professionals, and, in Indiana, even wrestlers had to document their loyalty. Colleges policed students' political activities. . . . Entertainers faced a 'blacklist.'" The sources of McCarthyism already existed. "Now all that was needed to put the anti-Red crusade into high gear was a politician ready to commit himself with reckless, career-dominating totality to the Communist issue. The junior Senator from Wisconsin would fulfill this role."[10] As Halberstam observes, "McCarthy's carnival-like four-year spree of accusations, charges, and threats touched something deep in the American body politic, something that lasted long after his own recklessness, carelessness, and boozing ended his career in shame. McCarthyism crystallized and politicized the anxieties of a nation living in a dangerous new era. He took people who were at the worst guilty of political naïveté and accused them of treason. He set out to do the unthinkable and it turned out to be surprisingly thinkable."[11]

The fear of communism and the revelations of actual Soviet espionage brought McCarthy diverse support from diverse sources. "What gave the 'ism' its bite was the political dynamic that obtained at mid-century, accentuated by the anxieties germinated by the Cold War."[12] Republicans had been out of power for twenty years and still could not accept their surprise defeat by Harry Truman—the subject of the next chapter—in the 1948 presidential election. New issues were needed to bring victory to the party; anticommunism served as both a genuine concern and a suitable strategy. Robert Taft, the ethical but partisan leader of the Republican right, exemplified the tactics. At first, he considered the charges "reckless" and "nonsense." But soon he was encouraging new attacks, advising McCarthy that "if one case doesn't work out, bring up another.... Keep it up, Joe."[13]

On more philosophical grounds, two articulate conservatives, William Buckley and Brent Bozell, found the senator's means necessary to the basic goal:

> America . . . has turned to the offense against Communism. We are at war, and there are many strategies, many tactics, many weapons, many courses of action open to us. . . . One thing is certain: Communism will not be defeated—any more than freedom was won—by postulating the virtues of democracy and of Christianity as evident truths and letting it go at that. McCarthyism, then, is a weapon in the American arsenal. . . . As long as McCarthyism fixes its goal with its present precision, it is a movement around which men of good will and stern morality can close ranks.[14]

Building on the nation's anxieties and resentments, McCarthy cast himself as a lone crusader against the destruction of America. Yet even as he stormed the alleged bastions of subversion, he often seemed to be acting a role—part villain, part crusader, even part comic, but never the diligent investigator. One informed journalist saw through the charade: "Joe couldn't find a Communist in Red Square—he didn't know Karl Marx from Groucho."[15]

McCarthy's charges and investigations would dominate American politics for the next five years and affect the nation for decades. A professor at Johns Hopkins University was "revealed" to be the "top Russian agent." President Truman's actions in the Korean War were explained as drunkenness, the influence of "bourbon and benedictine." McCarthy told the secretary of state to "remove yourself from this country and go to the nation for which you have been struggling and fighting so long." George Marshall, the architect of America's victory in the Second World War, was denounced for his procommunist activities, in "a conspiracy so immense and an infamy so black as to dwarf any previous venture in the history of man."[16]

But McCarthy's impact went beyond individual slander. His agents inspected overseas libraries of the State Department, leading to the removal and occasional burning of books by such "subversive" authors as Mark Twain. Government employees were encouraged to raid official files, including confidential records, to provide material for his crusade. Citizens, military officers, and civil servants were denounced in public and in Senate speeches, humiliated in testimony, and driven from their jobs. Prodded by McCarthy, both the Truman and Eisenhower administrations developed security programs that removed thousands of persons from government service. "McCarthy created a national environment of fear and suspicion, evident in all branches of government," Senator Margaret Chase Smith remembered. "McCarthy had created an atmosphere of such political fear that people were not only afraid to talk but they were afraid of whom they might be seen with. Dozens of State Department employees were pilloried by McCarthy under the cloak of senatorial immunity with unproved accusations and smeared with guilt-by-association and guilt-by-accusation tactics. This great psychological fear even spread to the Senate, where a considerable amount of mental paralysis and muteness set in for fear of offending McCarthy."[17]

McCarthy's baleful influence extended more broadly, into the entire society—to the mass media, private corporations, universities, and even the sports world—bringing with it "loyalty" investigations and ruined careers. To summarize his political effects: "He held two Presidents captive. . . . He had enormous impact on American foreign policy at a time when that policy bore heavily on the course of world history. . . . In the Senate, his headquarters and his hiding place, he assumed the functions of the Committee of the Whole; he lived in thoroughgoing contempt of the Congress of which he was a member, of the rules it made for itself and—whenever they ran contrary to his purposes—of the laws it had enacted for the general welfare."[18]

McCarthy gained added power as the result of widespread perceptions regarding his electoral influence. Senator Millard Tydings of Maryland chaired an investigation of the first accusations of communist influence in the State Department, dismissed the charges as baseless—and then lost his bid for reelection after McCarthy campaigned against him. Senator William Benton of Connecticut took the lead in denouncing McCarthy and then also lost his next election. In all, McCarthy was credited (or blamed) for the replacement of eight liberal Democrats by conservative Republicans. Later analysis would show, however, that McCarthy's support was essentially coextensive with that of the Republican Party, that he had little independent effect on his opponents' races, and that he was "more dependent on his party, and personally much less effective at the grass roots than has been commonly supposed."[19] At the time, however, the belief in McCarthy's electoral potency was more important than the realities revealed by later academic analysis.

The Defeat of McCarthy

As an individual, Joe McCarthy was probably doomed to fail, although the antisubversive cause he exemplified would persist. The Wisconsin senator had no comprehensive political program and no secure political base, and he lacked the extensive organizational skills needed to launch and sustain a long-term movement. In retrospect, we can see that McCarthy's decline resulted from a combination of long- and short-term factors. The simple passage of time reduced the threats that he exploited. Whatever the extent of actual subversion within the national government, and however it was exaggerated, the nation prospered economically and maintained a strong international position against the communist world. If McCarthy's political demise was likely, however, it was not predestined. It awaited human intervention through institutional processes; it required democratic heroism.

Margaret Chase Smith involuntarily demonstrated that necessity. A Republican from Maine, Smith was the first senator to speak out against McCarthy. Only three months after McCarthy's first foray, she found his charges baseless and deplored "the way in which the Senate has been made a publicity platform for irresponsible sensationalism." Recruiting six other Republican senators, she issued a "Declaration of Conscience." In it and in her first speech to the Senate, she defended "basic principles of Americanism—the right to criticize; the right to hold unpopular beliefs, the right to protest; the right of independent thought"—while opposing unnamed Republicans for their "selfish political exploitation of fear, bigotry, ignorance, and intolerance."[20] The reference to McCarthy was clear, although Senate rules would not allow him to be identified.

Smith's avowal was hailed by the liberal press, earning her a cover story in *Newsweek,* and was also commended, albeit off the record, by a number of senators. In the context of the times, it was courageous simply to endorse schoolbook virtues and to criticize McCarthy even in an indirect manner; all but one of Smith's cosigners soon ran for cover. Her action, however, was not an unalloyed expression of pure principle. Both Smith and the declaration itself criticized the Democrats and President Harry Truman as much as

McCarthy and accepted his premise that subversives had infiltrated the government. The Maine senator reiterated her criticisms in the following years, but she led no campaign against McCarthy. Instead of winning praise, she met rejection by the national party as a possible vice-presidential nominee and suffered isolation in the Senate, where she was required repeatedly to defend herself against McCarthy's petty retaliations, including the denial of her preferred committee assignments.[21]

In 1950, Smith's sex alone excluded her from the Senate club, where she was the only woman. (Illustrating the exclusion, there were no conveniently located lavatories for female senators until the 1990s.) McCarthy felt safe in ignoring her charges and in ridiculing the signers of the declaration as "Snow White and her Six Dwarfs."[22] At the time, women were generally rare in political office. Smith was the first of her sex to be elected to the chamber without a previous appointment as a widowed successor, and she shattered gender stereotypes by becoming expert in military affairs. Eventually, she became a respected figure in the Senate and briefly attempted a presidential candidacy. Smith's career opened up politics for other women, but these larger political opportunities would come only later, after her own defeat for reelection in 1972.

Smith had seen herself as a hero in the McCarthy struggle, "battling the forces of darkness, a script which had all but vanished for women with V-E day. . . . It was an extension of her search for a larger life, and the natural outcome of decades spent in pursuit of a quest plot."[23] But Smith, however admirable personally, could not be the hero who would defeat McCarthy. The time was not yet right, because McCarthy was regarded as too powerful to oppose and because he served the partisan interests of Republicans. Moreover, the person was not right, in the institutional context of the Senate. Smith was only a freshman, barely into her second year, and she was belittled because her political career had begun, in the House, as the congressional successor to her late husband. Removing the McCarthy threat would require a senator who better fit the institutional mold. It would, in those days of unquestioned gender inequality, require a man, and particularly a man like Arthur Watkins.

That effort would wait four years, however. The political environment changed significantly after the election of Dwight Eisenhower in 1952, when McCarthy confronted a Republican administration. His antigovernment campaign no longer served the interests of his party, and to levy charges of subversion against the commander of the triumphant military forces of World War II would be ludicrous. Eisenhower tried at first to accommodate McCarthy, although this later gave way to silent scorn. In fact, during the presidential campaign, the Republican candidate had gone so far in his accommodation as to delete a defense of his mentor, General George Marshall, from a speech in Wisconsin. Refusing to "get down in the gutter with that guy," the new president also sought to neutralize McCarthy, writing in his diary: "I believe nothing will be so effective in combating this particular kind of trouble-making as to ignore him. This he cannot stand."[24]

Then, in early 1954, the proper occasion for action arose, as McCarthy's standing declined in public opinion polls; unfavorable opinions now led favorable comments by 47 percent to 32 percent.[25] In a reckless move, he assailed the United States Army for alleged laxity in its antisubversive actions, particularly those of a base commander, General Ralph Zwicker. Attacks on entertainers or civil servants might be tolerated, but the military was held in far greater esteem. When McCarthy "took on another pillar of national virtue and responsibility, the United States Army," he became endangered—and "he was especially vulnerable because he struck at the army in a way that seemed to involve a self-interested game of extortion."[26] McCarthy, it developed, had tried to gain favored treatment for his committee aide, David Schine. The resulting controversy led to two months of televised hearings before the very Senate subcommittee usually chaired by McCarthy.

At the hearings, Richard Fried commented, "Joe came across as boorish, disruptive (with incessant 'points of order'), and anarchic. . . . It was brute soap opera, not a civics lesson. Poll data showed few viewers reaching civil-libertarian conclusions; rather, they saw McCarthy as a bad guy, a bully, and a loser."[27] The climax came when the senator attacked a young assistant to Joseph Welch, the army's lawyer, for alleged subversive activities. Welch's televised outrage destroyed McCarthy's moral authority: "Until this moment, Senator, I think I never really gauged your cruelty or your recklessness. . . . Little did I dream you could be so reckless and so cruel as to do an injury to that lad. . . . I fear he shall always bear a scar needlessly inflicted by you. Let us not assassinate this lad further, Senator. You have done enough. Have you no sense of decency, sir, at long last? Have you left no sense of decency?"[28]

Behind the scenes, Eisenhower helped the anti-McCarthy forces. He participated in development of a chronology of McCarthy's interventions with the army, in a maneuver to change Senate committee rules so as to end McCarthy's ability to issue subpoenas unilaterally, and in preparation for Army Secretary Robert Stevens's testimony. As the hearings became "a marathon televised exposure of McCarthy's uncivil comportment," the president found surrogates—including anticommunist avatar Richard Nixon—who would directly attack McCarthy, while the president remained above the fray, refusing to engage in personal attacks.[29] McCarthy was wounded, but not yet fatally. Americans still believed that there were communists in the government and that they presented a significant danger to the country, and substantial proportions would accept McCarthy's rather than Eisenhower's views on the subject.[30] The defeat of McCarthy would come not from defending abstract principles concerning civil liberties, but from defending the institution of the United States Senate.

Condemnation of McCarthy began with a resolution proposed by a Republican moderate, Ralph Flanders of Vermont, who proposed to censure McCarthy and to strip him of his chairmanship. The penalty was too severe for senators worried about McCarthy's presumed electoral clout and too personally threatening to Southern Democrats, long-serving beneficiaries of the principle of seniority. Instead, a list of specific charges was developed and then referred to a special committee chaired by Arthur Watkins. The anti-McCarthy forces were dismayed by this plan, since "virtually everyone assumed" that McCarthy "would dominate this hearing by the force of his aggressive personality and his take-over tactics, as he had every other proceeding." As a Washington joke had it, "the lion has been thrown into a den of lambs."[31] But Watkins was a different animal.

The panel was deliberately composed of noncontroversial figures, many with judicial experience, who had been approved by both parties' leaders. Most of them were drawn from southern and mountain states where McCarthy had limited support, and none faced immediate reelection. The outcome was thus uncertain. In the opinion of the *New York Times,* "Senator McCarthy's greatest danger, in the view of veteran Senators not necessarily against him now, would come to him if he made any attack on the integrity of the panel."[32] But McCarthy failed to heed the warning.

Watkins set firm rules for the hearing, based on judicial rules of evidence, and banished television cameras. He established that either McCarthy or his counsel, but not both, could speak to any particular point and that all statements must be pertinent to the charges. Despite the rules, McCarthy attempted to begin the proceedings with an attack on one of its members. Watkins firmly indicated that he would insist on these strict procedures: "I pounded the gavel, and continued to pound the gavel as Senator McCarthy tried to speak. . . . Finally, he gave up the attempt, (I believe) flabbergasted. After the recess, he was recorded as saying: 'This is the most unheard of thing I ever heard of.' . . . Having silenced Senator McCarthy for speaking out of turn and ruling that material not pertinent to the inquiry could not be injected, we set the tone for the remainder of the hearings."[33]

The committee pared the indictment against McCarthy to five general charges. While critical of his conduct, it did not recommend censure on three of these grounds: encouraging federal employees to send him confidential material, unlawful use of FBI files, and personal abuse of Senator Flanders. It recommended censure on two counts: contempt toward the Senate Privileges and Elections subcommittee that had investigated McCarthy after the 1950 election, and abusive treatment of General Zwicker.[34] The report was filed in late September 1954, but the Senate waited to act until the fall elections were over.

The defeat of several pro-McCarthy candidates provided new evidence of the senator's declining standing with the voters. Opinion polls also now supported Senate action in defense of the institution itself. Over a third of the respondents (37 percent) said that McCarthy's activities had decreased their respect for the Senate, but the public was now paying attention to the Senate's response (55 percent knew about the Watkins report) and, by a 49 percent to 24 percent margin, thought the committee had been fair. There was no groundswell of sentiment in the nation, but the public now supported censure, 47 percent to 34 percent.[35] The Senate could now accept the political risks.

McCarthy made the task simpler by his vitriolic characterizations of the committee and of Watkins: "deliberate deception," "fraud," "a lynch party," a "kangaroo court," a "packed jury," "cowardly," "stupid," and "the involuntary handmaidens," "involuntary agent," and "attorneys in fact" of the Communist Party. Watkins later came to believe that McCarthy "deliberately began to seek censure," in hopes "of becoming the political leader—the nationalist hero—of a cross-party-lines faction or even a third party."[36] Whatever his ambitions, McCarthy would not give senators an easy way out by simply agreeing to sign an apology for his remarks. Instead, he threw the pen offered to him across the room.[37] He did concede sarcastically that it was not "proper" to describe the Watkins committee as communist "handmaidens"—but only because handmaidens were women, while all the committee members were men.

In the formal debate, Watkins called his colleagues to account, virtually shaming them into supporting the censure resolutions. In his concluding speech, he invoked the honor of the Senate:

> Mr. President, I regret that I do not have a voice as heavy and as loud as have some of the speakers who have preceded me in this debate. If I attempted to make it possible for everyone present to hear me, I would have to shout, and then it might be thought that I was angry. I should like to be dispassionate in this discussion, even though it involves my own honor. I wish to speak in tones of moderation. . . .
>
> Senators have seen what I have called to their attention, an attack on their representative, their agent. They have seen an attack made on that agent's courage and intelligence. They have heard the junior senator from Wisconsin say that I am both stupid and a coward.

He concluded with a simple challenge: "I am asking my colleagues: What are you going to do about it?"[38]

Senators finally accepted the challenge, but reluctantly, and on the narrowest grounds. The Senate "defined the issue as disruptive behavior and violations of decorum, not 'McCarthyism' in the broad sense. The key participants in the debate were not the liberals who might have waged a fight on such grounds but instead members of the Senate inner circle who emphasized how McCarthy had damaged the Upper Chamber's dignity."[39] At the last moment, the count involving General Zwicker was dropped, replaced by a new count denouncing McCarthy's attacks on the Watkins committee itself.

On December 2, 1954, by a vote of 67 to 22, McCarthy was "condemned," without specific use of the synonym, "censured." All forty-four Democrats who voted supported the resolution, along with exactly half of the forty-four voting Republicans, and one Independent. Two other Democrats stated their support, matched by two Republicans declaring their opposition. Two unannounced senators worried about McCarthy support in their home states: Alexander Wiley of Wisconsin, the Republican chair of the Foreign Relations Committee, and John F. Kennedy, who ironically would soon publish *Profiles in Courage,* a history of senators who had voted their consciences in defiance of public opinion.[40]

The Senate action by no means constituted a ringing endorsement of civil liberties; beyond the respect for principle, the vote evidenced political timidity. Senators continued to worry about the possible harm from the censure to their careers. Even Watkins tried to appease a McCarthy follower, describing the vote as simply a "formal slap on the wrist, a pointed reminder" of unacceptable conduct, while expressing the disingenuous belief that, if McCarthy changed, he could do "an even more effective job of coping with Communists than he did before." Still, the deed was done. "With this thin stick, the dog of McCarthyism was beaten. . . . The censure wrote *finis* to McCarthy's five years as a figure of moment. Though it condemned him only for violating Senate 'club' rules, it marked a point of no return."[41]

McCarthy's influence ebbed rapidly. President Eisenhower had ostentatiously stayed out of the censure debate, reiterating up to the day of the vote that, "this is a matter of the Senate . . . determining what is required in the preservation of the dignity of the Senate, and no one else is in it." The day after the vote, however, Eisenhower invited Watkins to the White House, praised his handling of the hearings, and arranged for publicity concerning the meeting, including photographs of the president congratulating Watkins. McCarthy retreated to the Senate floor, to "apologize" for his "mistaken" belief that the Republican administration would wage a "vigorous forceful fight against Communists in government." With this implicit attack on Eisenhower, "McCarthy's prominence virtually dissolved. . . . Other senators immediately fell into the traditional pattern of ostracism, refusing to talk to him or even answer his questions."[42]

Politicians avoided and pitied him but no longer dreaded him. Eisenhower told his cabinet a new joke: "McCarthyism was now 'McCarthywasm.'" The only senator not invited to formal White House receptions, he was now also ignored by the press that had fueled his rise to fame. In a reversal of fortune, former associates shunned him as avidly as acolytes had once cheered his inquisitions and as fearfully as fence-sitters had avoided his wrath. Nixon dropped him from a campaign event in Milwaukee in 1956; FBI Director J. Edgar Hoover ended his contact with McCarthy. Less than three years after the Senate censure, heavy drinking led to McCarthy's death, at the age of forty-eight, from cirrhosis of the liver. By then, the press had come to ignore the erstwhile headliner. In death as in life, "If nothing else, he had illuminated the timidity of his fellow man."[43]

Watkins himself lost his next election, in 1958, despite Eisenhower's strong endorsement, when a former governor, well financed by conservatives, drew a quarter of the vote. He was then nominated by Eisenhower to chair the Indian Claims Committee and was unanimously confirmed "within minutes" by the Senate. As he happily reflected later: "I found a quieter, more healthful life, and greater net income."[44] In that calm environment, Arthur Watkins might remember how he overcame his own timidity to become an ordinary hero.

The Senate as an Institution

The decline of McCarthy was not only the result of a personal effort but also a historic demonstration of the character of the Senate, which again illustrates the interaction of individuals and institutions. At that time, far more than today, the chamber paid special deference to "Senate men" who displayed particular personal traits: "tolerance for others, courteousness, prudence, and willingness to help others, to work hard, to compromise, and to keep one's word."[45] These traits were certainly not evident among all senators, or even among all effective senators, but they were the features of the idealized legislator. Watkins exemplified these characteristics, while McCarthy provided a marked contrast. Closely related to these traits was the behavior expected of senators. Writing shortly after the McCarthy years, Donald Matthews defined the interpersonal rules of the Senate as the "unwritten but generally accepted and informally enforced norms of conduct in the chamber."[46] McCarthy had violated almost all of them, and these violations were the core of the Senate's condemnation.

Senate norms are similar, although not identical, to those of the House. In many respects, these norms are even more important in the upper chamber, because the Senate is less structured, smaller, and comprises more prominent individuals.[47] With fewer and more prominent members, personal interactions become more intimate and more delicate. With less structure, informal norms become more important than formal rules in regulating behavior. The character of the Senate as a legislative body is encapsulated in the traditions of unlimited debate and the filibuster, which allow these solons wide latitude in pressing their particular interests. To make the Senate effective, the members must exhibit considerable self-restraint and mutual consideration. Senate norms alone, however, were insufficient and unenforceable as restraints on McCarthy. Their limitations had been demonstrated by the futility of Senator Smith's attack. Her judgments might be both right and righteous, but her colleagues ignored the protest. Good words would fail until senators such as Watkins were ready for good acts.

Matthews listed six basic norms of the chamber. "The first rule of Senate behavior—and the one most widely recognized off the Hill—is that new members are expected to serve an unobtrusive apprenticeship. . . . The new senator is expected to keep his mouth shut, not to take the lead in floor fights, to listen and to learn. Like children . . . [to] be seen and not heard." But McCarthy had made his first charges only three years after taking office and was most clamorous during this first term. In addition, as in the House, Senate esteem is gained by "highly detailed, dull and politically unrewarding" legislative work. "Those who do not carry their share of the legislative burden or who appear to subordinate this responsibility to a quest for publicity and personal advancement are held in disdain." In contrast, McCarthy subordinated any legislative work, including the chairmanship of his own subcommittee on investigations, to his personal quest. Furthermore, according to the norms a senator "ought to specialize, to focus his energies and attention on the relatively few matters that come before his committees or that directly and immediately affect his state." McCarthy did little for his state. While he cast himself as a specialist in internal security, he roamed widely through the government, encroaching on foreign policy, the military, and the full range of cabinet departments.

Courtesy is "a cardinal rule of Senate behavior," mandating that "political disagreements should not influence personal feelings." As McCarthy eventually learned, "personal attacks, unnecessary unpleasantness, pursuing a line of thought or action that might embarrass a colleague needlessly, are all thought to be self-defeating. . . . They also suggest, despite partisan differences, that one senator should hesitate to campaign against another." His direct electoral attacks on colleagues—thought to be successful—made McCarthy a dreaded figure, but also intensely disliked. Along with courtesy, another basic principle in the chamber is reciprocity. "Every senator, at one time or another, is in a position to help out a colleague. The folkways of the Senate hold that a senator ought to provide this assistance—and that he be repaid in kind. . . . The spirit of reciprocity results in much, if not most, of the senators' actual power not being exercised." In contrast, McCarthy pushed his powers as committee chair to the limit.

Institutional patriotism, the most important norm, was a critical factor in the McCarthy censure. "Senators are expected to *believe* that they belong to the greatest legislative and deliberative body in the world. They are expected to be a bit suspicious of the President and the bureaucrats and just a little disdainful of the House. They are expected to revere the Senate's personnel, organization and folkways and to champion them to the outside world. . . . One who brings the Senate as an institution or senators as a class into public disrepute invites his own destruction as an effective legislator." McCarthy's disrespect for the Senate, not his attacks on individuals or his assault on civil liberties, brought about his downfall. Watkins pressed this institutional concern when he presented the censure resolution, and he continued to emphasize the issue years later in his autobiography:

> Every Senator has the duty to respect and maintain the dignity, honor, authority, and powers of the Senate. . . . When a Senator takes the oath of office to defend and support the Constitution of the United States, that pledge is not merely with reference to a document containing certain words. When a Senator does or says things which injure those institutions, he is violating his oath to defend and uphold the living Constitution of the United States.

It was not McCarthy's insufficiencies of character, as appalling as they may well have been, but scorn for senatorial courtesies and procedures, for his actions and words on the floor of the Senate of the United States, and for his abuse of his fellow senators—who were discharging their committee responsibilities—which were condemned by his fellow Senators.[48]

McCarthy obviously did not conform to the norms of the 1950s' Senate. His dissidence stemmed partially from his personality but also from his political position. Norms develop because they promote the goals of an institution—in the case of the Senate, the articulation of constituency interests and effective legislation. They will persist, however, only if they serve the goals of the individual members—reelection, advancement in the Senate, and the success of desired public policies.[49] McCarthy did gain advantages from some Senate practices, particularly seniority, which protected his subcommittee chairmanship. The unspoken norms, however, were of little importance to him. He had few specific legislative goals, so he could disregard norms of apprenticeship, specialization, hard work, reciprocity, and courtesy. His ambitions were primarily reelection or national leadership, and his policy focus was on the executive branch, giving him little reason to boost the institutional standing of the Senate. Indeed, he might have thought to use his contempt toward the Senate to bolster these alternate ambitions.

Even in his time, nonconformity was more likely to be seen among those senators seeking higher office, those seeking political change, and those opposing "the status quo in the chamber [and] generally conservative policies."[50] McCarthy's challenge to Senate norms was consistent with his developing national ambitions. Moreover, although McCarthy would be considered an ideological conservative, in institutional terms he was a radical, and therefore less accepting of established practices. For its part, the upper chamber had few means to enforce its norms. The Senate did not choose its own members, and it certainly lacked the will, or even the legal justification, to expel him.

McCarthy, despite his condemnation and rapid decline, contributed to a change in the Senate, for good or ill. He was ultimately an unwelcome alien in the Senate; nevertheless, he may have initiated the construction of an alternative and valued senate role, that of the "outsider," soon exemplified by his Wisconsin successor, William Proxmire.[51] Like the policy liberals he scorned, he was "dependent on the support of broad, often unorganized groups which can be reached only through the mass media." He may have pointed the way to later changes in the Senate norms, related to the spread of party competition, the greater role of the mass media, and larger constituencies.[52]

Today's Senate is a different chamber, because of changes in the political environment, such as the expansion of interest group activity, the increased role of the mass media, and the rise of new issues. The seniority principle of the 1950s, and virtually all of the norms except personal courtesy, are far less evident. While the chamber has become a more open forum for the articulation of diverse interests, it has become less effective in making decisions. In the contemporary body, writes a leading political scientist, "members are accorded very wide latitude. . . . The typical senator no longer specializes; he becomes involved in a broad range of issues, including ones that do not fall into the jurisdiction of his committees. . . . He is also more active on the Senate floor and often makes use of public arenas as well. He is less deferential to anyone and much less restrained in using the powers granted to him by the rules of the Senate."[53] In today's Senate, McCarthy's behavior would still be reprehensible, but it would be less strange. We can only speculate whether this different, less autonomous institution would also be less ready than it was in 1954 to defend itself against a new McCarthy.

McCarthy in Retrospect

Nearly half a century later, the baleful effects of McCarthyism can easily be forgotten. Indeed, the Wisconsin senator has been rehabilitated by some who seek to continue the cold war even after the disappearance of communism. Recent revelations from Soviet archives provide definitive documentation of communist espionage in the United States carried out by Alger Hiss and other Americans.[54] The proof of communist spying is used to validate McCarthy's investigations. Later events, such as protests against the Vietnam War, then become the senator's real-world nightmare: "American liberals and radicals allying themselves with domestic Communists on one side and with foreign totalitarians on the other."[55]

This rehabilitation is weakly grounded, however. The Soviet archives actually provide no evidence of disloyalty on the part of McCarthy's particular targets that would exonerate him or excuse his attacks. McCarthy accused persons who were not spies, while the true spies were not found by McCarthy. What remains as his harmful heritage is the damage done by his investigations to the quality of American policymaking. McCarthy's definitive biographer, David Oshinsky, renders the most charitable, but still negative, verdict available when he finds McCarthy's impact limited: "He had no desire to lead a movement, to run for higher office, or to formulate a program that went beyond the simple exposure of Communists. . . . He was not a would-be dictator. He did not threaten our constitutional system, but did hurt many who lived under it."[56] Yet there were great and real costs.

Loyal citizens, both prominent and common, were slandered, harassed, and driven from their jobs and denied personal security. Beyond the costs to individuals, there was major damage to the United States. Many able people were discharged, depriving the nation of their talents and advice. Those who remained in government service became more cautious and less venturesome in their actions. Moreover, American foreign policy toward the communist world after McCarthy was rigidified in a posture of hostility. "Democrats would spend the next thirty years proving that they were not soft on Communism, and that they would not lose a country to the Communists." A basic explanation for the disaster of American intervention in Vietnam was the fear of a Democratic president, Lyndon Johnson, who remembered "how Truman lost China and then the Congress and the White House. . . . Johnson was not going to be the President who lost Vietnam and then the Congress and the White House."[57] In the end, however, the United States not only "lost" Vietnam, but over fifty thousand of its youth.

Most importantly, McCarthy—and his allies—curbed the free speech that is critical to democratic self-government. Dissent and disagreement became disloyalty and danger. McCarthy thus left a base legacy to America. He brought a new word to the nation's language, "McCarthyism," as he illustrated its corrupting meaning: "the practice of publicly accusing a person or persons of procommunist activity, corruption, or disloyalty to the government, such charges being made usually without substantiating evidence," or, more broadly, "unethical investigative techniques."[58] Others would adopt the practice, some continuing the anticommunist crusade from the right, others pursuing political correctness from the left.

McCarthy's censure, however, did bring improvements. Some reputations were rescued, some persons were able to return to their careers. In calmer times, the Supreme Court loosened some of the restrictions of the 1950s.[59] Republican and Democratic presidents alike moved the nation toward détente with the communist powers until the Cold War ended with the collapse of the Soviet Union. The Senate returned to its decorous ways, able to handle even the Clinton impeachment with relative dignity and courtesy. Ironically, McCarthy may also have contributed to the later defense of civil liberties. In grave contrast to his unsubstantiated anxieties, the terrorist hijackings of September 11, 2001, were truly destructive attacks on the United States. Those attacks could have brought severe repression and did, in fact, lead to the passage of legislation and administrative actions by the attorney general that threatened to violate individual rights. Even in this real emergency, however, legislators and judges recalled the excesses of McCarthyism and held the potential repression in check.[60] The nation remembered the lessons learned from McCarthy, and from Watkins as well.

Arthur Watkins has neither a dictionary entry nor any material memorial to mark his role in initiating these liberating trends. He simply took on the task, reluctantly but dutifully, of defending the Senate, the exemplar of open and respectful debate. He did the heroic job of guarding an institution of a free America.

Chapter Five
Harry Truman

A Hero as President

Of all American institutions, the presidency would seem most likely to house the traditional hero, the exceptional individual of outstanding talent. Presidents embody the myths of the United States. Washington exemplifies honesty in his apocryphal admission that he felled a cherry tree. Lincoln personifies the nation's commitment to equality and democracy. Theodore Roosevelt speaks forever of American daring. Franklin Roosevelt symbolizes successful struggle against both personal disability and foreign enemies. We enshrine presidents in monuments and mountain carvings, see their faces daily on our currency, and define our history by their terms in office.

As head of state, the president commands the dignity and respect paid to a crowned king. Expected to embody the loftiest virtues, he is the high priest of the American civil religion—comforting the distressed in times of catastrophe, asking the blessing of God while invoking the national faith in rituals of patriotism, forgiving sins through an unrestricted power to pardon criminals. Once inaugurated in office, much like a deity, his personal name is never spoken: his identity is merged with the impersonal role of "Mr. President." His home is a national landmark, he has a large individual police force, and his arrival is heralded by the honorific music of "Hail to the Chief."

At the same time, the president is the head of the government.

The Constitution endows him with a panoply of powers—chief executive, the sole American voice in diplomacy, commander-in-chief of the armed forces, caretaker of "the state of the union." Legislation adds to these powers, giving the president authority to appoint the federal government's administrators, to force strikers back to work, to prosecute crimes, to issue regulations that affect almost every life, even to initiate world destruction through nuclear war. We credit and blame presidents for the major events of our history. By such individual accounts, Washington was father to his country, Lincoln saved the Union and freed the slaves, Hoover caused the great Depression and FDR ended it, George H. W. Bush won the Gulf War, and Bill Clinton created the longest economic expansion in U.S. history.

The portrait of the president as storybook hero was skillfully drawn by Woodrow Wilson, who wrote as a scholar of the presidency before he himself assumed the office: "His is the only national voice in affairs. Let him once win the admiration and confidence of the country, and no single force can withstand him, no combination of forces will easily overpower him. His position takes the imagination of the country. He is the representative of no constituency, but of the whole people. When he speaks in his true character, he speaks for no special interest. If he rightly interprets the national thought and boldly insists upon it, he is irresistible."[1]

But in fact presidents are unlikely to be supermen—nor will future women presidents be superwomen. Some presidents have indeed been exceptional people, and sometimes they were personally responsible for exceptional actions. But the general point of this book remains true. No nation, including the United States, can survive if it must depend on the chance that a Lincoln will be available in every crisis as significant as the Civil War. Successful government must be based, as Madison insisted, on ordinary leaders doing well in their accustomed jobs.

The presidential hero of this chapter was not a superman. After a limited education and an unsuccessful business career, he came to the White House uninformed and unprepared for the decisions he would face. He was mocked by the opposition party, which controlled both houses of Congress as it confidently prepared to oust him from office, and was also attacked by strong factions within his own party. He was often coarse in his language, inelegant in his appearance and speech, and nasty toward his critics. When he left office, he had one of the lowest public opinion ratings in the history of the presidency and few defenders even among his party's leaders.

Yet Harry S. Truman was a hero, because he made one of the most important decisions in presidential history, the creation of the Marshall Plan for European recovery after the Second World War. An ordinary man did what he modestly called "that job in the White House"—with extraordinary benefit to the nation and the world.[2] Truman was not likely to achieve his goal because of his personal allure. An artillery officer of modest rank in the First World War, his return to Missouri brought business failures and then a political career through the sponsorship of Tom Pendergast, the state machine's "boss." Elected to the U.S. Senate in 1935, he gained the quiet respect of his colleagues and of political insiders as the chair of a committee that oversaw defense contracts during World War II. Despite this achievement, however, and his standing as a member of the liberal wing of the Democratic party, he lacked a national constituency.

He became president through a combination of party compromise and historical chance. Truman was nominated as vice president in 1944 as the result of closed dealings among party bosses and over his own objections, simply because he was an acceptable substitute for the erratic incumbent, Henry Wallace.[3] "As so consistently through the Truman career, it had been the system of politics, the boss system, that counted in deciding his fate. There had been no

President Harry S. Truman

popular boom for him for Vice President. Nor had personal ambition figured."[4] After Roosevelt's election to a fourth term, Truman became an "accidental president," succeeding to the office on FDR's death in April 1945. In his brief tenure as vice president, he visited the White House infrequently and was scarcely informed on vital national issues, most dramatically the development of the atomic bomb.

As he sadly assumed the presidency, Truman exhibited personal modesty, even spending nights away from the White House for a time. On his first day in office, he spoke to reporters:

> "Boys," I said, "if you ever pray, pray for me. . . . I felt like the moon, the stars, and all the planets had fallen on me. I've got the most terribly responsible job a man ever had."

"Good luck, Mr. President," said one of the reporters.
"I wish you didn't have to call me that," I told him.[5]

That modesty was also evident as the Marshall Plan was being drafted and submitted to Congress. Writing to his wife, Bess, he wondered: "I can't see why it was necessary for me to inherit all difficulties and tribulations of the world—but I have them on hand and must work them out some way—I hope for the welfare of all concerned."[6]

To his critics, such humility was appropriate. A sarcastic columnist lamented: "For twelve years we had the champion of the common man in the White House. And now we have the common man." Truman likewise deprecated his strengths: "Without my glasses I was blind as a bat, and to tell the truth I was kind of a sissy. If ever there was any danger of getting into a fight, I always ran."[7] Any chief executive coming to office after the titanic figure of FDR would appear diminished, but Truman exaggerated the difference. In place of the aristocratic, confident, and dominating victor in depression and war, the occupant of the White House would now be a commonplace, admittedly uncertain man without breeding, a college education, or any special achievement outside of politics, and a politician who lacked an electoral mandate. Even a sympathetic scholar has to conclude that Truman "was no Roosevelt. . . . He communicated no vision to the nation of how he proposed to address its domestic woes. His addresses lacked dramatic flair, his delivery was halting, and his flat Missouri accent contrasted painfully with Roosevelt's deep senority."[8]

Beyond these personal limitations, the historical moment did not auger well for an attempt on Truman's part to assume leadership on policy. The American government had been transformed under his charismatic predecessor, FDR, but new initiatives would probably have to await new times. The nation had reached a consensual plateau on public issues, "an environment of policy and politics marked by a high degree of continuity."[9] Truman's historical moment resembled that of other times of relative consensus, when the president would not be expected to transform the nation but, less ambitiously, as Skowronek writes, to "galvanize political action with promises to continue the good work of the past and demonstrate the vitality of the established order in changing times."[10] Truman would be expected at most to articulate and consolidate the programs of the New Deal and to press toward final victory in war. Minimizing the impact of Truman's tenure as president, two major scholars conclude: "The list of great presidents ends with FDR. . . . [Truman] represented the consolidation and continuity of FDR's project, not change. Indeed the election of Harry Truman in 1948 is best understood as FDR's greatest political triumph."[11]

The immediate political situation was also unpromising. Within his own party, Truman was unpopular and feuded openly with Secretary of State James Byrnes, who had been his unsuccessful rival for the vice-presidential nomination. Worse, the Democrats had suffered a severe defeat in the 1946 congressional elections, losing control of both houses, as Republicans gained 13 seats in the Senate and 55 in the House. The common assumption at the time was that Republicans would certainly win the 1948 presidential election, with Truman "relegated, thereby, to the role of caretaker-on-term."[12] Yet Truman was an avowed partisan, with little regard for the Republicans. Even as he would seek their support for the Marshall Plan, he would privately complain to his wife: "Here I am confronted with a violently opposition Congress whose committees with few exceptions are living in 1890. It is not representative of the country's thinking at all."[13]

Truman's success on the Marshall Plan differs considerably from his record on other issues. He failed to gain passage of any significant measure in his domestic Fair Deal program. Clumsiness on the part of his administration contributed to the narrow failure of the effort to win repeal of the new Taft-Hartley labor law, a central issue in the 1948 election (and the one that brought Peter Rodino to the House).[14] On another issue, by instituting a loyalty program in the executive branch, he provided ammunition for Joseph McCarthy's rampage, described in the previous chapter.

The president also made mistakes in foreign policy. The best example is his response to the invasion of South Korea, or the Republic of Korea, by communist North Korea in June 1950. With the sanction of the United Nations, Truman immediately committed American troops to repel the communist aggression. Within three months, after a daring military maneuver by General Douglas MacArthur, the invaders were turned back. Then military triumph turned into political tragedy. Relying on MacArthur's overconfident analysis, Truman changed the war's aim from ending the communist aggression to unifying Korea under a noncommunist government. The administration ignored warnings of Chinese intervention, which soon followed, almost driving American troops from the peninsula. American policy was based on assumptions of communist passivity, a strategy that was "hopelessly fallacious. There was never any real chance that things would come to pass as it predicted."[15] It would take months of military bloodletting to restore the preinvasion division line, two years and a new administration to reach an armistice, and the rest of the twentieth century to open any prospects for permanent peace throughout Korea.

Truman erred in his Korean policy because he neglected to question his advisers, to consider the consequences of the expanded war aim, and to limit the military campaign. He "walked into such a corner facing front; he was not pushed, he chose."[16] Once the Chinese attacks came, he then missed the opportunity to gain bipartisan support for the more difficult war effort, deprecating the Republican position "that the President [make] no move whatsoever that was not first cleared with them" as "a one-way street."[17] Limiting consultations with Congress, Truman never asked for a specific congressional resolution of approval, —in contrast to Lyndon Johnson on Vietnam and both Bush presidents on Iraq—which he surely could have gained. That neglect made the war a partisan issue, contributing to national disunity, erratic shifts in tactics, and eventually the end of the Democrats' control of government.

These failures show that Harry Truman was not a sure leader or certain of success. He did accomplish a heroic result in the Marshall Plan, despite unfavorable circumstances and his own limitations. That achievement was not inevitable, even if we now recognize its historical importance. Great political opportunities are not always grasped when offered; indeed, "the lost compelling moments recorded in history would add up to quite a respectable span of time."[18] Nor was it certain that Truman would deal effectively with the situation leading to the Marshall Plan. His administration would eventually be seen as severely flawed; as one expert put it: "This seemingly average man turned out to be no better than an average President."[19]

Truman could not rely on his individual standing, his inherent personal qualities, or on the trappings of his office. Instead, he had to employ in an excellent manner the institutional qualities of the presidency to achieve an excellent result. Truman did his work well because he did his job as a leader working within an institution, not because he embodied the qualities of a titanic figure.

The World After War

World War II stands as the most important event of the twentieth century, a turning point in the history of the world. Until then, military conflicts had been confined to particular nations or regions, even if they were as destructive as the Crusades in the Middle East or the trench warfare of Europe in World War I. Between 1939 and

1945, however, the war became truly worldwide, involving every continent and bringing death and destruction by sea, air, and land to every major nation. In contrast to traditional warfare, this was not a clash of armies alone but a conflict of entire populations. Soldiers would still die on battlefields, but they would not be alone. Tens of millions of civilians too would perish, in concentration camps, death marches, and air raids and from lack of the food and fuel that had been destroyed in the conflict. The end of the war came with the dropping of two atomic bombs on Japan, new weapons that threatened the ultimate extinction of the entire human race.

For the United States, too, the conflict transformed society. Sixteen million American troops fought in the islands of the Pacific, the deserts of Africa, the fields and cities of Europe—and a million would become casualties of war. Government expenditures rose to unprecedented levels, amounting to 44 percent of the nation's total economy (twice the government's share in 2001), and the national debt increased to 123 percent of the total national product—equivalent to $16 trillion in today's values (five times greater than the actual national debt in 2001).[20]

The necessities of war also brought severe constraints on Americans' freedom. Taxes rose and, for the first time, were withheld from paychecks. Although jobs were plentiful, strikes were outlawed, wage increases were limited by government directive, and overtime hours were mandated in many industries. Consumption was limited by government allotment of basic foods, and personal travel was restricted by severe rationing of gasoline as well as military requisitions of public transportation. Censors controlled news reports from the battlefields as well as personal correspondence with servicemen. Dissidents were liable to prosecution, and tens of thousands of Japanese Americans were forcibly relocated to desert camps.

Americans of "the greatest generation" bore these deaths, costs, and privations with remarkable patience, endurance, and cooperation.

By war's end, however, the nation wanted relief. In the 1946 congressional elections, Republicans successfully asked voters, "Had enough?" The ballots were a clear renunciation of continued deprivation and sacrifice. The times were not politically auspicious for a new American effort to aid other nations.

Yet the need for such an effort became increasingly evident to national leaders. The worldwide conflict had brought worldwide distress. Exactly two years after the end of hostilities in Europe, the undersecretary of state, Dean Acheson, began a move to win public support for relief. Speaking in place of the president, Acheson described the continued plight of the European continent: "Planned, scientific destruction of the enemy's resources carried out by both sides during the war has left factories destroyed, fields impoverished and without fertilizer or machinery to get them back in shape, transportation systems wrecked, populations scattered and on the borderline of starvation, and long-established business and trading connections disrupted." More fundamentally, he defined the political dangers of these economic burdens: "Not only do human beings and nations exist in narrow economic margins, but also human dignity, human freedom, and democratic institutions."[21]

This political threat was critical to the emerging American policy. Europe was seen as vulnerable not only to economic distress but also to the advance of communism. World War II had been won through an uneasy alliance of the Western democracies, primarily the United States and Great Britain, along with the Soviet Union. Following the victory, American policy had been premised on continued cooperation among the wartime allies and their joint stewardship of the new United Nations organization.

The premise was false. Even before the final defeat of Nazi Germany, the alliance was riven by differences over the postwar settlement. As its armies drew an "iron curtain" through Central Europe, the Soviet Union established subservient communist regimes, eliminating competitive political parties and elections. A series of diplomatic conferences demonstrated that there would be no agreement among the erstwhile allies on a postwar settlement and reconstruction. A military conflict was possible in southern Europe, and communist parties came close to electoral victory in France and Italy. The United States faced the prospect that the ultimate victor of World War II would be not democracy but an antagonistic and authoritarian Soviet Union.

The first major American response was a resort to traditional techniques—diplomacy, money, the use of force, and threats.[22] Truman called for military and economic assistance to the weakened nations of Europe, beginning with Greece and Turkey. While not specifically naming the Soviet Union, he denounced countries that "sought to impose their will, and their way of life, upon other nations" and articulated what came to be called the "Truman Doctrine": "the policy of the United States to support free peoples who are resisting attempted subjugation by armed minorities or by outside pressures."[23]

Traditional techniques might work for a while and in some places, but they could not solve the entire problem of European devastation. Military action was unlikely, economic aid could not meet all the needs, and the nation was not likely to support America's role as "the world's policeman" after the ordeal of the war. The United States needed not simply to react to an imminent particular crisis but to design a long-term foreign policy.

In the aftermath of the war, the nation debated various options.[24] The devastation of Europe might be alleviated simply by calling on the generosity of Americans to provide charity, that is, by pursuing the idealistic goal of alleviating hunger through unilateral action—a position advocated by former president Herbert Hoover. A different, "realist" policy stressed such national interests as markets for American goods or military security. It would use unilateral action to meet the threat of communism by building a "Fortress America" based on military strength—an idea advocated by Republican Senate leader Robert Taft. A third position favored multilateral action, which entailed subordinating American sovereignty to a world government such as the new United Nations—the position of former vice president Henry Wallace.

Charitable aid surely would have won broad public support. In keeping with American traditions of generosity, a year after the end of the war 96 percent of the nation was prepared to send "as much food as we can" to alleviate "widespread starvation among the people in Europe." Even more notably, after experiencing deprivations of their own, close to half of all Americans (41 percent) were ready to "make sure that we send enough food even though it means rationing most food items in this country again."[25] The alternative route of a "Fortress America" would also have had ready advocates, since it would be based on traditions of national isolation from foreign nations and would have tangible and dramatic expression in weaponry. Even the idealistic policy of reliance on the United Nations might have won support on the basis of its utopian vision of world government.

The Marshall Plan represented a different combination. It marked a historic change in American foreign policy, turning the nation away from its traditional isolationism toward a permanent involvement in world affairs. It was not a purely idealistic policy, unlike the unilateral approach of traditional charity or the idea of allowing national policy to be guided by an international body such as the United Nations. Instead, it used multilateral strategies to pursue both idealistic goals—aid to the Continent and the preservation of European democracy—and national interests, such as expansion of American markets and the defeat of communism.

The new American initiative would affect not only the nation but the entire planet for the rest of the twentieth century. It was a rarity in politics, a policy based on a comprehensive worldview. The policy combined economic, strategic, and ideological elements. Economically, the Marshall Plan focused on the growth of free trade throughout the developed world by the creation of "a new system in which multilateral arrangements put a limit on competitive nationalisms, market forces and coordinating mechanisms worked to integrate economies, and economic integration cleared a path to stable growth and international harmony." Strategically, the plan assumed that "an integrated economic order, particularly one headed by supranational institutions, would help to control German nationalism, reconcile Germany's recovery with France's economic and security concerns, and thus create a balance of power in the West sufficient to contain Soviet power in the East."[26]

The national interest in free trade and the containment of the Soviet Union paralleled American commitment to the principles of democratic government. Democratic regimes were seen not only as better trading partners and firmer allies but also as more politically legitimate and more morally acceptable. American leaders combined these various objectives into a new international stance, based on a conviction that aid to Europe "is necessary if we are to preserve our own freedoms and our democratic institutions. It is necessary for our national security. And it is our duty and our privilege as human beings."[27]

The plan was launched on June 5, 1947, when Secretary of State George C. Marshall delivered the commencement address at Harvard University. Considering its eventual impact, relatively limited attention was paid to the speech at the time. Marshall accepted the Harvard invitation only a week in advance, his advisers opposed using the occasion to announce the new European policy initiative, and no advance billing was provided to the American press, foreign nations other than Britain, or even most officials in the State Department. Nor was the speech's historic importance immediately grasped. According to legend, the British Embassy in Washington, in order to save money, did not cable the speech to London but economized by using the diplomatic pouch.[28]

In terms of its rhetoric, Marshall's speech itself was understated. Marshall explained the economic deterioration of Europe as involving more than the physical destruction of war or the immediate privations caused by food shortages and bad weather. The basic and immense need was economic reconstruction, which in turn would have political benefits. "Our policy," Marshall declared, "is directed not against any country or doctrine but against hunger, poverty, desperation, and chaos. Its purpose would be the revival or a working economy in the world so as to permit the emergence of political and social conditions in which free institutions can exist." To achieve this goal, the policy would require cooperative effort across Europe, which could include the nations of the Soviet bloc. Marshall rejected the idea of unilateral aid simply to alleviate immediate distress in individual countries: "There must be some agreement among the countries of Europe as to the requirements of the situation. . . . The initiative, I think, must come from Europe. The role of this country should consist of friendly aid in the drafting of a European program and of later support of such a program so far as it may be practical for us to do so."[29]

Marshall's language was cautious, and there was no guarantee that his plan would actually be implemented. He had challenged Europe to develop a cooperative plan, but the continent had been accustomed to national rivalries and conflict for hundreds of years. Success could be achieved only with the economic reconstruction of Germany, the country that had been responsible for the very destruction now to be repaired. One purpose of the plan was to halt the advance of Soviet communism, but Marshall had invited the Soviet Union and its satellites to share in the promised aid. At home, the plan required substantial financial and political support from American voters and taxpayers, who might well be reluctant to commit their nation to a new foreign enterprise, particularly one that would benefit their former enemy, Germany, and their emerging competitor, the Soviet Union.

The Soviet Union unwittingly provided help in gaining support for the plan among the American population. Seeing the plan as a threat, it withdrew from the negotiations and forced the withdrawal of its submissive neighbors. These actions resolved the ideological ambiguity of the plan, which could now be supported as both a humanitarian and an anticommunist program.[30] Even Truman himself gave the Soviets credit: "Hell, that wasn't Truman's foreign policy; that was Stalin's foreign policy. I never could have got those things through Congress if it hadn't been for Stalin."[31]

Despite the many obstacles, the Marshall Plan became a reality. European meetings began a month later and were followed by a detailed proposal, including provisions for a common economic authority, at the end of September. President Truman held a large meeting with congressional leaders only a week later, called a special session of Congress in November, and submitted a detailed program before Christmas. On April 2, the legislation authorizing the plan cleared Congress, committing 12 percent of the federal budget and 2 percent of the nation's total output to the task.[32] Within two weeks, Europe received the first aid grants.

The plan has been praised, reputedly by Winston Churchill, as "the most unsordid act in human history." Altruism was one motivation, to be sure, but Harry Truman and other American leaders were also pursuing U.S. national interests.[33] They deserve commendation as much for their political abilities as for their humanitarianism. In only a few months, Truman led the United States to reverse its traditional stance toward the world, garnered large resources for the new course of action, and won the support of both political parties and the general electorate. Politics, not simply good intentions, accomplished a daring and innovative foreign policy.

The President and the Presidency

Presidential choices certainly reflect the personal characteristics and the governing style of the individual men, like Truman, who make them. Such decisions are also critically shaped by the institutional character of the office and the circumstances of their historical period. Truman exemplifies these relationships. He would later offer a pithy description of the job of the chief executive: "I sit here all day trying to persuade people to do the things they ought to have sense enough to do without my persuading them. . . . That's all the powers of the President amount to."[34] His terse description was particularly appropriate to the Marshall Plan, a program clearly of benefit to the United States but one that required adroit use of the bounded powers of the president. It illustrates well "the tensions in the American system that exist between restraints deriving from the institutional framework on the one hand and programs of action and presidentially driven solutions on the other."[35]

Of course Truman did not bring the Marshall Plan to life by himself. He was neither its intellectual creator nor its sole political sire. A president is not a biblical prophet or a divine lawgiver, a single, all-powerful individual who delivers truth and justice to a receptive people. Rather, a president is a democratic politician who must take ideas, wherever found, and win consent from a contentious citizenry. That was Truman's task—and his achievement.

The presidency has been evaluated in very different ways in American history and scholarship. We often rank presidents according to their "greatness," placing Washington, Lincoln, and the two Roosevelts at the top, with Buchanan and Harding at the bottom. We can describe the president's powers in Woodrow Wilson's expansive terms: "The president is at liberty, both in law and conscience, to be as big a man as he can be. His capacity will set the limit."[36] Or we can minimize them, in the words of James Lord Bryce, as "the same in kind as that which devolves on the chairman of a commercial company or the manager of a railway."[37]

While analysts often see the office as the central institution of American politics, their perspectives differ considerably. Some champion presidential leadership, some worry about an "imperial presidency," some criticize constraints on the chief executive.[38] One group of scholars has concentrated on the legal powers of the institution.[39] Others have focused on the persons occupying the office, examining topics as diverse as individual psychology, medical conditions, and personal style.[40] The most incisive research looks at the interactions between the individual president and the institutional framework, which both offers opportunities to and places limitations on the chief executive.[41]

The most important aspect of the institutional presidency is its centrality in American politics. At the hub of all American politics, the president is easily characterized as a "chief" of many tribes, as the nation's leading diplomat, legislator, commander, economic manager, partisan, administrator, and public figure.[42] He holds vast formal authority; he (along with his chosen running mate) is the only person elected by the entire nation; and he receives more media attention than any other person in the world.

The centrality of the presidency creates the potential for presidential power, but it does not assure it. The hub of a mechanism is not necessarily the source of its power; automobile tires, for example, spin around their hubs, but the energy comes from other parts, such as pistons and axles. As Neustadt emphasized in his classic work, *Presidential Power,* the formal powers of the president, in and of themselves, would make him only a clerk, serving the needs of other politicians. To be a leader, the president must take advantage of the uniquely broad and extensive vantage points he commands from his central position. From these vantage points he may, with skill, be able to persuade—not force—"other men to do what he wants done."[43]

With the benefit of half a century's hindsight, the wisdom of the Marshall Plan seems evident. At the time, however, its prospects were uncertain. Its adoption would depend on Harry Truman's skillful performance in his job as president. In this task, and in contrast to his later mistakes in the Korean War, he did heroic work.

A president has the unique ability to set the national agenda. As John F. Kennedy would later say, "The function of the President is to set before the people the unfinished business of our society . . . the agenda for our people, what we must do as a society to meet our needs in this country and protect our security and help the cause of freedom."[44] Simply by focusing attention on the Marshall Plan, Truman guaranteed that it would at least be seriously considered. So that the plan would receive priority attention, Truman made the choice to downplay other problems. Because of his focus on Europe, he gave less consideration to American policy in Asia. Within the constraints he imposed on the federal budget because of the large cost of European aid, Truman provided less money for the military. Truman "assumed that Congress would place a strict limit on national security spending and opted to divert as many resources as possible into foreign economic aid."[45] That difficult choice exemplified the job of the president, to establish national priorities.

After setting the agenda, a president must win support. Using the prominence of his position, Truman repeatedly backed the Marshall Plan in speeches and press conferences. For the most part, he worked indirectly, delivering only one national radio address on the subject. Instead, he bent his efforts to winning support in Congress, while endorsing the idea of using a variety of organizations to mobilize public support.[46] As Marshall had recognized, public support in the United States would be of critical importance, but it was not assured. A month after the Harvard speech, those who were aware of the plan were strongly supportive, by a 57 percent to 21 percent margin—but only half the public had heard or read about it. Fewer

Americans than in 1946 favored aid to Europe; only a third of the nation would now cut their own "food and supplies to help the European countries get back on their feet." The public was also unclear on whether the plan's main purpose was economic aid or the fight against communism.[47]

Public opinion responded to the efforts of Truman and his allies: the nation became better informed and positive in its response. By November 1947, when the program was submitted to Congress, two-thirds of the country had heard of it, and they were strongly supportive (56 percent to 17 percent). A year later, over four-fifths of the nation knew about the plan, and support was even greater (62 percent to 16 percent). Moreover, almost every respondent could correctly describe the Marshall Plan, at least superficially.[48] In later years, public support would fluctuate in reaction to international events, yet the program consistently won majority support.[49] Considering the typical public disinterest and frequent ignorance about foreign policy, this is a remarkable pattern of mass support, and a remarkable instance of open democratic leadership.

The president's preeminent position usually provides him with public prestige, a resource in winning support. By 1947, Truman had lost this prestige, standing low in public opinion. He met this problem by borrowing prestige from Marshall, deliberately identifying the plan with the secretary of state rather than with himself as president. Truman publicly reported this decision as simply reflecting an altruistic desire to acknowledge Marshall's contribution: "I said to him, 'General, I want the plan to go down in history with your name on it. And don't give me any argument. I've made up my mind, and, remember, I'm your Commander in Chief.'"[50] But a close adviser quotes Truman as revealing a more political strategy: "We have a Republican majority in both the Senate and the House and anything that goes up there with Truman's name on it is going to die. I've been thinking about this, and I agree, this is going to be big and it will have a real impact on the world. I think what we're going to do—I will first talk to Dean [Acheson] about it—is give it to General Marshall and have General Marshall do it. He is completely nonpolitical, he's neither a Democrat or a Republican. He's honored by the American people. Up on the Hill they will attach no political significance to it if General Marshall is associated with it."[51]

A related political resource of a president is his electoral strength: he alone can claim to be the choice of the entire national electorate. Truman lacked this resource as well, since he had not won election in his own right and seemed destined for defeat in 1948—if he could even manage to win the Democratic nomination over developing opposition. Truman also turned this problem to advantage, however. He repeatedly used the "bully pulpit" of the presidency to support the Marshall Plan but placed responsibility to adopt the program on the Republican Congress, so that "his own endorsement of it stayed on the right side of that fine line between the 'caretaker' in office and the would-be candidate."[52] In this way, his electoral weakness actually helped. Since it was "obvious" that he would soon leave office, Truman's programmatic advocacy was not seen as endangering the inevitable Republican victory in the 1948 election.

Truman also used the standing of the president as the nation's "chief legislator," exemplified in the chief executive's authority to submit bills and veto proffered legislation. While severely limited by Republican control of Congress in winning the necessary approval for the Marshall Plan, Truman still adroitly used the powers of his position. He won overwhelming backing among Democrats, invoking both personal and party loyalties:

> I called in all the favors I was owed, and we got it through. I called in [Speaker of the House] Sam Rayburn and when I told him what we had in mind, he just wouldn't believe it. He said, "Mr. President, it will bust this country." . . .

> And then he kind of swallowed hard, and he says, "Harry, how much do you figure this thing is going to cost?" . . .
>
> I looked him right in the eye, and I said, "It's going to cost about fifteen, sixteen billion dollars, Sam."
>
> Well, his face got as white as a sheet, but I said to him, "Now, Sam, I figure I saved the people of the United States about fifteen, sixteen billion dollars with that committee of mine, and you know that better than anyone else.
>
> "Now we're going to need that money, and we can save the world with it."[53]

Success would require more, particularly Republican and conservative Democratic support. In confidence, Truman disdained these "squirrelheads. All of 'em are living in 1890 when a billion-dollar Congress beat the Republicans in 1892."[54] But he kept his partisanship to himself as he worked to win the critical support of the opposition party.

To provide evidence on the devastation of Europe, Truman used a report prepared by Herbert Hoover, possibly the Republican he most disliked. He encouraged personal visits to Europe by nearly half of the members of Congress, and "almost all came back converts." One conservative congressman was reported to have shed tears and given away most of his wardrobe to ragged unfortunates."[55] Truman cooperated in the mobilization of the business community and other interest groups under the leadership of Republicans, such as FDR's secretary of war, Henry Stimson.

A particular object of Truman's advocacy was the Republican leader on foreign policy, Michigan Senator Arthur Vandenberg. Before the war, he had been a commonplace isolationist. As he came to accept an active international role for the United States, his former position gave him credibility within his party. His reputation was further buttressed among Republicans by his previous contentious relationship with FDR and his insistence on preserving the constitutional role of the Senate in foreign policy through approval of treaties and appropriations. Vandenberg led Republicans along the path to an internationalist but realist foreign policy. In its Mackinac Island declaration of 1943, the party supported "responsible participation by the United States in a post-war cooperative organization." Vandenberg subsequently became the chief author of the 1944 Republican platform's foreign policy plank, favoring an international organization of sovereign states while insisting on Senate approval of treaties. By January of 1945, he had moved even further along the internationalist path. Changing to FDR's position, Vandenberg accepted the creation of the United Nations before peace treaties were concluded and supported the possible use of military force by the U.N. and the president without prior Senate approval.[56]

Truman, advised by Acheson, cooperated in a recurrent stratagem of Vandenberg's, "to enact publicly his conversion to a proposal, his change of attitude, a kind of political transubstantiation. The method was to go through a period of public doubt and skepticism, then find a comparatively minor flaw in the proposal, pounce upon it, and make much of it; in due course propose a change, always the Vandenberg amendment. Then, and only then, could it be given to his followers as true doctrine worthy of all men to be received."[57]

Recognizing Vandenberg's critical importance, Truman courted the Michigan senator from the beginning of his own term in office, when Vandenberg served as a member of the U.S. delegation to the founding conference of the United Nations. The new president called on the friendship they had developed in the Senate and took his former colleague's advice to formulate a comprehensive, rather than piecemeal, approach to the problems of Europe.[58] Once the Marshall Plan was announced, Truman used his powers as president to "smooth the way for Vandenberg":

> The Senator insisted on "no politics" from the Administration side; there was none. He thought a survey of American resources and capacity essential; he got it.... Vandenberg expected advance consultation; he received it, step by step, in frequent meetings with the President and weekly conferences with Marshall.... When the Senator decided on the need to change financing and administrative features of the legislation, Truman disregarded Budget Bureau grumbling and acquiesced with grace. When, finally, Vandenberg desired a Republican to head the new administering agency, his candidate, Paul Hoffman, was appointed despite the President's own preference for another [Acheson].[59]

Throughout his campaign for the Marshall Plan, Truman necessarily relied on the institutional powers of the presidency. He was both politically too restricted to invoke support on the basis of his individual prestige and personally too modest to make the attempt. His tactics were grounded as well in his view of American institutions: "He had an enormous veneration and respect for the institution of the Presidency."[60] He could, and did, build on the president's responsibility to assess the "state of the union," to call attention to the critical problems of European reconstruction and the emerging communist threat. He could, and did, build on the president's constitutional positions as commander-in-chief and the diplomatic voice of the United States to define the national interest. He could, and did, use the president's budget authority to make foreign economic aid a national priority. He could, and did, use his power as chief executive to appoint supportive officials and to achieve unified support throughout the administration. He could, and did, use his legal powers to present proposals to Congress and negotiate consensual legislation.

By his reliance on institutional powers, Truman avoided the faults Lowi finds in "the plebiscitary presidency," which exaggerates the individual power and mystique of the White House. He worked with his subordinates instead of seeking to be the single "star." He used the developing skills of American diplomats instead of bypassing the foreign policy experts. He held the administrative pluralism of American government in check instead of condoning bureaucratic incoherence. And, while he did emphasize the perils facing Europe, he did not engage in flagrant exaggeration and oversell.[61] In these actions, Truman reconstructed both Europe and the presidency.

Americans might take pride in the unprecedented generosity of the Marshall Plan. As Truman boasted: "In all the history of the world we are the first great nation to feed and support the conquered."[62] They might be even more satisfied with its enormous historical impact. Europe's ancient conflicts were diffused through economic cooperation, leading to rapid recovery, broad-based prosperity, and a common market. The continent's history of bloody conflicts ended, replaced by a common defense through the North Atlantic Treaty Organization. Political disunion was replaced eventually by the European Union's open borders, integrated market, and single currency. Communist parties in western Europe declined, and Russian expansion was halted and then eventually reversed by the fall of the Soviet Union and the democratization of its erstwhile satellites.

These heroic achievements resulted from the skillful use of institutional powers by an ordinary man, Harry Truman, who occupied the presidency. He himself wrote the appropriate conclusion to this chapter. "He observed once that he hoped he would be found deserving of a tombstone inscription allegedly seen in a cemetery in a town on the western frontier: 'Here lies N. N.—he tried his damnedest.' To anyone who knew or knows Harry Truman, there can be little doubt that he offered as an epitaph what he had clearly always viewed as his motto."[63] In establishing the Marshall Plan, President Truman did his job—very well.

Chapter Six
Wayne Justice

A Hero of the Judiciary

Heroism seems unlikely in the judiciary. By the nature of their job, judges are insulated from the rough world of threat and conflict. Judges are well paid, awarded great deference, and cloistered against political attack. Yet, although protected, they are politically frail. With "no influence over either the sword or the purse; no direction either of the strength or of the wealth of the society, [exercising] neither force nor will," they can achieve results only through the fragile weapons of the printed words in their opinions.[1] In a democracy, judges would seem especially powerless against the will of the majority, the source of legitimate power.

In Texas, the judiciary does boast a hero, a federal district judge. Appropriately named William Wayne Justice, he has had a remarkable impact on the law and on the lives of Americans. His decisions have created or extended constitutional rights for many disadvantaged groups, particularly in Texas, including segregated students, juvenile offenders, prisoners, and Mexican Americans. His heroism is exemplified by a path-breaking decision that established the right of the children of illegal aliens to a free public education. To be sure, Justice refuses to consider himself a hero, which he defines as "someone who knows that there is a risk involved, but goes ahead anyway.... No, I don't categorize myself as a hero. I would be scared if somebody came in here with a gun. . . . I guess I've never been impressed by myself. I'll put it this way: I know what I am. I'm a country lawyer who lucked into a job, and tried to do the best I could. . . . It's been a fun job. It's interesting to be in a position when you can maybe right some wrongs."[2]

The Texas judge wryly adopts a friend's characterization: "Wayne isn't impressed by himself, but he sure is impressed by his job." He is plain as well in his personal attitudes. Although he insisted on decorum in his courtroom, he also allowed long-haired "hippie" defense lawyers to appear in ragged clothes. His office has few decorations or evidence of his achievements. The only photograph, aside from those of family members, is a signed portrait of former Justice William Brennan, the intellectual leader of the U.S. Supreme Court's liberal wing. The Texan is tellingly proud of the inscription: "For Judge William Wayne Justice, a very courageous judge who has rendered some momentous decisions in a very difficult environment." His commendations from the Texas Civil Liberties Union and the NAACP, and his Association of Trial Lawyers of America Award for Outstanding Federal Trial Judge are not displayed.

This modesty also appears in routine activities. In earlier years, when his court was in the more rural and traditional area of Tyler, Texas, Judge Justice had a special test for prospective law clerks. He would take them for an early breakfast to a country-music restaurant frequented by local farmers, literally rednecked thanks to their long hours in the sun, so that out-of-staters would know the persons likely to be in their courtroom. In the more sophisticated city of Austin, invited to lunch in the course of a four-hour interview, he chose a country-and-western roadside locale, advertised as "the best armadillo restaurant in the world." It has plain tablecloths and chrome chairs, and "entertainment" is provided by a radio talk show hosted by Jim Hightower, a populist and former state secretary of agriculture. Obliged to wait in a long line for a table, he never thought to ask for preferential treatment; he then recommended the house's meat loaf, corn bread, and black-eyed peas, and insisted on paying the tip on a $15 bill. Although he has received many death threats over the years, he parks on an unguarded rooftop where, he fatalistically observes, a sniper could easily shoot someone from the surrounding buildings.

Justice was certainly not born to greatness. His father won local recognition in Athens, Texas, as a defense lawyer and was politically active as a populist within the Democratic party, then totally dominant in one-party Texas. Wayne Justice's future was mapped out early, when his father added his seven-year-old son to the law firm's name. The young man followed this predestined path as he performed competently, but not brilliantly, in his small-town high school, at the University of Texas, and at Officers' Candidate School during World War II.[3] Wayne Justice had no combat experience in the war and returned home to practice law and to marry. As an active lawyer inheriting his father's practice, he inevitably became prominent in the community—even "a small-town stereotype—an overweight, cigar-smoking Rotary Club president whose career ascent was based on political patronage."[4]

With deep Southern and Confederate roots, Justice grew up in a segregated and unequal society. Still, he developed early sympathy for the underprivileged:

> I got kind of a worm's-eye view of life early on. My father was a tremendous criminal defense lawyer. He lived in a small town, but he was widely known. He had a reputation for getting everybody off. As a little boy I used to go around with him some. I was listening when he talked to clients. And nobody approved of his clients. So I got kind of a feeling that it's us against the world. I found that these so-called

Judge William Wayne Justice

criminals, they did these bad things, but I viewed them as individuals. Some of them were very nice people, in spite of the trouble they were in.

Then as a kid, I was healthy up until I was about four years old, and then I got a case of whooping cough that very nearly killed me. In those days you didn't go to the hospital until you were about dead. They took me up to the Bator Hospital; I stayed up there six weeks. I just barely survived. I was in really bad health up until I was about ten years old. I would get beat up pretty often. I wasn't strong enough to be a very good fighter. So I got a worm's-eye view there too. It kind of stayed with me. I can empathize with people that feel powerless.

He recognized racial injustice early, in the taunting of a black childhood friend, but he admits that he never expressed his opposition to segregation until he was safely on the bench. "I was married and I had a child. And if I had let my thoughts about integration be known, I would have no law practice. I am not all that brave. I wanted to continue to have a law practice. I was very timid about that.... [But] I thought *Brown v. Board of Education* [the 1954 decision outlawing school segregation] was right." He explains: "It just seemed so inequitable, the way we treated these human beings. The blacks are just as much a part of our society as the whites. I thought it was unjust. And when I read about this school decision, I thought, well that's right. Why are they going to this inferior school, Fisher High School and Fisher Elementary School? Why are they going there instead, getting second-hand books, ones that had been discarded by the white school? Totally unjust. You know my mother had told me, not that she was an integrationist, but she just impressed on me that you did things that were right. And that wasn't right to me."

The Democratic party at that time was sharply divided between a more conservative faction represented by President Lyndon Johnson and a more liberal wing led by Senator Ralph Yarborough. Justice was able to maintain cordial relationships with both groups, although he remembers the rivalry as excessive: "There would be bombs going off in Vietnam, or war in India, and the two of them would be arguing over who would be collector of customs in Port Arthur." When vacancies occurred in the positions of U.S. attorney and then of federal district judge, the rivalry worked to his advantage. Justice felt no qualms about advancing his own cause as a satisfactory consensus choice. In 1968, at the age of forty-eight, ordinary politics and ordinary patronage brought an ordinary man to the security of a lifetime job. He would do that job in extraordinary fashion.

His subsequent rulings were not popular. "He has been called the most hated man, the most powerful man in Texas and the real governor of Texas. . . . Many Texas politicians, who consider their state a republic unto itself, regard him as the symbol of federal intervention."[5] When Justice acted on his convictions to protect minorities, his neighbors reacted with disdain. "Construction workers walked off a remodeling job at his home. Social invitations sometimes were scarce. Almost 4,000 people signed an impeachment petition. Caravans of honking cars circled the courthouse. Obscene phone calls came with the hate mail. . . . 'You could put the letters on a single day in a bushel basket,' Justice said."[6] Yet he persisted.

Despite his major impact on the law, Justice was not seen as a crusader. One article in the *New York Times* described him as "a formal, bookish, elaborately courteous and hospitable man," who is "an unlikely hero and an unlikely villain."[7] Nor did Justice see himself as a crusader. In doing his work, he did not seek the notoriety he received: "I didn't ask for a single damn case that ended up on my docket. They just would just file them on my docket, and I had to dispose of them." Even as he sought to promote his vision of social equity, the Texan recognized the limitations placed on a judge's discretion and personal values. As he frankly described his operational procedure:

> I've tried not to let my feelings interfere with what I think are the facts, but I do my best to look at the facts right in the face. I decide cases all too often in a way that I consider to be [morally] wrong.
>
> I make no bones about it, when I listen to a case I try

to figure out who's in the right about this. What is fair and what is unfair. It is a very simplistic approach to things. What are the equities in this case?

I try to figure that out and if I decide that one side really ought to win this case, I will call my law clerks in and I'll tell them what I find the facts are. And I'll say, "See if you can find something that we can get upholding this." So they go out and look and look. And if they can't find anything that upholds me, I'm a professional; I look things in the eye. So I just decide the case the other way, if the law won't permit me to be fair.

The Law and Justice

Wayne Justice's judicial heroism was epitomized in a case that he "knew was going to be trouble." It brought a major extension of constitutional rights for a triply disadvantaged group, children of illegal immigrants (who, more gently, are often called "undocumented aliens"). Children lack the legal protections of adults, immigrants lack the protections of citizens, and illegal immigrants lack even the protections of aliens. The Texas legislature, having no reason to fear a political reaction from voteless aliens, decided in 1975 that these children would be barred from the public schools unless they paid yearly tuition of $1,000. Since the parents of such children were not only poor (with an average annual income of $4,000) but also legal fugitives, the statute in effect denied their children any educational opportunities. Joining school authorities in a thousand Texas districts, the Tyler superintendent, James Plyler, barred undocumented alien pupils from school.

To Wayne Justice, the social equities of the case were obvious: "I thought that the consequence of a failure to educate those children would be disastrous. We would have this subclass of young people, growing up without any education, fitted only for the most menial type of work. And you could predict that many of them would turn to a lawless way of living. And just having that kind of a subclass appeared to me to be a recipe for social disorder later on down the line. So I looked for a way to avoid that."

Judges, however, are tightly constrained by the institutional character of their position: they cannot simply do what is "right." There are two fundamental limits to judicial activism. First, there must be an actual case involving alleged injuries to particular, real people. Unlike a legislature, courts cannot pursue an abstract search for justice or good public policy. Second, courts must rule on the basis of legal doctrine, grounding their decisions in the reasoning of statutes and established precedents. Both limitations applied in the schooling of these children. The likely injury to the children was obvious, deprivation of education. But it is legally necessary for an aggrieved party to make a claim, to file a lawsuit. In this matter, any attempt by the parents—the appropriate persons to take action—to gain redress on behalf of their children carried great risks. As soon as they identified themselves in court, they became potential targets of federal prosecution. As illegal immigrants, they would be subject to deportation, loss of their jobs and homes, possibly prison. Even a sympathetic judge like Wayne Justice would be required to enforce the laws against illegal immigration.

While Justice knew that he wanted to uphold the right of the children to a free public education, he was further constrained by institutionalized legal doctrines, which raised considerable obstacles to providing relief. Courts are generally reluctant to overturn state legislation, and a state court had already upheld this particular statute. Moreover, the U.S. Supreme Court had recently ruled on the Texas educational system and had declared that there was no constitutional right to education and no legal necessity for a state to provide equality in state funding for different districts or different kinds of children.[8]

Judge Justice was required to accept this doctrine, which had been promulgated by the highest court in the land.

To reach his decision, Justice could pursue three lines of legal reasoning.

Preemption. First, and least important to the eventual outcome, he could determine that federal legislation on immigration took precedence over any state law, a doctrine known as "preemption." He might attempt to draw a parallel to federal laws regulating trucks on the highways, which take precedence over any state regulation.

Equal Protection/Rational Classification. The second possible basis for a decision lay in the Fourteenth Amendment to the Constitution, which requires that states provide "equal protection of the laws" to "any person within its jurisdiction." Because the Fourteenth Amendment speaks of "persons," it might be applied even to undocumented aliens, just as it had been previously interpreted to protect citizens, legal immigrants, and even "artificial persons" such as corporations.[9]

But, in the law, equal does not mean identical. Generally, the courts have been deferential to state legislatures, allowing them to assign people to different classifications and then to give disparate treatment to the various groups. The discretion left to the states is quite broad: "The Fourteenth Amendment permits the States a wide scope of discretion in enacting laws which affect some groups of citizens differently than others. The constitutional safeguard is offended only if the classification rests on grounds wholly irrelevant to the achievement of the State's objective. State legislatures are presumed to have acted within their constitutional power despite the fact that, in practice, their laws result in some inequality. A statutory discrimination will not be set aside if any state of facts reasonably may be conceived to justify it."[10] This doctrine, called "rational classification," is sometimes denigrated as "toothless," because the justices will accept almost any legislative classification under this standard if it could conceivably advance any legitimate state interest.

For example, a state can decide to limit the driving age to eighteen, even if others believe that it should be seventeen. The Supreme Court used this relatively lax standard in the case upholding the right of Texas to award different amounts of educational aid to different school districts.

Despite the courts' usual deference to legislatures, there have been some laws that they have invalidated for lack of any "rational basis" for distinguishing one group from another. Illustratively, the Supreme Court has lately become particularly wary of gender classifications. Historically, distinctions based on sex won the approval of the courts. Early in the twentieth century, for example, the Supreme Court upheld a law restricting the number of hours women — but not men — could work. In language that today would provoke feminist scorn, the Supreme Court found that a woman "is a delicate organism, and like that of a child's hers is a defenseless nature." Therefore, "she is properly placed in a class by herself and legislation designed for her protection may be sustained, even when like legislation is not necessary for men and could not be sustained."[11]

Since the early 1970s, a more "evolved" Court will not sustain these laws or even less blatant differentiation. Establishing a new standard of "heightened scrutiny," it now requires that gender-based laws serve an "important" state interest. A good example of this changed perspective is found, interestingly, in bars. In the more traditional 1940s, the Court found it rational for states to prohibit women from working as bartenders. With the advent of women's liberation came new attitudes regarding women and libations. The Court struck down an Oklahoma law that allowed presumptively cautious eighteen-year-old women to purchase 3.2 beer, while prohibiting presumptively impulsive men to consume any form of alcohol until the age of twenty-one.[12] In rulings of larger import, laws "protecting" women from employment in "dangerous" occupations no longer pass judicial muster.[13] In light of these rulings, Judge

Justice thought it might be possible that the children of illegal aliens might also benefit from the "heightened scrutiny" principle that was newly being applied to women.

Equal Protection/Strict Scrutiny. The Fourteenth Amendment also provided a third possible avenue of attack on the Texas statute. In certain distinct circumstances, the courts reverse their usual deference to legislatures and instead employ the judicial doctrine of "strict scrutiny." They use this tougher standard when legislation establishes a "suspect classification," typically one based on prejudice. When the courts determine that a group classification is "suspect," they will approve a law only if serves a "compelling state interest." For this reason, almost no legislation would be acceptable, for example, that distinguished groups on the basis of race. A state therefore cannot write a law that treats interracial marriages differently from those of whites.[14]

The "strict scrutiny" test has also been applied to laws that curtail "fundamental rights," such as suffrage, travel, the free exercise of religion, and the right to criminal appeal.[15] State laws on these subjects will receive exacting judicial examination. This test may be particularly relevant when a group is unable to meet its needs through the normal political process. Perhaps, the Court said in a famous footnote, there are occasions when "prejudice against discrete and insular minorities may be a special condition, which tends seriously to curtail the operation of those political processes ordinarily to be relied upon to protect minorities, and which may call for a correspondingly more searching judicial inquiry."[16]

On all of these grounds, arguably, a focus on undocumented aliens might also be considered a "suspect classification," and the law restricting their children's education might deserve the strict scrutiny of the courts. Legislative classification on the basis of citizenship had already drawn court skepticism. Free public education could, moreover, be considered a fundamental personal right. Certainly, illegal Mexican immigrants were objects of prejudice who could not resort to the normal political process. And "the political powerlessness of undocumented alien children is even more severe, of course, because they are unable to rely on their parents to protect their interests."[17] It might be worth a try.

A Heroic Decision

Eventually a lawsuit—in legal terminology, *Plyler v. Doe*—on behalf of the children was filed within Wayne Justice's jurisdiction in Tyler, along with suits in sixteen other districts. A statewide injunction temporarily halted the exclusion of these children from school, but the main action would take place in Justice's courtroom, where his "findings of fact" would become the evidentiary record for later decisions. Justice delayed action until he could develop an extensive factual case. As he heard the evidence, he also made efforts to protect the parents who, just by bringing the lawsuit, were calling attention to their illegal immigration into the United States. The plaintiffs were identified only by the anonymous legal pseudonyms of "Doe, Roe, Boe, and Loe." Court proceedings were held at the quiet hour of 6:00 A.M., when reporters or publicity seekers were unlikely to be roaming the courthouse, and the plaintiffs used a private entrance. The judge did inform the federal authorities, who voluntarily took no steps to enforce the immigration laws against the parents.[18]

In his effort to find relief for the alien children, the Texan engaged in judicial strategizing:[19] "My law clerk and I got together and analyzed the various personalities on the Supreme Court. I was trying to figure out what would happen there, and we correctly predicted that Justice Powell would be the swing vote. I decided that maybe the case would be upheld because Justice Powell had been known for his sympathy for children, and it had been expressed in a couple of his opinions. And that is the way it turned out. We had gotten [accurate predictions for] all but two judges." Judge Justice employed all three possible approaches in his opinion, successfully betting that at least one line of argument would be acceptable to higher courts. Preemption was a minor point. There were considerable weaknesses in this approach. It was illogical to argue that federal authority over immigration gave immigrants immunity from general state laws, such as those governing driving regulations, zoning statutes, and school attendance. Justice nevertheless included preemption in his opinion because "I was just trying to cover all my bases." The major focus was on the competing interpretations of the Fourteenth Amendment.

The first hurdle in reaching a decision, the "threshold issue," involved bringing the children within the scope of the Fourteenth Amendment, giving them some of the protections of the Constitution of a nation whose laws they had violated with their first entrance. Although established doctrine provided some procedural safeguards for illegal aliens, their overall constitutional position was uncertain. Justice's first contribution was to bring these children fully under the Fourteenth Amendment's "equal protection" clause. Once the children were included, the central issue became the appropriate degree of protection to accord the group. Judge Justice wanted to include illegal aliens as a "suspect class" since they could easily fit the established definition of a group "saddled with such disabilities, or subject to such a history of purposeful unequal treatment, or relegated to such a position of political powerlessness as to command extraordinary protection from the majoritarian political process."[20]

The Texan found a number of reasons why the law affecting these children might come under strict scrutiny. By denying them an essential benefit, education, the law would deprive each child of the basic skills necessary to participate in the political process. Moreover, this deprivation affected only poor people, who might be considered a suspect class. Third, using a strategically deliberate quotation from Supreme Court Justice Lewis Powell, the law would "penalize and stigmatize children who are not in a position to prevent the wrongful acts of their parents," making the statute "contrary to the basic concept of our system that legal burdens should bear some relationship to individual responsibility or wrongdoing." Finally, Texas had implicitly welcomed the aliens into the state to exploit their labor but had then left them "virtually defenseless against any abuse, exploitation, or callous neglect." In effect, Justice had built a moral case against the Texas statute. Yet he could not push established law far enough to declare undocumented aliens a "suspect class." Having made his argument, he adopted a safer, even conservative, judicial attitude. He reserved the high ground for a direct, scornful attack on the statute, an approach that rendered the "suspect class" issue moot. Since there was no "rational basis for the state law or the local policy," he argued, "it is not necessary to resolve finally the difficult conceptual problems."[21]

The judge remembers his deliberations:

> I had a very brilliant law clerk. And we argued back and forth about all that. I told her, I said, I want you to categorize them as a suspect class, and so she did. That was in my preliminary injunction. And before we got down to the trial of the case itself, I listened to all the evidence in the case, and I began to worry that no one had ever held them to be a suspect class.
>
> I began to retreat. She was with me on that. We decided that there just was simply no rational basis for the legislation. It didn't accomplish what it set out to do. So I gave all the arguments for suspect class, but just at the last minute I said it's not necessary for me to decide on this issue. We'll just go on and say it has no rational basis. I think that this circuit,

as I remember, came out full blast for suspect class. The
Supreme Court put these undocumented alien children in
the same category as women, or virtually so. They called for
"heightened scrutiny."

The state law was, in truth, an easy target. Its defenders made
claims, easily refuted, that it would save money (although the children
involved constituted only 40 out of 1,600 pupils), that their parents
paid no taxes (although they obviously did pay sales tax, the basic
revenue source in Texas), that they came to Texas for education
(rather than jobs), that undocumented children were particularly
likely to transmit communicable diseases, and that the law would
relieve the need for special education programs such as bilingual education (although these costs were overwhelmingly paid by the federal
government and actually spent on other Mexican American children,
who were citizens or legal aliens). Disdaining these paltry defenses,
Judge Justice moved to "invalidate state efforts that fail to demonstrate a rational basis and that make scapegoats of a defenseless
group, chosen in an arbitrary or even invidious manner."[22]

Justice's careful strategy succeeded on appeal. The circuit court
did not accept his minor argument, that federal legislation had pre-
empted state action. Otherwise, it essentially adopted his reasoning,
and even some of his fervor. It unequivocally brought undocumented
aliens within the "equal protection" clause. It, too, considered the
possibility of their categorization as a "suspect class" but ultimately
shied away from taking this step. On the basic issue, however, it
clearly set limits: "A state's desire to save money cannot be the basis
of the total exclusion from public schools. . . . Texas may not justify
its discrimination by a mere desire to discriminate."[23]

The ultimate test would be the U.S. Supreme Court, for only
it could transform Judge Justice's views into the authoritative "law
of the land." On the vital threshold issue, the reach of the constitu-

tional protections, the Supreme Court—speaking through Justice William Brennan, writing for the Court, —adopted the Texan's position, firmly declaring that "the protection of the Fourteenth Amendment extends to anyone, citizen or stranger, who is subject to the laws of a State, and reaches into every corner of a State's territory."[24] The Supreme Court was unwilling to treat illegal aliens as a suspect class, and it would not declare education to be a fundamental constitutional right. Yet its sympathies were clearly on the side of the children, who bore no personal responsibility for their illegal residence. Contrary to that principle of fairness, Brennan wrote, the law "imposes a lifetime hardship on a discrete class of children not accountable for their disabling status. The stigma of illiteracy will mark them for the rest of their lives. By denying these children a basic education, we deny them the ability to live within the structure of our civic institutions, and foreclose any realistic possibility that they will contribute in even the smallest way to the progress of our Nation."[25]

The Court would accept these heartless consequences only if they could be shown to further a "substantial state interest." In the understated language of the judiciary, Brennan concluded: "It is difficult to understand precisely what the State hopes to achieve by promoting the creation and perpetuation of a subclass of illiterates within our boundaries, surely adding to the problems and costs of unemployment, welfare, and crime. . . . Whatever savings might be achieved by denying these children an education, they are wholly insubstantial in light of the costs involved to these children, the State and the Nation."[26]

By a five-four vote, the Court upheld Wayne Justice and overturned the Texas statute. The decision in *Plyler v. Doe* was narrow in some respects, applying only to children and to public education. It did not end all of the disadvantages faced even by legal immigrants; still less did it remove the taint of criminality from undocumented aliens. But it did bring even this unloved group under the protection of the Constitution. That legal determination alone "made a significant advance in constitutional jurisprudence," which would "shield [undocumented aliens] from the baldest forms of discrimination."[27]

The *Plyler* decision had a broader impact than the extension of rights and opportunities to these few children or the extension of limited protections to their parents. Soon after the decision, an amnesty was offered to illegal entrants to the United States, opening citizenship to millions of undocumented aliens, surely including the very parents and children involved in this case. The legal principle established in *Plyler v. Doe* continues in effect to the present day, although the "heightened scrutiny" it inferred has not been applied to other situations.[28] The decision has been cited extensively (873 times by 1996) in subsequent decisions, particularly in regard to the rights of aliens and of students within the public schools.[29] Its egalitarian effect is evident in other important actions, including the reversal of attempts, as recent as 2002, in California and New Jersey to deny education to the children of illegal immigrants.[30]

More generally, Wayne Justice's effort embodies a basic American principle, cultural pluralism. It accorded Mexican immigrants, even if illegal entrants, the same right to equal protection available to citizens, to the freed slaves for whom the Fourteenth Amendment was written, and to the European immigrants who were later included in its coverage. The political significance of the decision is even greater. *Plyler* was a rare victory for Hispanics, long a powerless ethnic minority in the United States. Ensuring a minimal education, even for illegal entrants, created the possibility for eventual participation in the political process. In Justice Harry Blackmun's concurring words: "If a class cannot participate effectively in the process by which those rights and remedies that order society are created, that class necessarily will be relegated, by state fiat, in a most basic way to second-class status."[31]

Not far into the new century, Latinos have become the second largest ethnic group in America, surpassing African Americans. They already constitute the largest minority in the critical states of California, Texas, and Florida, and their ascent in politics is evident in the selection of such prominent persons as the speaker of the California Assembly, in the intense efforts to learn Spanish made by presidential aspirants, and in the rapid increase in naturalization and voter registration by immigrants from Mexico and other Latin American nations. America has already become a multicultural society. If it is to preserve its established democratic institutions, Hispanics must become part of the American political experience. The decision of Wayne Justice constituted a vital step in that direction.

Judicial Review and Democracy

The *Plyler* decision demonstrated how a judge could further social ends while working within the severe restraints imposed by the judicial system. It also raises general issues about the role of the judiciary in a democracy.

Wayne Justice's other decisions have also been far ranging:

- By ordering school desegregation throughout the state of Texas, his court was responsible for more school integration than any other district court in the nation in the aftermath of the Supreme Court's 1954 decision in *Brown v. the Board of Education*. Even when later modified on appeal, his desegregation order "remained the most comprehensive such order in history, encompassing over one thousand school districts and two-thirds of the Texas student population."[32]

- He ordered all Texas school districts to provide instruction in Spanish at all grade levels for Mexican-American children deficient in English, along with remedial instruction in English. Although later reversed on appeal, Justice's order stimulated an extensive improvement in the state's bilingual education.[33]

- In an attempt to establish juveniles' constitutional right to rehabilitative treatment, Justice took control over the state's juvenile prison system. Rejecting partial measures, he appointed a supervising attorney and pushed a negotiated settlement that eventually resulted in "the elimination of physical abuse and an individualized program plan for each inmate," along with "due process procedures for discipline, the end to racial segregation, . . . the hiring of trained professional staff members, the redesign of the physical plant to afford youths privacy and personal security, and the development of a recreational system."[34]

- For over two decades, Justice has supervised an almost total reform of the state's prisons. In 1979, after a trial extending over twelve months, Justice found that Texas prison conditions violated the Constitution's prohibition of "cruel and unusual punishments." His orders were somewhat restricted on appeal, but they still resulted in major improvements in regard to overcrowding, prisoner safety, due process, hygiene, and health care. "The decision is regarded by many as the most successful prison reform case in the country," and the issue remains the major item on his docket.[35]

Granted, the judge has not been completely successful in achieving his policy goals. School desegregation slowed soon after his decision and has been unsuccessful in the major metropolitan areas. He admits that he handled the case ineffectively, largely by trying to manage the complex issues himself: "I was inexperienced in class action in those days, and I didn't know how to do it. If I had appointed a good special master, if he had gone over there and sat over there in that agency every day, and had gone through their records and pointed out things they should have been doing that they weren't doing, I think we would have gotten a lot done. But I didn't know to do that. I just didn't know. We could have done wonders with that case in the way of integration, if I had some kind of special master. But I just didn't know, I didn't have any experience. I still didn't grasp the concept."

The process of judicial review, so vigorously exercised in these cases, nonetheless raises basic issues of democratic practice. How can we justify the power of an unelected (and decidedly unpopular) judge to overturn the decisions of an elected legislature, which surely acted in accordance with the views of the state's majority? In his *Plyler* dissent in the Supreme Court, Chief Justice Warren Burger raised precisely this question. The chief justice, personally a decent man, was also critical of the Texas law: "Were it our business to set the Nation's social policy, I would agree without hesitation that it is senseless for an enlightened society to deprive any children—including illegal aliens—of an elementary education. I fully agree that it would be folly—and wrong." Burger, however, argued that his responsibilities as a judge were limited and that the Court should not attempt its own "speedy and wholesale formulation of 'remedies' for the failures—or simply the laggard pace—of the political processes of our system of government."[36]

The issue is not easily resolved. Some judges, such as Burger in this case, simply put their trust in the political process, believing that popular majorities and government officials will generally do right. Others are comfortable in restraining the political branches of government. Wayne Justice, for example, is suspicious of legislators: "They respond to influence, because they need influence to win elections." He makes no apologies for intervening to protect minorities: "Well, you know, we live in a democracy all right. But it is a democracy that is limited by our Constitution. The majority cannot oppress the minority under the terms of our Bill of Rights. So I have not felt the slightest twinge about remedying unjust situations just because the majority wanted it that way, because the Constitution requires it otherwise. The idea that, well, he is going against the majority—well, of course I am. I am doing it because I am supposed to. If the majority is not following the Constitution, they have to be reined back."

Judicial review has been both long established and continually controversial in American history. The framers of the Constitution made it "the supreme law of the land" and assumed—but did not specify—that it was the duty of judges "to declare all acts contrary to the manifest tenor of the Constitution void."[37] The suggestion was accepted by the first great U.S. chief justice, John Marshall, who declared that "the constitution controls any legislative act repugnant to it" and that "it is emphatically the province and duty of the judicial department to say what the law is."[38] Philosophically, judicial review has been praised as "the chief means at hand for making real in the world the idea of the limitations of the power of the State itself."[39]

Others have disputed the judiciary's power, including Presidents Jefferson, Jackson, Lincoln, and Franklin Roosevelt. Judicial review has been condemned as a defense of conservative interests, not of personal liberties, and an undemocratic "check on elections, a nullification of the powers of government by the consent of the government."[40] Robert Dahl incisively states the problem raised for democratic theory: "We cannot simultaneously lodge the authority to make laws and policies exclusively in the hands of elected officials who are, at least in principle, accountable to citizens through elections and at the same time give the judicial branch the authority, in effect, to make crucial public policies."[41]

Wayne Justice, an advocate of democratic government and certainly not a conservative, readily defends judicial activism. He argues "a lawyer's duty as an advocate requires him or her not only to contemplate, but actually to participate in the development of the law."[42]

He bases his position on three related grounds. First, Justice finds activism inescapable, because the Constitution requires interpretation. Although he reveres the Constitution, Justice argues that the framers themselves believed "that the words had their own intrinsic meaning; and if interpretation was called for, it was for the judge to decide what the meaning was, regardless of what the authors may have intended." As he also points out, interpretation will inevitably involve the judges' own values:

> All of the judges are their background; they are victims of their upbringing, products of their upbringing. We all enter the trial of a case with a different attitude. If you just decided on the law alone, why is it we have these 5 to 4 decisions on the Supreme Court? I don't believe that. And they say, well, the law is plain. There is nothing that is plain about the law that I've found yet. You look at the same words, and they mean different things to you. If that were true, if we were all capable of arriving at the same meaning by looking at the words, [why] do we have so many different denominations founded on the Bible, different readings of the Bible? It is just not so.

In a second defense of judicial review, Justice focuses on the purposes of court intervention. "The Court must ask itself, 'For what human purpose—to what end—should these property rights be recognized as constitutionally protected?'" Proper activism should exemplify "the most basic concern of rights decision-making, the protection of human dignity."[43] Acknowledging that "the judicial task is necessarily a normative one," the Texan still endorses a fundamental criterion, both lucidly moral and almost naive in its simplicity: "the ultimate test of the Justices' work must be goodness."[44]

The Texan also presents a third, procedural defense for his own activism. Justice defends his practice as "remedial activism," which he supports as "completely consistent with the obligation of a district court judge to determine the existence of constitutional injuries and impose appropriate remedies based upon the evidence adduced in the case."[45] Justice's argument here is simply the legal adage that there must be a remedy for every wrong. An active judiciary is necessary to develop remedies because the political branches of government are subject to inertia and may thus initially resist progressive change, such as desegregation.

Recently, however, the power of the judiciary has been disputed not only as normatively improper but also as empirically futile. Gerald Rosenberg argues that court action is neither necessary nor sufficient to achieve significant social change, instead emphasizing the impact of the elected branches of government, social movements, and the "current" and "tide" of history. After examining the role of the courts in major issues, including racial desegregation and abortion, Rosenberg concludes "U.S. courts can *almost never* be effective producers of significant social reform." He belittles their contribution as "akin to officially recognizing the evolving state of affairs, more like the cutting of the ribbons on a new project than its construction."[46]

In contrast, Wayne Justice believes that his activism has had significant effects—and his critics would unhappily agree. His career suggests a broader perspective on judicial activism. The courts' review of the elected branches of government, properly understood, can be defended as neither an improper infringement or a necessary restriction on majority rule, but on grounds of democracy itself. The actions of the courts may facilitate democratic government by broadening the political process to include new *people,* new *considerations,* and new *issues.*

The prodemocratic role of the courts is most obvious when judges' rulings open the political process to fuller participation. In implementing school desegregation, Southern district and appellate judges created new opportunities for African Americans.[47] In overturning once-segregated primary elections in the South, the Supreme Court enabled blacks to participate in the most critical contests in these one-party states. By requiring equal populations among legislative districts, the Supreme Court enabled urban and suburban majorities to control state legislatures.[48] Even though it is not an elected, majoritarian institution, in taking such actions the Court promoted "the fundamental rights that are necessary to the existence of a democratic political system."[49]

The judiciary can also serve democracy by facilitating public discussion of considerations that go beyond the immediate controversy over some issue. Properly handled, "judicial review brings principle to bear on the operations of government," argues Alexander Bickel. "Their insulation and the marvelous mystery of time give courts the capacity to appeal to men's better nature, to call forth their aspirations, which may have been forgotten in the moment's hue and cry."[50] When, for example, the Supreme Court declared school desegregation unconstitutional, it did limit the power of state legislatures by denying them the right to create a particular kind of educational system. At the same time, it compelled the states, and indeed the nation, to consider the full meaning of equality—the founding principle of America—and to confront historical racism.

Courts may also promote democracy when they bring new issues into the political process, and encourage, even require, voters and elected bodies to wrestle with previously neglected matters. "Providing effective access to participants who wish to take part in decision making, placing issues on the agenda of public opinion and of other political institutions, providing an imprimatur of legitimacy to one side or another . . . these are all important parts of the policy-making process."[51] For example, the Supreme Court recently considered the putative "right to die" of terminally ill patients. Declining to reach a final conclusion, it neither approved nor disapproved the practice of assisted suicide. Although its decision left the issue in the hands of state legislatures, the Court's review gave the problem greater prominence on the public agenda.[52]

Contrary to Rosenberg's argument, these examples show how the courts can foster social change. Legislative and executive action were needed to make court rulings on desegregation effective, but those actions were "rendered compelling policy, and probably passed constitutional muster because *Brown* had already established desegregated public education as a substantive right protected by the Equal Protection Clause."[53] As desegregation and other issues illustrate, "the judiciary's real power and efficacy lies in how its decisions influence our political language and the way we think about political and social issues. The Court's decisions have tremendous sway over the way we think about politics, providing the opportunity and impetus for action."[54]

In our major example, the *Plyler* case, Wayne Justice promoted democracy in all three ways. Providing free education for the children of illegal aliens would enable them better to participate in the political process when they became adults. By demonstrating the unfairness of their exclusion from public schools, Justice brought considerations of principle to the issue. His own decision put the issue of their education onto the legislative agenda. An apparent and short-term restriction on democratic majority rule in truth created a long-term expansion of democratic principles.

William Wayne Justice exemplifies the heroism that is possible within the judicial institutions of American government. His virtues are those of a judge, not a missionary. He emphasizes hard work, careful research, and persistence. "I did not skimp the work. Everybody I was associated with during those years knows that. I was getting by on about a half a day a week doing the essential personal things, like buying groceries and paying bills, and things like that. And maybe go to the movies. The rest of the time I was working—Saturdays, Sundays. Having a caseload that was so terrific in those days—I had one time 1,157 civil actions—and a substantial criminal case going, and juggling about three or four class actions at the same time. They just didn't leave me any time."

Justice's passion for hard work was rewarded in his favorite case, *Plyler v. Doe*. At many points in both the circuit and U.S. Supreme Court decisions, the reviewing judges refer to the extensive factual record developed in his courtroom. Since factual judgments are usually accepted on appeal, this accumulation of detail strengthened the conclusions he drew from the facts that he established at trial. But Justice makes light of this devotion to his work. "I would be bored to death if I didn't have cases to do," he explains simply. Yet he also finds another motive for his commitment in his favorite Bible verse, Matthew 6.34: "Take therefore no thought for the morrow: for the morrow shall take thought for the things of itself. Sufficient unto the day is the evil thereof."[55]

William Wayne Justice does not present an image of a storybook hero. Like our other figures, he emphasizes his duty to his job, while focusing on his responsibility to protect the disadvantaged. "I worked like a slave. I gave the best I had. If it worked out, that is good; if it didn't—well, still I did the best I could." By giving his best, this judge has made America more just.

Chapter Seven
Frances Kelsey

A Hero of Bureaucracy

Can bureaucrats be heroes? The common view of these workers in public administration would rule out the possibility. They are often regarded as unfeeling time-servers, automatons ensnarled in "red tape," using pointless rules to complicate our lives for no good reason. Encountering bureaucracy, citizens often feel like Joseph K., Franz Kafka's pathetic victim in *The Trial*, who never knows what his offense is or wins vindication.

Like it or not, bureaucracy is one of the major institutions of American politics. Indeed, it is the largest of these institutions. The Constitution simply vests all executive power in the president and only vaguely suggests the possible creation of "Executive Departments." Yet the two million bureaucrats of the national government vastly outnumber the elected and appointed members of the Congress, the presidency, and the courts. If ordinary heroes are vital to the American democratic process, they should certainly be found among the bureaucrats.

Frances Oldham Kelsey, a bureaucrat, is one such hero. In 1962, while working as a staff scientist for the Food and Drug Administration, she prevented the introduction of the drug thalidomide into the United States. Sold abroad as a mild sedative, widely used to treat morning sickness in pregnant women and insomnia, it had become the third-largest-selling drug in Germany and was available in forty-six countries, often without a prescription. This drug, if taken during early pregnancy, was eventually found to cause serious harm to fetuses. Ultimately, twelve thousand children would be born worldwide with major defects, most commonly without arms and legs, a condition called phocomelia.[1]

By taking action, Dr. Kelsey prevented similar damage from occurring to thousands of other children born in the United States. She spared these unborn children and their parents immense pain, as well as the potentially immense expense of caring for such children. In recognition of her work, Dr. Kelsey won promotion, a presidential citation, and international recognition. Her work led to major legislation, giving the FDA authority to monitor the effectiveness, as well as the safety, of new drugs. Her achievements, however, are more than the accomplishments of a life-sustaining individual. Kelsey is a hero of the bureaucratic institution.

Frances Kelsey and the FDA

Frances Oldham Kelsey offers a sharp personal contrast to Peter Rodino, our first subject: a female scientist-bureaucrat rather than a male lawyer-politician, a reserved Canadian from the Midwestern plains rather than a gregarious Italian American from Newark's dense streets. Our interview took place in a standard government-issue office without plaques and degrees, still laden with packing boxes after two-and-a-half years' occupancy, rather than a congressional office decorated with the photographs and flags that symbolize power. Despite their individual differences, however, both are democratic heroes.

Raised on Vancouver Island, Canada (where a middle school now bears her name), Frances Oldham was educated at McGill University and received her Ph.D. from the University of Chicago. She then went on to medical school at Chicago, and thinks it possible that she avoided sexual discrimination in admissions because of her first name, which is easily confused with its male counterpart, Francis. Ten years of medical research, practice, and teaching in Chicago and South Dakota followed.

Like our other exemplars, Kelsey resists efforts to depict her work as heroic. She avoids probes into her personal feelings or motivations, talking readily only about her career.[2] In her earlier years, she had been involved in another notable inquiry, when her graduate adviser found that the base of a sulfa elixir was essentially antifreeze (diethylene glycol) and had consequently been responsible for serious injuries and even deaths, particularly among children.[3] In related work, she tested the effect of synthetic substitutes for quinine, the antimalarial drug, on rabbits. "She found that rabbits metabolized quinine rapidly, but pregnant rabbits had less ability to break down the drug, and embryonic rabbits could not break it down at all."[4] This study, on which she and her future husband, Fremont Kelsey, collaborated, was one of the first "to call attention to the fact that some drugs which adults can take safely can be dangerous to embryos in the womb."[5] An amateur psychologist might speculate that these investigations made her a crusader for children's health and that her zeal was further stimulated when she later became the mother of two. Yet even when she was working on embryo metabolism of new drugs, she said her motivation was "just scientific interest." In her opinion, her most significant research was work on the pituitary gland and on antimalarial drugs.

Throughout her career, Kelsey emphasized the ordinary canons of scientific investigation. In her first job after graduating from medical school, she had worked for the *Journal of the American Medical Association* as an editorial associate, reviewing drug studies submitted for publication, and was struck by "the poor quality of the studies that came in." Later, at the FDA, this experience aroused her skep-

Dr. Frances O. Kelsey

ticism, when "many of the studies in support of safety of the new drugs were done by investigators whose work had not been accepted for publication in the *Journal*. I found that those were the ones doing the studies on drug applications."[6]

Kelsey came to the FDA in 1960, when her husband took a position at the National Institutes of Health. At the time, the FDA received an average of 693 applications for new drugs annually but had very limited resources available for review. A small staff of only seven full-time and four part-time physicians, and similar numbers of chemists and pharmacologists, faced a sixty-day time limit for approval or rejection of the drug applications. Moreover, even before these potentially dangerous substances were licensed, manufacturers were allowed to conduct field trials of new drugs. Kelsey succeeded another woman physician, Dr. Barbara Moulton, who "had quit in disgust because her superiors had repeatedly overruled her decisions. . . . She was particularly critical of the close relationships between FDA officials and drug makers and the way agents of the drug companies were permitted to harass FDA doctors and scientists with constant phone calls and visits."[7]

The status of the Food and Drug Administration in 1960 was uncertain. Its role was certainly important, ensuring safety in foods and medicines. This vital mission, however, did not immediately win the FDA strong political support. Approval of safe medicines is a "collective good," one desired by everybody but that has no identifiable individual beneficiaries.[8] Patients who do *not* receive an unsafe drug never know that their lives have been spared and therefore have no reason to give support to the FDA and its review procedures. Drug companies, however, have an obvious interest—market share and profit—in limiting FDA supervision and in moving their products quickly toward licensing approval.

Because of this imbalance, bureaucracies tend to seek political protection by developing close relationships with "their" constituency, "those groups, both governmental and nongovernmental, whose interests must be taken into account." As a result, "administrative agencies tend generally to act in accordance with the dominant interests in their constituency. . . . If an agency is to survive it must be able to obtain enough political support from non-opposing groups to offset adversary groups."[9] Government officials and private businessmen consequently develop close personal relationships. These connections are often facilitated by overt roles given to regulated groups within the very bureaucracy responsible for their regulation. "Most but not all interest groups and occupational clusters have some organizational expression in the departments, agencies, bureaus and divisions of the national government, the leadership of which is expected to be responsive to the group to a greater or lesser extent."[10]

In some cases, these relationships result in the "capture" of the bureaucracy. Rather than restricting businesses, the government's power is turned to the industry's self-interest, as administrators "use their discretion to serve the interests of the regulated sector."[11] For example, the Federal Energy Regulatory Commission has often shown more concern for maintaining the profitability of power companies than in limiting the prices consumers pay for electricity. More often, though, a bureaucracy is open to multiple influences, seeking support through a complex "issue network" of interests, experts, administrators, and elected officials. But even this "loose-jointed play of influence" does not assure that general public needs such as drug safety will be met.[12] The imbalance between a general but passive public interest and specific and vocal special interests had been evident throughout the history of food and drug regulation in the United States, giving the FDA "a reputation for excessive sensitivity to industry."[13] Efforts toward the control of dangerous substances have tended to be sporadic, typically occurring only after a human tragedy has aroused the nation.

There was no federal regulation at all until 1906, when Upton Sinclair's muckraking novel *The Jungle,* which depicted the dirt, danger, and disease in the meatpacking industry, was published. The Food and Drug Act, passed that same year, prohibited interstate shipment of adulterated food and drugs but gave enforcement powers to the Department of Agriculture, an agency without strong commitment to the undertaking. Moreover, the law's reach was limited: "False therapeutic claims for patent medicines were basically unregulated [and] standards for food purity and content were nonexistent." Regulation received new impetus in a drug tragedy of 1937. Sulfa drugs had been developed to fight strep throat and similar infections, and one manufacturer had developed a liquid form to simplify giving the drug to children. This was the elixir that Kelsey and her adviser found to be deadly, but not before 107 people, many of them children, had died in severe pain. But the chemical company that "had produced an unsafe pharmaceutical problem did not violate any existing law." New legislation in 1938, and subsequent amendments, moved the Food and Drug Administration into more supportive cabinet departments focused on public health. This legislation required that new drugs be scientifically proven safe before they could be marketed and that consumers be warned of potential hazards. It would take the next tragedy, thalidomide, to make these requirements truly effective.[14]

Thalidomide: The Wonder Drug

With the clear vision of hindsight, the history of thalidomide demonstrated the need for independent governmental supervision of new drugs. At first, the medicine apparently provided great benefit to certain individuals, and its side effects seemed limited. Consumers, however, had no way of knowing the dangers; to ward off tragedy, political action would have been required, as London's *Sunday Times* observed: "The knowledge and scientific procedures to give protection were available. The disaster might well have been averted everywhere. Arguably, the havoc wrought could have been much less than which occurred."[15] But ensuring the safety of consumers could only come through the collective power of government.

The regulation of drugs exemplifies the need for government bureaucracies, which develop, as Anthony Downs explains, because "important social functions cannot be performed adequately by market-oriented organizations." Drug safety involves an "external benefit" that "does not reflect itself in market prices." It is an "indivisible benefit. As soon as it exists, everyone is able to benefit from it regardless of whether he himself has paid for it." To achieve these benefits, nonmarket bureaucracies are required to provide resources for such social functions as national defense, education, and medical safety. They are also needed to control monopolies, such as a pharmaceutical company that holds patent on a drug. Most relevant, government can provide the "protection of consumers from their own ignorance or incompetence."[16] All these theoretical efforts were necessary in the real case of the use, and misuse, of thalidomide.

The drug was originally distributed in 1958 as a nonaddictive sedative, to relieve insomnia; its additional ability to alleviate morning sickness was soon noted. In the highly competitive market for sleeping pills, thalidomide was vigorously promoted by a German company, Chemie Gruenenthal. No controlled tests were conducted to assess its effects on women in the critical first trimester of pregnancy, but claims of complete safety were made on the basis of reports from women in the later stages. Commonly sold without prescription, the sedative soon accounted for nearly half the company's gross profits.

Doctors in many nations, however, soon suspected a connection between thalidomide and a condition called peripheral neuritis, a loss of sensation in toes and legs, which could be "followed by severe muscular cramps, weakness of the limbs, and a lack of coordination." In rebutting these charges, Gruenenthal tried many strategies, conceding only that individuals who developed these symptoms should stop using the drug. As more reports accumulated, however, the company "lied when doctors wrote [about the symptoms]"; "denied all causal connection between thalidomide and peripheral neuritis"; "tried to conceal the number of cases that had been reported"; "tried to suppress publication of reports"; "sought to counter critical reports [through] money ... influence, and ... distortion"; and "fought to prevent the drug's going on prescription."[17]

Eager to expand its market to the United States, Gruenenthal licensed thalidomide to an American pharmaceutical company, Richardson-Merrell, which adopted the brand name Kevadon. By the middle of 1959, before U.S. drug trials, Kevadon was widely distributed to doctors, a procedure then permitted under the law. Merrell claimed the drug could treat at least twenty-four different medical conditions, including sexual ailments ranging from menopause to premature ejaculation. "If thalidomide were not an elixir to cure all the ills of mankind," wrote the *Sunday Times,* "then it was certainly intended to make them incomparably easier to bear."[18] As Kelsey wryly remembered, "one of the claims or the mentions in the brochure included several cases in which persons had tried to commit suicide and been unable to do so," which led to "a later comment that, had thalidomide been on the market, Marilyn Monroe would be alive today."[19]

The claims were based on data that were at best faulty, and at worse fraudulent. The only animal tests cited had been conducted abroad, and some evidence of fetal damage had been ignored. Instead of conducting further animal tests, Merrell embarked on a human "investigational program," distributing over 2.5 million pills of Kevadon to 1,267 doctors and over 20,000 patients, including thousands of fertile women. The program ignored scientific standards: there were no control groups, nor any requirement that doctors keep records, and therefore no list of patients receiving the drug.

In fact, the investigation was not even conducted by Merrell's scientists, but by its sales force, which was instructed to see the campaign as a means to acquire publicity, not data: "You can assure your doctors that they need not report results. . . . Appeal to the doctor's ego—we think he is important enough to be selected as one of the first to use Kevadon."[20] After a year, Merrell was ready to seek FDA approval. But it was not prepared to meet Frances Kelsey.

Thalidomide v. Kelsey

In September 1960, one month after joining the FDA, Kelsey was assigned her first drug review, of thalidomide, heading the usual three-person team of a physician, chemist, and pharmacologist. The job appeared to be a routine review, an easy way to introduce her to her new duties. In the context of her job, Kelsey is best seen as a scientist, working for a bureaucracy, and trying to further the purposes of that bureaucracy—safe drugs. For the FDA, the review of thalidomide was but an example, ultimately exceptional in its consequences, of standard practices. Illustrating these bureaucratic routines, Kelsey and her associates first delayed approval of thalidomide for purely technical reasons, as demonstrated in this matter-of-fact list of detailed objections drawn from "Denial of Approval for Thalidomide in the U.S.": "the animal data were not reported in full detail"; "the chronic toxicity data were incomplete"; there were "deficiencies relating to details of the manufacturing process"; "the asymmetrical carbon atom in the molecule [an indicator of possible problems] was noted"; "insufficient cases had been studied"; "the claims of safety were not adequately supported."

After these technical issues were raised, the drug company submitted a new application, only to meet with new objections. A bureaucratic pattern developed. Limited to sixty days for its review, the FDA team would reject Merrell's application, thereby beginning a new cycle. Merrell would submit new data, the reviewers would raise new objections, and the clock would start again. In the meanwhile, Kelsey had also begun to worry about the possible connection between thalidomide and peripheral neuritis. Her doubts were based on a research note in a British scientific journal that she had found almost by accident as she was checking references on another drug. The manufacturer, Merrell, still wanted to go ahead with Kevadon, merely adding a warning label to the medication. "Dr. Kelsey shook her head. She pointed out that they were only talking about a sleeping pill. It was not a cure for some hitherto incurable disease from which people were dying daily. As she saw it, giving Merrell a license to make people sick would be inexcusable."[21]

The FDA team's repeated objections brought complaints from the manufacturer, Kelsey remembered, that she was "dragging [her] feet . . . nit-picking and asking for unnecessary stuff. There were some raised eyebrows." Merrell appealed to Kelsey's superior, then went up the bureaucratic ladder to plead with the head of the agency's medical division, and finally went to the top, visiting the head of the FDA. As Kelsey puts it, rather mildly: "I guess they were a little aggressive on it. You sort of expect that, they were anxious to get it on the market." Writing about *Women of Courage,* Margaret Truman is more forceful: "It was a subtle way of applying pressure by letting Dr. Kelsey know that Merrell had access to much more important people in the FDA."[22] In the circumstances, the politically prudent action would have been to accept the manufacturer's assurances and its promises of careful marketing.[23]

Kelsey remained obdurate. Throughout the review, her focus was on professional precision, not on a sentimental protection of children. She disdained the Merrell application because it was "sloppy." It lacked complete data on the tests that had been employed, as well as on the samples, the controls, and the company's scientists, and it even included mistranslations of the original German research articles. Procedures were easily abused. "We got the impression from a new drug application that maybe forty or fifty doctors had the privilege of trying it out," Kelsey said. But Merrell, instead of following the usual practice of focused testing, "came back with a list of over a thousand doctors all over the States. . . . They didn't bother keeping records."

In May 1961, spurred by Merrell's failure to disclose its available information on peripheral neuritis, Kelsey wrote a straightforward summary of her objections, its dispassionate tone disguising her growing personal concern: "In particular the application does not include complete reports of adequate animal studies nor sufficiently extensive, complete and adequate clinical studies to permit an evaluation of the toxic effects of the drug which have been manifested by reports of cases of peripheral neuritis. . . . Detailed case studies with adequate follow-up studies will be required to determine whether the condition is reversible. . . . The burden of proof that the drug is safe—which must include adequate studies of all the manifestations of toxicity which medical or clinical experience suggest—lies with the applicant."[24]

By September 1961, she had begun to wonder about the long-term effects of the drug, particularly on fetuses—something that had never been tested. Her skepticism increased in the absence of any data on the use of thalidomide during the early months of pregnancy, since Merrell's reports applied only to the last trimester (and even those reports were tainted). "Recalling how quinine had affected adult rabbits and fetuses differently, Kelsey wondered what effect thalidomide may have if used during pregnancy. She suspected that a drug that could damage nerves could also affect a developing fetus."[25] Backed by her superiors, Kelsey insisted on new animal tests, and the FDA warned that pregnant women should be excluded from further tests of Kevadon.

Kelsey now wanted the drug to be withdrawn, and she achieved her goal in November 1961. Before the FDA could act on its own, reports came from Germany, Australia, and Britain of teratogenic defects in babies born to mothers using thalidomide: "Many children had foreshortened limbs, often no more than flippers like casual addenda to the trunk. Eye and ear deformities were common. . . . There were babies with malformed kidneys, others whose genitals were missing or deformed. It was as though the jigsaw of life had been jumbled and the pieces forced into places they could not fit or simply left out altogether."[26]

Although the German manufacturer continued to resist, to deny a causal connection between thalidomide and these birth defects, and to suppress evidence, following a German newspaper report in late November, the German government forced Gruenenthal to withdraw the drug. Only now did Merrell conduct appropriate animal tests, using rabbits, not mice. These tests provided evidence of the dreadful side effects, which led to the formal withdrawal of Merrell's application in March 1962. But the company's action came too late—at least seventeen deformed children had already been conceived in the United States. In the rest of the world, where the sale of drugs was typically less closely regulated, the toll was tragically far higher. Lawsuits brought by consumers were successful in most of the world, but only one jury trial was ever held in the United States. It initially resulted in a $2.75 million award for damages, later reduced on appeal to $500,000.

Kelsey had prevented an American catastrophe, even though she had focused not on fetal damage but on adult symptoms of peripheral neuritis. Perhaps her qualms were only lucky guesses, but good luck is the residue of good preparation. As she put it, "there was something that I just didn't like about the drug. Maybe that's woman's intuition or something foolish, but I don't think so." In fact, her caution stemmed from informed professional judgment, not inexplicable intuition: "I was not prepared to see the type of applications that were submitted, because I lived in sort of an academic dream world, I guess.... It was so superficial and so anecdotal." Overall, "what emerges from the record is that she got it right largely for the right reasons. True, she did not *predict* that thalidomide would cause birth deformities, but she *did* ask the question."[27] And the nation got the right answer.

Kelsey's action has sometimes incurred criticism, and even ridicule, in a way that illuminates, although unintentionally, the character of her bureaucratic heroism. Dr. Steven Harris, an opponent of FDA regulatory practice, correctly points out that the FDA already had nominal authority over the safety of drugs even before thalidomide and that the later statutes added power over efficacy, not safety (although they also made it easier for the FDA to assess safety). "It was only by the sheerest chance that the red-tape" delayed thalidomide until the connection was made to birth defects, he argues. Rather than a hero, he denigrates Kelsey as only "a delay-causing bureaucrat" who allowed Europeans to serve as first-class 'guinea pigs' for Americans, in a case where (quite literally) guinea pigs themselves would not have done an adequate job."[28] He regrets the new powers gained by FDA as a result, arguing that the agency has harmfully delayed many desirable drugs and has limited patients' access to experimental therapies.

Harris's policy position has some validity, and complaints about FDA delays have recently led Congress to require speedier trials. At the same time, he minimizes the difficulties in FDA safety regulation at the time of thalidomide. In criticizing Kelsey for her caution, moreover, he ironically praises her "ordinary" virtues. We expect a good bureaucrat—and a good scientist—to be careful, to apply objective rules, to act on the basis of the relevant evidence. As a scientist, Kelsey waited for reliable data, which could have been provided by proper clinical tests, as Merrell's tardy efforts demonstrate. Her caution was particularly appropriate at the time, given the absence of any system for the international exchange of information about new drugs. For example, German scientists had some suspicions about birth defects, but the manufacturer's promotional material said that the drug was widely used in North America—meaning Canada. When the German scientists checked with U.S. hospitals, they didn't know that thalidomide had not been approved for use in this country; therefore they found no unusual cases and dropped their investigation. Nor did

Kelsey experiment on humans, European or American, but the terrible human results justified her bureaucratic posture.

The Effects of the Thalidomide Controversy

Major consequences followed on the heels of Merrell's withdrawal of thalidomide. The FDA did not itself publicize the thalidomide case, refraining from making political capital of the incident. "In those days," Kelsey explains, "it was just different, you just didn't air those things." Even later, when famous, Kelsey herself published only two short medical journal articles about thalidomide.[29] Instead, the story was broken by the *Washington Post* on July 15, 1962, under a headline, "'Heroine' of FDA Keeps Bad Drug Off of Market," and subsequently received broad coverage in the media. In August, President John Kennedy awarded Kelsey the highest honor in the government, the Distinguished Federal Civilian Service medal. A year later, after reorganization at the FDA, she became chief of the Division of New Drugs. After successive promotions, she was still working at the end of the century, at the age of eighty-six, as the director of Scientific Investigations. In 2000, she was inducted into the National Women's Hall of Fame.

The thalidomide publicity engendered major legislative change. Kelsey, although not active in politics, makes a shrewd political judgment: "If you want the law to change, you have to have something that affects children. Because that did it overnight." After years of inaction, a Senate subcommittee chaired by Estes Kefauver could use the near tragedy to gain support of its efforts to amend the drug safety laws. Kefauver had been primarily concerned with the price of drugs, and with the monopolistic implications of the cozy relationships between the drug companies and the American Medical Association. The concern was that the companies held tight control over the manufacture and distribution of new drugs while insulating themselves from medical criticism by spending millions on advertising in the association's journal. Kefauver's investigations and hearings went on for two years, but reform legislation faced uncertain prospects. A tepid measure had been worked out between the Kennedy White House and conservative legislators, but Kefauver found it of little value. "The best things that could be said for the new bill," he remarked sarcastically, "was that it did not repeal the Food, Drug and Cosmetic Act of 1938."[30] Once the thalidomide story became news, however, the focus became drug safety rather than drug prices. The administration and congressional opponents quickly changed their positions in favor of stricter regulation. Amendments to the existing act were swiftly and unanimously passed, giving the FDA jurisdiction over the effectiveness, as well as the safety, of new drugs. Furthermore, standards for drug safety were also extended. Three months after the news of thalidomide broke, President Kennedy signed the new law.

Under the new law, the FDA would have to give approval even to experimental studies, the departmental secretary was required to give specific approval to any new drug and could also order a drug off the market instantly if evidence arose that it was unsafe, informed consent was required of patients taking medications, unqualified doctors could be removed from trials, and manufacturers were required to report adverse reactions publicly. "Back then," Kelsey recalled of the early 1960s, "most applications were about four volumes in size. Today, they are about a hundred to two hundred volumes." FDA resources were also expanded considerably; over two hundred medical officers are currently on the staff and are now insulated from pressures by the industry.[31] Before marketing a drug, the manufacturer must now submit detailed data on both safety and efficacy. In contrast to the situation at the time Merrell applied for licensing of thalidomide, data from other tests cannot be substituted for U.S. trials, and extensive animal tests are required before controlled human trials. Prior screening of drugs is the most stringent in the world, so much so that the agency is most likely to be criticized for its strictness and for insufficient monitoring after drugs have cleared these already high barriers. In short, "the FDA has certainly used its muscle."[32]

There was still another consequence to this story, unintended but large. One American woman, a pregnant Arizona broadcaster named Sherry Finkbein, borrowed thalidomide from her husband, who had used it for insomnia on an overseas trip. When Ms. Finkbein learned in 1962 of the likely deformities of her fetus, she flew to Europe to have the abortion that was then illegal in the United States. Finkbein publicized her problems with thalidomide, not her abortion. But her case spurred the movement to legalize abortion, probably the most divisive political issue of the last three decades.

The ironic epilogue to this story is the return of thalidomide. In the past four years, the drug has been found to be effective in treatment of a variety of serious illnesses, including leprosy, pancreatic cancer, and AIDS.[33] One prominent patient is Geraldine Ferraro, the Democratic vice-presidential candidate in 1984, who is receiving thalidomide treatment for multiple myeloma, or bone-marrow cancer.[34] The new uses of thalidomide offer another testament to the virtues of the bureaucratic process. The FDA insisted on scientific studies to explore the drug's basic chemistry. The studies found that the drug inhibits the growth of new blood vessels, an effect that explains both its effect on fetuses and its recent successes.

If these investigations had been conducted decades earlier, there probably would have been no horrific births. As it is today, the FDA has approved the limited distribution of thalidomide, with strong marketing controls, including monthly testing on women of childbearing age. With these controls, developed after consultation with its surviving victims, "thalidomide is now the strictest regulated drug in U.S. history, and so far there have been no fetal exposures."[35]

One leader in developing these regulatory guidelines was Frances Kelsey, who followed the scientific evidence that allowed the return of thalidomide. Still committed to the principles of effective regulation, "she provided the moral and scientific backbone to the group."[36]

The American Bureaucratic Institution

The thalidomide controversy illustrates the character of bureaucracy, the newest and largest institution of American government. Bureaucracy often works well—as it did in this case—but the ways it works often differ from theoretical expectations.

Complex administrative organizations are ubiquitous in modern society; bureaucracies exist not only in government but in most private organizations as well. "Groups, federations, insurance companies, corporations, and government agencies share at least one common trait: they impose an administrative process on as much of their internal structures and on as much of their environments as they possibly can."[37] In government, as the work of the FDA illustrates, bureaucracy is usually "indispensable in translating abstract intentions into workable programs of action, in performing the substantive work associated with executing a policy intention, in providing information based on institutional memory and continuity, in offering practical advice on what can be done, and in giving some accounting of what is being done."[38]

Kelsey was successful because she insisted on adhering precisely to bureaucratic routines—to the impersonal procedures of the FDA. Extensive formal rules are necessary and inevitable in bureaucracies, for reasons that Anthony Downs elaborates. Because they operate outside of a market context, bureaucrats cannot gauge the effect of their actions in greater or lesser profits, wages, or similar measures of business success. Instead, bureaucracies rely on "formal rules to help individuals decide their behavior." Rules promote an "efficient means of coordinating complex activities. If no such rules existed, each bureau member could respond to any given situation in whatever manner appeared appropriate to him at that time." Regular procedures also promote fairness in interactions with the public. "If no formalized rules governed such decisions, the bureau's responses to similar conditions might be quite different for different clients," which could lead to charges of discrimination and personal favoritism.[39]

Bureaucratic procedures can become burdensome, of course, as almost anyone who has filed a health insurance claim would agree. "The heavy reliance on rules, regulations, and canons of procedure can, and sometimes does, have the consequence that the bureaucrat is so preoccupied with procedural niceties as to lose sight of substantive goals. . . . A similar criticism of bureaucratic procedure is the inordinate amount of routine paperwork that characterizes any sizable office. . . . 'Red tape' is a universal bureaucratic component of inefficiency."[40] Over the course of the thalidomide review, the manufacturer did complain vigorously about the procedures and "red tape." But Merrell's real complaint was that it did not get quick approval, whatever the rules. It wanted a substantive result, not procedural regularity. In this case, "red tape" was simply an abusive term for the bureaucratic virtues of established and depersonalized procedures.

The classic description of bureaucracy was written by Max Weber, who was probably the most important sociological theorist of the twentieth century. In Weber's theory, bureaucracy is characterized by a specialization of function among officials, a hierarchy of positions in the bureaucratic agency, and "the 'objective' discharge of business . . . according to *calculable rules* and 'without regard to persons.'"[41] To Weber, the bureaucrat is an esteemed person, to whom "office-holding is a 'vocation,'" for which a long period of training is needed, and is founded on "an acceptance of a specific obligation of faithful management in return for a secure existence." In modern bureaucracy, "loyalty is devoted to impersonal and functional purposes," which require "the personally detached and strictly 'objective' expert, in lieu of the master of older social structures, who was moved by personal sympathy and favor." Efficient administration "develops the more perfectly the more the bureaucracy is 'dehumanized.'"[42]

Frances Kelsey exemplified many of the characteristics of Weber's bureaucrat, and the FDA, probably without reference to Weber, certainly tried to follow the model of the ideal bureaucracy. American public administration, however, fits the Weberian model only slightly. Certainly, American bureaucrats do not enjoy the esteem that Weber postulated. Any politician can find an easy target in "faceless bureaucrats." The suspicion of bureaucracy is evident in unfavorable comparisons of government agencies to corporations as well as by efforts, particularly noticeable in recent years, to give private employers rather than the government the power to provide social services, even in the case of such essential functions as airport security or public education.

The egalitarian traditions of the United States also conflict with the bureaucratic principles of expertise and hierarchy. A nation based on the declaration that "all men are created equal" is reluctant to acknowledge that some men and women have become more skilled and more competent than their presumed peers. Consequently, there is deeper political penetration in the American bureaucracy than in other nations, with elite "experts" having less authority, and elected and appointed "outsiders" more. The administrative branch shows considerable turnover in personnel and is based on a system of broad, democratic recruitment. "American bureaucracy is not run by a privileged group, but by men and women of diverse backgrounds. It is not separate from the community at large, but an integral part of it."[43]

The traditional model of organizational structure assumes, as Emmette Redford explains, a single hierarchical line of responsibility, where each level of the bureaucracy sets binding rules for those at subordinate levels. In reality, public administration consists of "a web of interrelationships"—with both the president and Congress seeking to control the administrative branch, bureaucrats establishing ties across agencies that have overlapping jurisdictions and also to relevant congressional committees, and with lower-level bureaucrats often able to exercise autonomous power within departments. Thus, "administrative relationships are multi-directional: they flow upward and downward and laterally in varied channels. . . . In the American polity, administration is not a function solely of the executive branch; it is a continuing function of both legislative and executive branches. . . . Every position, whether in Congress or in the executive branch, has its own official role or sets of roles and every actor has his own stakes . . . . Every line is a two-way channel of communication . . . every line of communication is a potential channel of influence for the interests represented in both the official roles and the personal stakes of actors."[44]

Rather than a hierarchical chain of command, American bureaucracy is a complex institution framing multiple contests for the power to command. Those contests can be seen even in the relationships between the president and his cabinet appointees, presumably his most loyal subordinates: "Half of a President's suggestions, which theoretically carry the weight of orders, can be safely forgotten by a Cabinet member. And if the President asks about a suggestion a second time, he can be told that it is being investigated. If he asks a third time, a wise Cabinet officer will give him at least part of what he suggests. But only occasionally, except about the most important matters, do Presidents ever get around to asking three times."[45]

The political complexity of American bureaucracy provides many other opportunities for influence. Interest groups can press their case, as the drug companies did with the FDA. Agencies with strong outside support can become insulated from control by their nominal superiors, even including the president, as was true of the FBI under J. Edgar Hoover. In many policy areas, "iron triangles" develop, in which "cozy little groups of congressmen, bureaucrats, and interest group representatives make numerous day-to-day policy decisions."[46] A classic example is the cooperation among the Army Corps of Engineers, local interests, and congressional appropriations committees in distributing the "pork barrel" of river and harbor construction projects.[47]

The regulatory commissions constitute a major part of the federal bureaucracy, governing much of American life. They are legally "independent" of both the president and Congress, but often lack clear statutory guidelines to their decisions beyond a cloudy commitment to "the public interest, convenience, and necessity," to quote the vague mandate of the Federal Communications Commission. "The fact that agencies rely on the case-by-case approach in the development and implementation of policy adds to the confusion caused by vague rules or lack of rules."[48]

In short, American bureaucracies live in a world of political uncertainty and political compromise. The realities of democratic government prevent them from meeting the ideal prescriptions of technical rationality, hierarchy, and professionalism.[49] Instead, they evince a pattern of "fragmented and decentralized administration," where "the proliferation of groups is the almost inevitable tendency of successfully enacted policies unwittingly to propagate hybrid interests." Government becomes less subject to the control of elected office holders and more open to penetration by technical experts operating through "specialized subcultures composed of highly knowledgeable policy-watchers."[50]

These complexities provide opportunities for individual bureaucrats. They can use their expertise and their secure positions to manipulate the flow of information and to shape the policy decisions of their superiors, or even to ignore or subvert directives they oppose.

Moreover, administrators "not only possess the skills and resources to formulate policy decisions but are explicitly relied upon to do so."[51] As they implement public policy, they must interpret laws and executive directives, and in so doing inevitably apply their individual knowledge, procedures, and values. The outcome can sometimes be arbitrary and sometimes beneficial, as in the case of thalidomide, but it is never a purely objective, Solomonic result.

The activities of bureaucrats differ considerably from one policy controversy to another. Most administrative decisions involve distributive policies, which typically engender relatively little conflict, because the government's benefits—such as tariffs, construction, defense contracts, or new drug approvals—can be widely distributed. "A billion-dollar issue can be disaggregated into many millions of nickel-dime items," and an administrative agency can spread these benefits with little public notice. Regulatory policies do invite conflict, however, because they involve "a direct choice as to who will be indulged and who deprived"—which groups will be allowed to vote or to work, for example, or whether pharmaceutical companies or patients will assume the risks of experimental drug trials.[52]

In the thalidomide case, the bureaucratic process changed from one kind of politics to another. When Merrell submitted its application, it was acting in a world of distributive politics, where each manufacturer routinely received approval of its products, without any political involvement on the part of its economic competitors or any awareness by patients—and still less by future children—of the stakes potentially involved. In this world of quiet micropolitics, "individuals, companies, and communities seek benefits from the larger polity for themselves."[53]

In opposing the thalidomide application, Kelsey promoted a more egalitarian ethic, which "requires that decisions regarding such interests be made with consideration of their effects on related or competing interests, and on the diffused interest of the community as a whole." When the effects of thalidomide became known, the process was transformed from distributive to regulatory politics, as Congress openly debated and strengthened drug enforcement policy. Her actions exemplify the means by which bureaucracy can limit the inequalities of restrictive micropolitics. As Redford describes the process: "Create a rule or standard that will govern in most or all micro decisions. . . . sink in administrative process the application of policy to particular situations" that establish an authoritative record and decision, and "seek judgment by persons who act expertly and impersonally. . . . In sum, the primary route to reduction of micropolitics is bureaucratic administration."[54]

Bureaucracy worked in the thalidomide case because Kelsey and her colleagues displayed the virtues of bureaucrats. They showed how bureaucracy can enhance life, quite literally, and extend individual freedom. "It is true," Downs points out, "that bureaus place far more restraints on the average man today than they did formerly." However, today's citizens also enjoy a much greater choice than they would have had in earlier times. These two trends are closely related, because "increased bureaucratic regulations are actually one of the causes of . . . greater freedom." Drug regulation, in particular, fosters longer, safer and more productive lives. As Kelsey demonstrated personally, "greater bureaucratization is one of the inherent costs of greater freedom of choice."[55]

What made Frances Kelsey a hero? She was a typical scientist and bureaucrat, not a person of rare talent. Her actions were part of her customary work, not glorious exceptions to her quotidian routine. Her colleague in the thalidomide investigation, Lee Geismar, voiced the standard refrain of these individuals: "It was just my job. I just went to work and did my job. I never set out to do anything extraordinary."[56] The heroism of Frances Kelsey is found in her ordinary deeds, which yet had exceptional impact. By her devotion to the high standards of the scientific enterprise and her commitment to the objective procedures of effective bureaucracy, and by doing her job well at an exceptional time, this exemplary administrator became another democratic hero.

Chapter Eight
Thurlow Weed

A Hero in Party Politics

Party politicians are not heroes in America. One cynic expressed a common belief when he defined the politician as "an eel in the fundamental mud upon which the superstructure of organized society is based.... As compared with the statesman, he suffers the disadvantage of being alive."[1] Officials, even though elected as Republicans or Democrats, proclaim their disdain of "partisan politics," and voters assert their own independence from party loyalty.

To political scientists, by contrast, party politicians are essential to a free society. Almost all share a belief "that the political parties created democracy and that modern democracy is unthinkable save in terms of the parties."[2] In the modern world, open competition between political parties has become the hallmark of effective democracy. Citizens accomplish their control over the government through their choice of party politicians. As politicians search for votes, they are compelled to satisfy the demands of the voters. In the words of Joseph Schumpeter, "democracy is the rule of the politician."[3]

Political parties are one of the institutions of American politics, although they are different from the institutions described in previous chapters. Parties are not included in the written Constitution, which regards them "like a scandal in polite society: they are alluded to but never discussed."[4] Nevertheless, parties are an integral part of the formal organizations of the government, shaping the workings of Congress, the election of the president, appointments to the judiciary, and policies of the bureaucracy. Their role as an established institution is recognized in statutes and constitutional law, just as their place is preserved in Americans' hearts and minds. Contrary to common expectations, even party politicians may become heroes, when their ordinary work is carried out in fitting historical circumstances. We can find such a circumstance in the greatest crisis of American history, the Civil War, and see heroism in the actions of a typical, and now unheralded, politician.

Thurlow Weed and the Civil War Crisis

Thurlow Weed is no longer remembered, but he was a major figure in American politics in the nineteenth century. Weed was the dominant figure in New York state politics for thirty years, first leading the Whig party and then taking a prominent role in the formation of the Republican party and its subsequent presidential victory at the onset of the Civil War. His actions during the war played a critical role in saving the Union.

Until the war, Weed was a typical politician of his time, although more successful than most of his colleagues and competitors. He was "a master politician with keen awareness of human nature; he knew instinctively when to use flattery and when to use force. He could bend a merchant prince . . . to his purpose as easily as he could an illiterate ward heeler."[5] As publisher of the *Albany Evening Journal,* he wielded a potent propaganda weapon at a time when the press was openly partisan and newspapers were unchallenged by other media. Despite his lack of formal education, as "the wizard of the lobby" he forged alliances and performed services for commercial interests that enabled him to rise from poverty to wealth.[6] Through

Thurlow Weed

the common techniques of patronage, government contracts, and election management, his Whig machine came to dominate the state's politics.

With New York as the largest state, he also gained considerable national influence. His support was critical in the Whig party's presidential nominations of William Henry Harrison, Henry Clay, and Zachary Taylor. Personally shy and modest, he held no public office above state assemblyman, but he wielded considerable influence behind the throne.[7] In his time, Weed "was a great power, if not a great man. Awe-inspired politicians knew him as America's most formidable political boss." With senators chosen during this period by state legislatures, not popular vote, "Thurlow Weed was a man who, when asked if he knew a certain senator, could snort, 'Know him! I created him.'"[8]

Weed had none of the personal characteristics of a storybook hero. Even a sympathetic biographer acknowledges "his proneness to coarse vituperation, his mastery of the art of evasion, his willingness to compromise his conscience for the sake of political advantage." Even his virtues were modest: "tactful and tireless, singularly gifted as an analyst of men's motives and reactions, candid with his friends and loyal to their interests."[9] In the crisis of the Civil War, Weed did not act alone, nor was his heroism evident in a single dramatic act. His service to the Union was surely unequal to that of Abraham Lincoln, his party leader and probably the greatest figure in American history.[10] Yet Weed's partisan work was critical to Lincoln's success on at least three occasions. Without his contributions, it is quite possible that the nation would be permanently divided and that slavery would continue in the independent Confederacy.

Weed's first contribution came at the time of the election of 1860. In the contest for the Republican presidential nomination, Weed had backed his state's senator, William Seward, who was the strong front-runner, while reportedly offering to support Lincoln as the vice-presidential nominee. Through clever maneuvering and some backroom deals, Lincoln defeated Seward, to Weed's great disappointment.[11] Nevertheless, as a faithful partisan, Weed loyally supported the party ticket. When Lincoln narrowly won the presidency (with only 39 percent of the popular vote), the South approached the brink of secession.

Weed bent his efforts to preserve the Union. In two days of consultation with Lincoln, he advised the president on the composition of his cabinet—which they likened to "properly-made December sausages"—and persuaded Seward to join his former rival's administration as secretary of state.[12] At Lincoln's request, he used an undetermined combination of persuasion and patronage to gain influential support for the war from James Gordon Bennett, the editor of the *New York Herald*.[13] As the secession movement developed, Weed also attempted to reach a compromise with the emerging Confederacy. But when Lincoln opposed these efforts, which also proved futile, he supported the war and the president.[14]

The Albany politician made even more important contributions in the early years of the war. Although he was privately opposed on political grounds to the Emancipation Proclamation, he vigorously supported Lincoln's policies in public and lent his voice to conciliation among the quarrelsome factions in the president's cabinet. When Lincoln wanted to replace Simon Cameron, the powerful but ineffective secretary of war, Weed discreetly persuaded Cameron to accept appointment as ambassador to Russia.[15] He also quietly undertook a diplomatic mission to Britain, despite the opposition of his ally, Secretary Seward. While in London, he successfully advised Lincoln to make amends for the forcible removal of Confederate envoys from the *Trent,* a British vessel.[16] Through the relationships he developed with the British government and with Queen Victoria, Weed significantly helped to avert the possible entrance of what was then the world's greatest power on the side of the Confederacy.[17]

The Critical Election of 1864

Weed's most important contribution, however, came in the presidential election of 1864, "arguably the most critical election campaign in our history."[18] Although it receives scarce attention in today's history books, that contest set the course of American history. In one sense, as Harold Hyman observes, "the most remarkable fact about the 1864 election is that it occurred."[19] Simply to hold the election amid the bloodletting of the Civil War demonstrated a commitment to the democratic process even in the worst circumstances. The balloting assured that elections would be a permanent institution in American government, come what may.

The significance of the election was substantive, not simply formal. At the time, it seemed quite possible that Lincoln might not even be renominated and quite probable that he would be defeated. In that case, the Union cause would be lost, slavery would continue, and the divided United States would lose its potential for political and moral world leadership. As late as August 23 of the election year, both Weed and Lincoln predicted defeat. The president made his dire forecast in a memorandum he circulated to the cabinet, requiring each member to sign it unread, committing them to the president's cause: "This morning, as for some days past, it seems exceedingly probable that this Administration will not be re-elected. Then it will be my duty to so co-operate with the President elect, as to save the Union between the election and the inauguration; as he will have secured his election on such ground that he can not possibly save it afterwards."[20]

Lincoln's defeat seemed likely because the North had become weary of the enervating war. Although Lincoln had issued the Emancipation Proclamation, the action was insufficient for radical Republicans, yet too extensive for those who sympathized with the Confederacy. The nation was not ready to fight on endlessly simply to end slavery, and the more popular cause of preserving the Union seemed fruitless, as one military loss and one ineffective field commander followed another. The pessimistic mood of the country was echoed in the popular song, *Tenting on the Old Camp Ground:* "Many are the hearts that are weary tonight, Wishing for the war to cease."[21]

The exigencies of war brought further problems. The military draft, once easy to evade, became more widely used, and more onerous. As war went on, government spending rose rapidly, and the national debt reached the figure, astonishing for the time, of $3 billion. Conspiracies designed to overthrow the national government were rumored in the Midwest, and persons as prominent as Horace Greeley urged secret negotiations for peace with the Confederacy.[22] These discontents were reflected at the polls. In the congressional elections of 1862, the Republicans lost control of the largest states, including New York, and salvaged only a thin majority of eighteen seats in the House of Representatives. Now the loss of national power appeared imminent. Panicked Republicans sought drastic remedies—the repeal of emancipation, a different candidate, even compromise with the states that had seceded. Beyond their partisan self-interest, "the basic impulse remained the reasonable conviction that a Democratic triumph would mean Confederate independence, the perpetuation of slavery, and the further fragmentation of the dis–United States."[23]

Weed played a critical role in overcoming these problems. With his reelection in peril, Lincoln turned immediately to the New York boss. In early 1863, at the White House, he asked Weed to raise money for the forthcoming campaigns:

> Mr. Lincoln, taking him by the hand in his cordial way, said:
> "Mr. Weed, we are in a tight place. Money for legitimate purposes is needed immediately; but there is no appropriation from which it can be lawfully taken. I didn't know how to raise it, and so I sent for you."
> "How much is required?" asked Mr. Weed.
> "Fifteen thousand dollars," said the President. "Can you get it?"
> "If you must have it at once give me two lines to that effect."[24]

The practical president soon followed this plea with a terse letter: "The matters I spoke to you about are important; & I hope you will not neglect them." At the bottom of the letter was a list of seventeen businessmen who had pledged $1,000 to Lincoln's reelection. That evening, Weed sent $15,000 to the White House. It was a tangible expression of Weed's sentimental support, expressed earlier in 1863: "I may not be able to do much good but all I am belongs to my Country and to yourself, as its President."[25]

Opposition to Lincoln was widespread, causing his private secretary to worry, "I hope God won't see fit to scourge us for our sins by any one of the two or three most prominent candidates on the ground."[26] The president and his managers attempted to rally popular support by presenting Lincoln "in the role of an outsider, who had the support of the people if not the politicians."[27] In contemporary American politics, that strategy would mean an emphasis on direct appeals to the voters in primary elections. In 1864, however, even a Lincoln required the support of professionals such as Weed.

Lincoln's opponents considered many potential candidates for the Republican nomination. An early boom developed for Salmon Chase, the secretary of the treasury, still unreconciled to his loss of the Republican nomination four years earlier. "Chase had employed the patronage of the Treasury Department to build a personal organization. By arranging for his portrait to appear on the one-dollar national bank notes, Chase placed 'a campaign picture in every man's pocket.' Over a three-year period, he wrote more letters about his political availability than about Treasury Department business."[28] Although Lincoln forced Chase to disavow his potential candidacy, the secretary remained ambitious to replace his chief.

Another formidable candidate was John C. Fremont, the Republican standard-bearer in 1856, the year of the party's first national campaign. Fremont was an unbending abolitionist who saw Lincoln as too cautious on emancipation. Even more to the point, he deeply resented having been removed as military governor of Missouri, as Lincoln sought successfully to keep the border state in the Union, as well as his dismissal from the army by Lincoln the following year. Seeking revenge and glory, Fremont became the candidate of a splinter group of Republicans, the "Radical Democracy." Lincoln rebuked them, with a biblical quotation, as a small group comprising "every one that was in distress, and every one that was in debt, and every one that was discontented."[29] But the president's humor could not eliminate the threatened loss of votes to this third-party candidate.

Weed was central in overcoming the various opponents. He did so primarily because of his commitment to the Union cause, but he also had personal motives in mind. He surely enjoyed besting Greeley, editor of the rival *New York Tribune,* and a chief supporter of the Radical movement. Patronage was also a consideration. Weed had been severely distressed with Chase's selections, in which Lincoln initially acquiesced, for lucrative positions at the New York Customs House. But Weed's support for the president was cemented when Lincoln rejected a Chase appointment, unexpectedly accepted Chase's ritualistic resignation from the cabinet, and then named friends of Weed to profitable offices in customs, the post office, and the treasury.

With these secondary considerations satisfied, Weed took a central role in Lincoln's renomination campaign. The first element of the strategy involved broadening the president's appeal. For this purpose, the Republican National Executive Committee—all patronage appointees or distributors—called for an early convention of a new and more inclusive Union party. The second step was to present the impending convention with popular mandates on behalf of Lincoln. A series of state conventions and legislative caucuses endorsed Lincoln, beginning with New Hampshire and Ohio (Chase's birthplace and home), followed by Connecticut, a Weed fiefdom. "At this time—during the first months of 1864—Thurlow Weed seems to have been one of the powers behind the scenes." As an opposition newspaper ruefully reported, Weed "rolled up his sleeves and went to work making his combinations." The New York "boss" brought loyal patronage appointees into the contest. "Through postmasters, provost marshals and other government officials getting elected to the Convention, the endorsement of Lincoln for another term was obtained."[30]

New York was obviously particularly important. "Weed, beneficiary of much patronage from Lincoln and a loyal supporter of the administration, scotched any attempt by the Chase forces to control the New York State Union convention by the use of Custom House patronage." While Chase supporters were absent, Weed won a Lincoln endorsement from the state Republican central committee, and then prevented any reconsideration by immediately distributing election circulars. In May, the party's state convention met, as "from every county [came] the internal revenue collector, the assessor, the sub-collectors, the provost marshal or his deputy, and the city and village postmasters." As Weed enforced their expected loyalty to party leaders, Lincoln received the state party's unanimous endorsement.[31]

The Union convention was sewn up for the president, who won unanimous ballots from all states but Missouri. Weed "hovered around the hallways and caucus rooms. . . . He was not a delegate to this convention, but was a looming presence nonetheless."[32] To ensure the outcome, he supported the admission of delegates from three reconstructed southern states to provide friendly votes. The only decision still left for the delegates was the selection of a vice-presidential candidate. The incumbent, Hannibal Hamlin of Maine, brought no apparent strength to the ticket. While Lincoln—in contrast to modern practice—declined to state his preference, Weed championed a war Democrat, Andrew Johnson of Tennessee, and vetoed the suggested designation of a New Yorker. As usual, Weed combined party and personal goals. Electorally, he saw Johnson bringing added support to the ticket from Democrats. At the same time, he acted to protect the position of his ally Seward in the cabinet and, not incidentally, bolstered his own control of New York patronage.[33]

With Henry Raymond of the *New York Times,* a longtime partner who chaired the reelection effort, Weed pressed the campaign. Lincoln sought total victory in the war and was now committed to full emancipation, and the Union platform endorsed a constitutional amendment to end slavery. But the prospects of electoral success seemed dim, as Lincoln faced two conflicting attacks. As the military campaign stalled, inflation soared, and a new draft of half a million men loomed, sentiment grew for an end to the bloodletting and for restoration of the Union on almost any terms. At the same time, conversely, radical Republicans called for draconian measures to punish the Confederate rebels, a severe reconstruction of the South under Congressional control, and immediate equality for all blacks.[34]

Dissident Republicans saw their opportunity. Congress passed a bill that would force harsh conditions on the Southern states, including immediate emancipation without constitutional amendment. When Lincoln pocket vetoed the bill, an unusual procedure at the time, its sponsors issued the Wade-Davis Manifesto, "probably the most scathing attack ever made upon Lincoln within his own party."[35] The radicals, spurred by Greeley, laid plans to replace Lincoln as the party nominee. Asked to participate, Weed was disdainful. According to John Hay, Lincoln's private secretary, "he replied that his only objection to Mr. Lincoln was his favor to such fellows as they & that he shd not join them against him."[36] Weed would soon triumphantly declare that "the conspiracy against Mr. Lincoln collapsed on Monday last."[37]

Defeating the Democrats and the growing peace sentiment took more effort. In August, the grim military and political news led Weed to inform Seward, in writing, Lincoln orally, that Lincoln's "re-election is an impossibility."[38] To salvage the contest, he and

Raymond devised a stratagem to undercut the Democratic opposition. They suggested making a peace offer to Jefferson Davis, the Confederate president, proffering a cessation of hostilities on the sole condition that the South acknowledge the supremacy of the Constitution. Davis could either accept the proposition and save the Union or, more likely, reject it, thereby incurring the blame for the continuation of the war. Lincoln played with the idea long enough to convince its proponents that it was both impractical and electorally useless, while keeping them in the fold.

At the end of the month, the Democrats held their convention, still hoping that war weariness would bring them victory. Their platform called for an immediate armistice and a restoration of the Union, with state control over slavery. For president, they nominated George McClellan, one of the incapable generals whom Lincoln had dismissed. McClellan soon demonstrated the Democrats' incapacity for government, as he repudiated the party's peace platform, while also acceding to the continuation of slavery. Lincoln's prospects further rose when the war news turned optimistic. Mobile fell to Union ships, Atlanta surrendered to the Union army, the final rebel assault on Washington was turned back. At last, at long last, the Confederacy was close to defeat.

The party politicians did not leave the election to the shifting tides of war. Lincoln took no public role, but he was busy "pulling wires, throwing levers, and twisting arms quietly behind the scenes—as was his way."[39] The Union Republicans used a variety of means to win the canvass, methods typical of politics at the time but some of them unacceptable by modern standards. Nevada was admitted as a new state to reinforce Lincoln, who had predicted that without this new support he would win by only three electoral votes. Deals were arranged without shame. Fremont was persuaded to withdraw, in return for the ouster of moderate Montgomery Blair from the cabinet. Chase campaigned vigorously for Lincoln after he was promised appointment to the Supreme Court. Lincoln hinted to Greeley that he would name the erratic editor postmaster general in the next administration.

To spur support, one million flyers were distributed among the troops and one hundred government clerks were detailed to send out campaign materials, while other federal employees were paid to go home to vote, assessed 3 percent of their annual salary for campaign expenses, and dismissed if they were working for the Democrats. Military contractors were directly solicited for contributions, with expected amounts specified, and unfriendly newspapers were denied government advertising. Voting by soldiers was encouraged, either in the field—which nineteen states allowed—or on furloughs that allowed them to return home to cast their ballots, with Lincoln winning the military vote 3 to 1. To prevent disruption at the polls, federal troops were sent to New York City, and Kentucky was put under martial law.[40]

The election was a decisive, but not overwhelming, victory for Lincoln. The popular vote increased substantially in the twenty-five states now in the Union. Lincoln carried 55 per cent of the four million popular votes and twenty-two states, garnering 212 electoral votes. McClellan won only three states—Delaware, New Jersey, and Kentucky—with 21 electoral votes. Yet the election was closer than it seemed. The Confederate states, surely Democratic, did not vote, and a shift of only one percent of the vote in certain states would have elected McClellan. Lincoln needed all the support he got; even with Weed's aid, he carried New York by fewer than seven thousand votes, less than one percent of the state's total.[41]

By these actions, Weed helped decisively to make Lincoln the mythic president, to preserve the Union, and to effectuate the federal emancipation of slaves that he had privately opposed. Lincoln himself was obviously central to his own victory. "By dominating his party, securing a renomination, and winning re-election, a superb politician had gained the opportunity of becoming a superb statesman."[42] Yet Lincoln could not have won by his own efforts. Concentrating on the war, he was also constrained by political norms of the time that restricted presidential campaigning. Weed provided the crucial help. His previous limited focus on pelf and patronage had become a broader vision of union and freedom. The party politician enabled the embattled president to write his second inaugural address—the finest political language in American history—and to begin the effort toward national reconciliation while bringing the war to a successful and moral close.

The election of 1864 vindicated the American democratic process. Even with his personal interest and the nation's existence at stake, Lincoln insisted on holding the vote, declaring: "We cannot have free government without elections, and if the rebellion could force us to forego, or postpone a national election, it might fairly claim to have already conquered and ruined us."[43] The campaign evidenced free discussion, open campaigning even by candidates with near-treasonous messages, and peaceful balloting. "In the midst of the western world's longest, most searching, and destructive war since Napoleon's surrender, the United States allowed ballots, many cast by soldiers, to determine basic civil and military policies and the destiny of millions of black people."[44] The election stands as a historic tribute to the heroism of party politicians in the mold of Thurlow Weed.

The Heroism of Party Politicians

Parties are certainly important, indeed indispensable, in American democracy. Their role as an informal institution is vital, yet paradoxical, in that they employ self-interested means to achieve public goals. Party politicians such as Weed hardly seem likely to be heroes. For the most part, they are ordinary men and women who characteristically seek power and profit, not altruists who pursue noble ends. Theories concerning party politicians generally accept, even overstate, the empirical importance of selfish ambition among politicians, assuming: "That they act solely in order to attain the income, prestige and power which come from being in office. Thus politicians in our model never seek office as a means of carrying out particular policies; their only goal is to reap the rewards of holding office."[45]

For analytical purposes, it is useful to accept this premise. In reality, though, the selfishness of politicians is exaggerated. Partisan leaders often do show a commitment to principles and do seek policies they believe to be in the public interest.[46] All the same, heroism would seem unlikely to be found in an institution founded on self-interest.

Weed fit the traditional model of the party politician: "The acquisition of political power became the master passion of his life, and in pursuit of this objective he became an adept in organization and the formulation of party policy." However, he was not committed to any particular cause. "His basic principle in politics, he confessed, was 'not to make or control pubic sentiment, but to ascertain the direction it was taking and to follow it.'"[47] Yet in the Civil War crisis Weed took heroic and decisive action. He did so as he displayed the qualities and virtues typical of the politician doing his job within the party institution. Shaped by the electoral environment, these traits include a realistic view of institutions and people, loyalty to leaders, devotion to electoral success, readiness to compromise, and attention to rewards.

Characteristically a realist, the party politician accepts the limitations of the political environment as well as the limitations of human beings. In the United States, the environment effects, as a classic text put it, "the persistence and ascendancy of the two-party scheme" and structures the "loose, supple, interest-directed, principle-shunning, coalition-forming nature of the two major parties."[48]

As is well known, the dominant institutional structure of American elective politics has indeed been the two-party system. The electoral system forces politicians' ambition into two, and only two, channels. For Congress and most other offices, a single person is elected, who needs only a plurality, not an absolute majority, of the vote. This structure gives the advantage to politicians who can unite behind a single candidate, regardless of their diverse views, while it punishes those who insist on maintaining their separate beliefs. The same effect is evident in presidential contests. To win this single office of supreme power, parties must forge coalitions in the electoral college, uniting diverse states, interests, and programs. The parties' drive to control the White House effectively restricts presidential competition to the polar choice of incumbents versus opponents.

Weed understood the basic character of American parties and worked within these environmental constraints. He disdained minor parties, and he left the Whig party only when he could build a new major party, the Republicans. The logic of American party dualism became evident in the election of 1864, as even Lincoln's detractors were forced to choose between him and McClellan. Thus Fremont withdrew "not to aid in the triumph of Mr. Lincoln, but to do my part towards preventing the election of the Democratic candidate"—although his distinction was only theoretical, since he still had to support Lincoln. The *New York Herald*'s editor, James Bennett, cynically but accurately foresaw the consolidating effects of a two-party system and the electoral college. Lincoln's opponents, he predicted, "will all make tracks for Old Abe's plantation, and will soon be found crowing, and blowing, and vowing, and writing, and swearing and stumping the States on his side, declaring that he, and he alone, is the hope of the nation, the bugaboo of Jeff Davis, the first of conservatives, the best of abolitionists, the most honest of politicians, the purest of patriots. . . . The spectacle will be ridiculous, but it is inevitable."[49]

Seeking to win office within the two-party framework, parties foster appropriate attitudes and behavior. Even though it is often scorned by those outside the profession, loyalty to the party and its leaders is a basic virtue to politicians because it contributes to victory. Weed demonstrated this characteristic in his support of Lincoln, despite the fact that Lincoln had not been Weed's preferred presidential candidate and, in the election of 1864, despite his earlier preference for a one-term limit for presidents. In both 1860 and 1864, Weed worked hard and effectively for the victory of his party's candidate. He could truthfully write to Lincoln: "I do not desert those in power who are faithful to their Country, or permit personal griefs, real or imaginary, to interfere with the discharge of any duty. If you will carry our Country safely through its great Trial—and I know you will if you can—I will serve, honor and bless you—with all my strength and my whole heart, as long as Life is given to me."[50]

Weed's partisan loyalty had been exemplified earlier in his devotion to the Whig party. He had been one of its founders in New York (suggesting that it be called "Republican"), and he stayed with it longer than most of his peers even as the slavery issue divided the party into regional factions and caused its death. Sectional division became predominant after the Kansas-Nebraska Act of 1854 extended the reach of slavery into the western territories, but Weed still tried to hold the Whigs together across the widening cleavage of North and South. He then faced a new opposition, the Know-Nothing or American party, founded on an anti-immigrant and anti-Catholic program. Weed attempted various strategies to counter the new threat, including infiltration of its secret councils. Favoring voting rights even for aliens and blacks, he resisted both the bigotry of the Know-Nothings and their electoral challenge. Finally, as his beloved Whig party grew moribund, he led it into fusion with the nascent Republicans.[51]

To be effective in the American political environment, a party must unite diverse interests and be able to moderate clashing opinions. In combining the Whigs with the new Republican party in New York, Weed was ready to compromise whatever principles he had and to fuse disparate factions. For Weed, "His own anti-slavery sentiments were sincere, but he was more desirous of getting anti-slavery men to accept Whig candidates than of committing the party openly to their cause; for the abolitionists who clamored for a party of their own he had nothing but scorn."[52] The emphasis on victory was exemplified in the Whig presidential nomination of 1848. Although Henry Clay had been the leading figure in the party since its founding, he had lost three national contests. Rather than stay with a loser, Weed worked on behalf of General Zachary Taylor, whose triumphs in the Mexican War had made him a celebrity. The Whig party, along with Weed, was so intent on victory that it dispensed with the adoption of a platform, thus avoiding taking a position on the emerging question of the extension of slavery to new territory.[53]

Weed's position on slavery emphasized party victory over his personal moral condemnation of the "peculiar institution." His support was essential in winning the Whig nomination in 1848 for Taylor, who was a slave owner and refused to specify any policy on the issue. As a growing abolitionist sentiment threatened the Whig party in the North, Weed and his ally Seward also condemned slavery. They opposed the Compromise of 1850, not simply because of it permitted slavery in the territories, but as much because they needed to find a campaign issue, knowing "they could mobilize voters only by differentiating themselves from Democrats."[54]

As regional conflict over slavery loomed, Weed looked for new means to win office for the nascent Republican party. "The Republican party had to expand its appeal from its antislavery position to a broader basis. . . . Although Seward and boss Thurlow Weed fought against nativism, they finally agreed to compromise sufficiently to win support of a large enough portion of the nativism-motivated voters."[55] Similarly, when Seward's position on slavery appeared too extreme to win the Republican nomination and the election in 1860, they became more conciliatory. These odd, even unsavory, combinations of sentiments were critical to the eventual election of Lincoln and thus to the ultimate achievements of preserving the Union and emancipating the slaves.

The lack of firm ideological commitment might disappoint those who want leaders to be consistently pure of heart. This characteristic, however, enabled Weed to put his talents into Lincoln's service as he adopted the president's causes. As a prototypical politician, his "basic interest was in pursuing power for its own sake. Yet, on occasion, Weed could be distracted by national issues to use his political machine for constructive purposes."[56]

Compromise is the means that artful politicians use to achieve, through incremental steps, their ultimate principled aims. Weed opposed slavery, but he gave first priority to preserving the Union. In 1861, he thought he could achieve both goals through tactical compromise. In the secession crisis, he was ready to allow the temporary continuation of slavery in the South in order to hold the border states. "I believed then, as I know now, that by insisting that the war was prosecuted to maintain the Government and preserve the Union, the Democratic masses, with some of their leaders, would remain loyal; while, on the other hand, if the whole Republican party proclaimed it a war for the abolition of slavery, a united South would prove too strong for a divided North."[57]

In Weed's view, the slavery issue had already been settled by the election of 1860, so that further controversy was both unnecessary, and in fact self-defeating:

> Assured that slavery's control in national politics was terminated forever by the growth of free soil feeling all over the

country, the preponderance of that feeling in the Northern States, and the election of Mr. Lincoln, Mr. Weed saw no good result to be gained by further agitation on the subject, at a time when the South was busily preparing for a trial of strength on a new issue: the preservation of the government.

"In abhorrence of slavery I am behind no man," he declared, but he had a still higher goal: "Our danger has been, and is, that abolition, by dividing the North and uniting the South, may enable rebellion and slavery to avert the penalty both so richly merit."[58]

And then the war came, and Weed abandoned compromise for his highest principle, the preservation of his country. "Strike! Strike hard! Arguments have been exhausted. There can be no settlement, no clamoring for peace, no sentimental whining about humanity, until the majesty of the American Union has been vindicated. . . . Let us hear the tramp of men and the sound of bugles. Let there be no peace until traitors yield unqualified submission."[59]

To achieve winning coalitions, parties must deal realistically with the ambition for power, the ruling passion of politics. Weed accepted this reality for, like many party leaders, he was more interested in the means than the ends of politics. Party politicians are prone to pursue politics as a "game," stressing the pleasure of the competition, rather than engaging in a "crusade" for transcendent goals. "Weed, a seemingly selfless and personally undemanding master of political management, was drawn to politics in this way," Stanley Kelley observes.[60] Henry Adams was struck by Weed's lack of egotism. "He grasped power, but not office. He distributed offices by handfuls, without caring to take them. He had the instinct of empire: he gave, but he did not receive. . . . Management was an instinct with Mr. Weed; an object to be pursued for its own sake, as one plays cards; he seemed incapable of feeling himself one of them. . . . Every card had a relative value. Principles had better be left aside; values were enough."[61]

To function, parties must provide rewards for their members. In the traditional party, material incentives—jobs—were the predominant rewards, and Weed devoted much of his managerial skill to getting and administering appointments for his followers. When Lincoln was constructing his cabinet in 1860, he joked that he needed advice because he "had never learned that trade." Weed readily replied that "though never a boss cabinet-maker, I had as a journeyman been occasionally consulted."[62] He was proud of these efforts, writing: "I have done something in my day towards Electing Presidents and Governors, none of whom have found me an expensive Partizan [*sic*]. Possibly some Gentlemen in Power may have derived advantage and found relief in a Friend."[63]

Weed's interest in patronage was not personal. As he told Lincoln's secretary, John Nicolay, in regard to a dispute over the choice position of collector of customs in New York, "the ambition of his life had been, not to get office for himself, but to assist in putting good men in the right places." To Weed, the artful use of patronage was critical to good government. Proper patronage appointments—selection of Weed's candidates—would make the administration coherent. But Weed feared that if Lincoln "were not strong enough to hold the Union men together through the next Presidential election, when it must necessarily undergo a great strain, the country was in the utmost danger of going to ruin." The president, Weed advised his private secretary, must appoint only true friends to office. Otherwise, he warned, Lincoln's administration would have an enfeebling reputation, "that you hold on with such tenacity to men once in office, although they prove to be incapable and untrustworthy."[64]

The argument was not strange to Lincoln, who made robust use of his appointment powers during the war and who eventually did replace the unsupportive placeholder with Weed's candidate.

Both Weed and Lincoln might well have agreed with a later New York politician, George Washington Plunkitt:

> I ain't up on sillygisms, but I can give you some arguments that nobody can answer.
>
> First, this great and glorious country was built up by political parties; second, parties can't hold together if their workers don't get offices when they win; third, if the parties go to pieces, the government they built up must go to pieces, too; fourth, then there'll be hell to pay.[65]

More than a century later, two Supreme Court justices would also endorse the desirability of patronage. To Justice Lewis Powell: "patronage appointments help build stable political parties by offering rewards to persons who assume the tasks necessary to the continued functioning of political organizations."[66] Even more ardently, Justice Antonin Scalia praised patronage as a system that stimulates "the local political activity supporting parties" and that "has been a powerful means of achieving the social and political integration of excluded groups." Patronage also promotes moderation in a two-party system, Scalia argued, because parties seeking office have "a relatively greater interest in appealing to a majority of the electorate and a relatively lesser interest in furthering philosophies or programs that are far from the mainstream."[67] Weed would agree; indeed, he exemplified these virtues.

In doing his job as a party politician, Thurlow Weed also did the work of a hero, endeavoring to keep his country united, to free its slaves, and to build its greatness. To Weed, as to most of his breed, party politics was more than self-interest. Instead, it was a means to induce citizens to submerge self-interest in larger causes. In its most glorious periods, "the party, as an institution, led voters a long step away from merely personal allegiance toward loyalty to the republic." In the decades of the slavery crisis, party loyalties contested sectional loyalties, as "party leaders tried, stubbornly and with some measure of success, to find a 'national solution.'"[68] Weed continued these efforts even while the Civil War raged.

In making these efforts, Weed was like many other Republican politicians who aided Lincoln's reelection and the Union cause. But he was also different. Because his influence was greater, his support had more impact. Weed's task was also personally more difficult. He changed from an opponent of Lincoln to the president's advocate, from one willing to compromise with the proponents of slavery to an emancipator, from a seeker of patronage to a champion of Union. He worked through an institution, the political party, that often appears to be based on selfishness and bombast, yet he avoided both the cynicism of Chase and the delusion of Greeley. Ultimately, he subordinated self-interest to the supreme national interest.

As he pursued his ambition, as he served his party, Weed also served his country. Patriotism, to Weed, necessarily involved party loyalty. Americans would do well to learn this lesson from a nineteenth-century review of his career: "A life like Mr. Weed's shows very clearly what a passion patriotism was in the days when the nation was gathering itself together. . . . Mr. Weed was a patriot. He believed in his country heart and soul; and while he was a thorough partisan, his party, in his mind, was the servant of the nation. This passion for his country ennobled his political energy and gave it bent and direction. . . . His counsels in the critical time after Mr. Lincoln's first election were the wise counsels of a patriot, and it is entirely just to revise one's judgment of his early career by a reading of his later."[69]

Thurlow Weed was a party politician in the ideal sense of the term. Certainly, his job involved some mundane, even unattractive, features. He resolutely sought power, often compromised his principles, and emphasized material rewards for party followers. But, in dutifully building his Whig and Republican parties, Weed also did the work of a hero, by enabling a young democracy to work its will and to extend its freedoms.

Chapter Nine
Ida Tarbell

A Hero of the Press

As the twentieth century opened, the United States faced a crisis of democracy. The crisis was not narrowly political. Formal equality had been won for white males; the vote would be extended soon to women and, later but eventually, to African Americans. The looming crisis was economic: the domination of American life by national corporations, the concentration of wealth in the hands of a small elite, the closing of opportunity for the tens of millions of entrepreneurs, farmers, and industrial wage earners in the nation's middle and working classes.

The United States was fast becoming a society dominated by the rich, worsening a problem that Alexis de Tocqueville had called attention to in 1835, when he cautioned that "the manufacturing aristocracy growing up under our eyes is one of the harshest that ever existed in the world." Corporate combinations, known as "trusts," held virtual monopolies, controlling prices and production in critical industries, including oil, iron and steel, copper, coal, railroads, beef, lumber, cement, hardware, sugar, milk, even whiskey and tobacco. By the start of new century, less than 10 percent of the nation's families held more than 70 percent of its wealth; the richest one percent alone may have held half the country's assets.[1] Inevitably, this economic transformation would undermine political democracy as well, Tocqueville had warned, as "the manufacturing aristocracy of our age first impoverishes and debases the men who serve it and then abandons them to be supported by the charity of the public."[2]

The trend toward economic oligarchy was halted, and considerably reversed, in the first four decades of the century, beginning with the Progressive movement and continuing through the presidencies of Theodore Roosevelt and Woodrow Wilson and the New Deal of Franklin Roosevelt. This renewal of democracy was spurred by the nation's press, another political institution—like the political parties considered in the last chapter—distinct from the formal bodies of government.

Among the journalists of this period, known as "muckrakers,"[3] Ida Tarbell, who wrote a critical series of articles on the Standard Oil Company, probably made the greatest impact. Her work led to the breakup of the Standard Oil monopoly and the restructuring of American capitalism. Her investigative reporting was of immense importance, but it also exemplifies the regular practice of the journalist's job. Her effect on the American economy was indeed "all in the day's work," the phrase Tarbell chose for the title of her autobiography.

A Woman Journalist

Ida Tarbell blazed trails both as a woman and as a news reporter, but she rejected the first role, that of a feminist pioneer, even as she illustrated the second, that of an investigative journalist. Tarbell grew up in the 1860s and 1870s, when women's opportunities were quite constrained, and she resented the limitations society placed on her mother and herself. "I would never marry; it would interfere with my plan," she resolved, as she set her sights on higher education and economic independence. "Above all, I must be free; and to be free I must be a spinster. When I was fourteen I was praying God

Ida M. Tarbell

on my knees to keep me from marriage."[4] Leaving home to become the first woman student at Allegheny College, she relaxed her social rules sufficiently to collect four different fraternity pins. But she kept her focus on her career.

After local stints as a teacher and newspaper apprentice, she moved to Paris for three years, where she became deeply involved in its vibrant salon culture. There she began to write seriously—sketches of the city's life (her first article sold for five dollars), interviews with notable intellectuals such as Louis Pasteur and Émile Zola, and a full-length biography of Manon Roland, a female hero of the French Revolution. In 1894, she returned home to join the staff of *McClure's* magazine, a new periodical that would become the sparkplug of the Progressive movement. With new studies of Napoleon and Lincoln, Tarbell established her credentials as a historian and a journalist, laid the foundation for her future fame, and began to gather ample resources for an independent life.

With this record of achievement, Tarbell could easily be considered a feminist icon. As the twentieth century ended, she would be honored by induction into the Women's Hall of Fame, and by inclusion in a U.S. postage series celebrating women journalists. Yet in reality she rejected most feminist goals and came close to repudiating her own career as a model for other women. Most strikingly, Tarbell opposed the great crusade of women during her lifetime, the call for the right to vote. "Suffragists said women with the franchise would cure all ills. Tarbell didn't believe that, so she argued against the vote."[5] She maintained that position even when other prominent women, such as Helen Keller, held public meetings to refute her arguments.

Instead of feminism, Tarbell championed a traditional role for women sharply different from her own. She disparaged the careerist, whom she termed the "Uneasy Woman." Instead, she argued that "for the normal woman the fulfillment of life is the making of the thing we best describe as a home—which means a mate, children, friends, with all the radiating obligations, joys, burdens, these relations imply." Women were basically different from men—neither superior nor inferior—and could serve society best by fulfilling the responsibilities of their nature. An unmarried woman without children, she would nonetheless define *The Business of Being a Woman* in traditional terms: "The central fact of the woman's life—Nature's reason for her—is the child, his bearing and rearing. There is no escape from the divine order that her life must be built around this constraint, duty, or privilege, as she may please to consider it."[6] But Tarbell's deeds sharply contradicted her words.

The Muckrakers

Tarbell's impact came not as a philosopher but as a working journalist, a prominent member of the muckraker press. "The role of the press was particularly important in this period of national reform," notes historian Richard Hofstadter. "To an extraordinary degree the work of the Progressive movement rested upon its journalists. The fundamental critical achievement of American Progressivism was the business of exposure, and journalism was the chief occupational source of its creative writers."[7]

The impact of journalism derived from the confluence of contemporary social and technical developments. The spread of high school education and the migration of rural residents and foreign immigrants created a broader audience for the press. New print technology—the use of wood pulp for paper and photoengraving for pictures—made newspapers more attractive and considerably cheaper for the growing readership. The press was also changing its stance toward politics. Previously, newspapers had been organs of political parties (as we saw in the case of Thurlow Weed). Now, they moved away from the parties and were thus free to conduct their own investigations—and to sell more papers through their crusades.

The practice of journalism also changed. Instead of simply reporting news, the press attempted to make it. "The papers made news in a double sense: they *created* reportable events. . . . They also *elevated* events, hitherto considered beneath reportorial attention, to the level of news occurrences by clever, emotionally colored reporting. They exploited human interest, in short." The change in practice also changed the internal structure of newspapers. "All this concern with news, interviews, exposure, and human interest set a premium on the good reporter and reduced the importance of editorial writing. . . . Bold reportorial initiative, good reportorial writing were now very much in demand." The new journalism found its most important outlet in innovative mass circulation magazines, "newspapers in periodical form," selling to millions of readers for as little as ten cents a copy.[8]

Of the new magazines, the most influential would prove to be *McClure's,* published by Samuel McClure, a businessman quick to recognize talent and provocative news. He assembled a staff unprecedented in its journalistic skill.[9] Among this talented group, said her colleague Lincoln Steffens, Tarbell was a leader and a conciliator: "When we were deadlocked we might each of us send for her, and down she would come to the office, smiling, like a tall, good-looking young mother, to say, 'Hush, children.' She would pick out the sense in each of our contentions, and putting them together with her own good sense, take away only the privilege of gloating. The interest of the magazine was pointed out, and we and she went back to work."[10]

These journalists who would change American society were generally dispassionate, focused on professional reporting rather than political action. These reporters did not offer a reform agenda. Their work was "factual, though critical. It was primarily directed at the social conscience of the nation. Its aim was to expose, not solve. The muckrakers were 'the publicity men of reform'; they were the press agents for the Progressive movement."[11] The reporters focused on doing their jobs, in keeping with rules remembered by Steffens: "Mr. McClure was interested in facts, startling facts, not in philosophical generalizations. He hated, he feared, my dawning theory. He had his own theories, like his readers. . . . I alone was not to give my theory."[12] As Tarbell explained to a friend, "we were after, as McClure always insisted, interesting reading material and if it contributed to the general good, so much the better."[13] Similarly, as she assured President Theodore Roosevelt, "we on *McClure's* were concerned only with facts, not with stirring revolt." Rejecting the muckraker label, she insisted on objectivity: "I was convinced that in the long run the public . . . would weary of vituperation, that if you were to secure permanent results the mind must be convinced. . . . Experience aroused me to questioning, qualifying even what I advocated, which no first-class crusader can afford to do."[14]

Standard Oil

Tarbell's greatest achievement, her heroic contribution, came in a series of articles on the Standard Oil Company. Originally, the editors planned only three installments, but as Tarbell's detailed accounts garnered extensive public attention, the number eventually grew to nineteen. (By now, her wages had also risen considerably, topping the *McClure's* staff at $4,000 an article—still decent pay for a journalist today.) The articles began to appear in November 1902; they were subsequently collected into a two-volume work, *The History of the Standard Oil Company*, published in 1904 and reissued in 1925. As the noted historian Allan Nevins summarized Tarbell's achievement:

> The time, the magazine, and the writer combined to make this serialized book the most spectacular success of the muckraking school of journalism, and its most enduring achievement. Theodore Roosevelt had now been in power for a year. . . . His annual message in December called for new weapons against industrial monopoly. S. S. McClure and John S. Phillips had given their monthly a circulation and prestige such as no magazine of equal solidity and literary quality had ever achieved. Directly or indirectly, it reached nearly the whole literate public of America. As for Miss Tarbell . . . into her work on the Standard she threw all her industry, earnestness, and skill. . . . Her labors were as searching as four years of toil and ample expense funds could make them.[15]

The series was first inspired by McClure, who saw some "educational value" in describing the nation's expanding business corporations, beginning with "the story of a typical trust to illustrate how and why the clan grew. How about the greatest of them all—the Standard Oil Company?" Although reluctant at first, preferring to investigate the sugar industry, Tarbell was the perfect choice to write the series. She had grown up in western Pennsylvania, the site of the first major oilfields in the world. Her father had been both an early entrepreneur in the industry, inventing a tank for transporting oil, and an early victim of the aggrandizing practices of Standard Oil and its leader, John D. Rockefeller, when he resisted their consolidation of oil refining in Pennsylvania. Those experiences had made Ida Tarbell believe that it was a "privilege and duty to fight injustice," but her zeal was appropriately focused. "As I saw it," she insisted, "it was not capitalism but an open disregard of decent ethical business practices by capitalists which lay at the bottom of the story." To tell that story, this practiced journalist decided that "I must go back to records, maps, reminiscences; that I must undertake a long and serious piece of investigation."[16] At the time Tarbell began to write, Standard Oil dominated the energy industry, the central enterprise of the industrial world and the twentieth century. As Nevins notes in his biography of John D. Rockefeller: "Never before in history had such an imposing array of industrial units been banded together in a single organization. Never before had any really great industry come under so nearly complete a control." Nevins underlines the company's impact: "Standard was the earliest, the greatest, and the most successful of the industrial combinations; its railroad bargains were the most notorious; its chieftains were the most mysteriously puissant."[17]

The first commercially viable oil well had been drilled in 1859 in Titusville, Pennsylvania, only miles from the log house where one-year-old Ida Tarbell was taking her first steps. Tarbell would later describe the scene in the first paragraph of her series, itself a model of the journalistic rule to begin a story with a colorful lead:

> One of the busiest corners of the globe at the opening of the year 1872 was a strip of Northwestern Pennsylvania, not over fifty miles long, known the world over as the Oil Regions. Twelve years before this strip of land had been but little better than a wilderness; its chief inhabitants the lumbermen, who every season cut great swaths of primeval pine and hemlock from its hills, and in the spring floated them down the Allegheny River to Pittsburg[h]. The great tides of Western emigration had shunned the spot for years as too rugged and unfriendly for settlement, and yet in twelve years this region avoided by men had been transformed into a bustling trade centre, where towns elbowed each other for place, into which three great trunk railroads had built branches, and every foot of whose soil was fought for by capitalists. It was the discovery and development of a new raw product, petroleum, which had made this change from wilderness to market-place.[18]

Prospectors, drillers, transporters by road and rail, merchants, prostitutes, and charlatans rushed into the area, bringing both growth and chaotic competition. Standard and Rockefeller brought order to this chaos, accomplishing feats of economic integration, unifying its growing portion of the oil industry from drilling well to household lamp. In 1870, when Tarbell began her tale, Standard Oil held 10 percent of the refining industry in the country; by the end of the century, it controlled 85 percent. The enterprise grew timber and manufactured barrels, refined oil, stored it in warehouses, and transported the fuel throughout the nation and around the world in its own ships and tank cars.

The fulcrum of the industry was the refinery. With a firm grasp on that point of leverage, Standard could extend its reach from the actual production of petroleum to its transportation from the fields to the nation's cities and ports and then to its eventual sale to consumers. To accomplish these goals, the corporation developed a system to control the prices of rail shipment, the predominant mode of oil transportation. Each railroad would be allocated a specified proportion of the available refined oil, to be shipped at a specified price. Standard and Rockefeller developed two ingenious schemes to gain critical advantages from these shipments. First, they won a rebate from the railroads on oil shipped from their own refineries; the rebate amounted to about a third of the listed price. Even more daunting, the railroads contracted to give the trust the same rebate, called a drawback, on oil shipped by their competitors. In effect, aside from paying a higher rate, its rivals were also paying Standard for the right to compete. As even Nevins, one of Rockefeller's more sympathetic biographers, concludes: "The rebate provision of the contracts were brutal, unjust, and outside the pale of business ethics even in that loose period. They ran counter to the essential spirit of fair play and democracy in American enterprise."[19]

With transportation, soon expanded from rail to pipelines, under its control, Standard now extended its domain through the entire industry, working through nine directors of fourteen interlocked companies. Able to regulate manufacturing prices, it undercut rival refiners. Faced with disproportionately high shipping costs and shrinking revenues, the independents could choose to join the conglomerate, or to accept a very limited market niche, or to die. Producers could try to withhold their oil from Standard's refineries, but they would quickly be bankrupt if they could not refine and ship the overflowing petroleum. They were soon forced to accept both controls on their prices and their production as Standard single-mindedly stabilized the industry to its own advantage. In

Daniel Yergin's authoritative account: "Rockefeller and his associates would approach their targets with deference, politeness, and flattery. They would demonstrate how profitable Standard Oil was compared to other refiners, many of which were struggling through hard times. . . . If all that failed, Standard would bring a tough competitor to heel by making him 'feel sick,' or as Rockefeller put it, by giving him a 'good sweating.'"[20]

Standard's gains came not only from its market dominance and strong-arm techniques. These economic advantages were reinforced by spying on other companies. Railroads sent copies of competitors' freight invoices to the trust. "Using this data the Standard could decide where to cut prices and by how much so as to drive a competitor from an area." This "organized illegal strategy," Tarbell recalled, "turned my stomach against the Standard in a way that the indefensible and robust fights over transportation had never done. There was a littleness about it that seemed utterly contemptible."[21]

Through her extensive research, Tarbell was able to figure out the tricks of Standard's trade, which she then explained to her magazine audience, spicing her journalistic account with an element of restrained passion. Her approach is well illustrated by her analysis, based on published oil prices over a period of four decades, of the conglomerate's manipulation of oil prices. "Rockefeller and a few of his friends," she wrote, "proposed . . . simply to get all of the refineries of the country under their control, and thereafter make only so much oil as they could sell at their own interpretation of a paying price." As Tarbell went on to explain, the price of oil was maintained at a highly profitable level, even as the costs of actual production and transportation fell, and even as technological advances created new products from previous waste material. When faced with limited competition, however, Standard would drop its prices, even below the cost of the original crude oil, to eliminate the independents. Once in control, the trust would raise the price to consumers—for example, in New York's frigid winter of 1902–3, charging eleven cents a gallon for heating oil, double Standard's production cost.[22]

Tarbell concluded her articles with an ardent summary:

> We have always paid more for our refined oil than we would have done if there had been free completion. But why should we expect anything else? This is the chief object of combinations. . . . As a result of the Standard's power over prices, not only does the consumer pay more for oil where competition has not reached or has been killed, but this power is used steadily and with consummate skill to make it hard for men to compete in any branch of the oil business. . . .
>
> Human experience long ago taught us that if we allowed a man or a group of men autocratic powers in government or church, they used that power to oppress and defraud the public. . . . And yet we have here in the United States allowed men practically autocratic powers in commerce. . . . As a natural result of these extraordinary powers, we see, as in the case of the Standard Oil Company, the price of a necessity of life within the control of a group of nine men, as able, as energetic, and as ruthless in business operations as any nine men the world has ever seen combined.[23]

Tarbell's Impact

By the time she completed the series of articles, Tarbell was exhausted: "I asked for nothing in the world but to get them into a book and escape into the safe retreat of a library where I could study people long dead. . . . There would be none of these harrowing human beings confronting me, tearing me between contempt and pity, admiration and anger, baffling me with their futile and misdirected power or their equally futile and misdirected weakness." For his part, Rockefeller attempted to ignore her attacks, ordering his staff: "Not a word. Not a word about that misguided woman." But Standard did in fact respond. It paid for wide distribution of the few critical reviews of Tarbell's series, including five million copies of a subsidized pamphlet accusing her of undermining the efficiency of the conglomerate and the economy of the nation.[24]

Tarbell's Standard Oil series had a great national impact. The book sold widely, receiving glowing reviews and extensive newspaper publicity, and led her to the first of many lecture tours across the country. Nearly a century later, a leading chronicler would call the work "the single most influential book on business ever published in the United States," a judgment with which Standard's successors would no doubt agree.[25]

Political action followed. Despite his wariness of the muckrakers, President Roosevelt "saw no harm in encouraging political rhetoric more extreme than any he would use on Congress himself."[26] After his reelection in 1904, he joined the muckrakers verbally, warning in a speech at that den of capitalism, the Union League Club: "Neither this people nor any other free people will permanently tolerate the vast power conferred by vast wealth . . . without lodging somewhere in the Government the still higher power of seeing that this power . . . is used for and not against the interests of the people as a whole."[27] Standard and Rockefeller were inviting targets for Roosevelt: "In his public utterance and private letters he repeatedly fulminated against Rockefeller, whom he regarded as still active director—nay, dictator—of the Standard's policies and acts" as well as against the conglomerate's attempt "to crush out every competitor, to overawe the common carriers, and to establish a monopoly which treats the public with contempt." In 1906, deeds followed words. Along with actions by a dozen states, the federal government filed suit against Standard under the antitrust laws. Replicating Tarbell's research, "the government charged that the Standard had gained its dominant position not by superior efficiency, but by unfair and immoral acts."[28] To increase the pressure, Roosevelt ordered the military to stop buying Standard's products.

The case against Standard continued beyond Roosevelt's term in office, accumulating by 1911 a record of fifteen thousand pages. By this time, Standard was the equivalent in contemporary terms to a combination of Exxon, Mobil, Chevron, Sohio, BP's American subsidiary, Amoco, Conco, ARCO, and Sunoco.[29] Faced with this record, the Supreme Court, while permitting the existence of some trusts, ruled that the Standard companies "constitute a combination in restraint of interstate commerce, and that they have attempted to monopolize and have monopolized parts of such commerce,— all in violation of . . . what is known as the anti-trust act of 1890." The Court ordered the division of the conglomerate, within six months, into thirty-eight separate and competing companies.[30]

Tarbell was skeptical that the decision would end the power of the oil and other trusts. But "within a decade, virtually all of the abuses she had pinpointed were proscribed," as new legislation regulated railroad rates, mandated equal rates for all shippers, and gave the Interstate Commerce Commission power over pipeline rates.[31] In Woodrow Wilson's administration, trust busting was extended, with the creation of the Federal Trade Commission to deter unfair competition and enactment of the Clayton Anti-Trust Act to further restrict monopolistic practices. Reinforcing the effects of legislation, competition grew in the oil industry with the spread of automobiles and the discovery of new fields in the southwest.

Tarbell had planned to write a third volume of her *History of the Standard Oil Company,* tracing the development of Standard since the court decision, and did complete 20,000 words intended for publication in a revived *McClure's*. But then the publishing enterprise failed, and her interest faded. "Perhaps it was just as well," she concluded, "both for *McClure's* and for me. Repeating yourself is a doubtful practice, particularly for editor and writer. I felt now there was no hope of recapturing the former interest in the former way. The result would have smelt a bit musty."[32]

Instead, she agreed to the republication of the original two volumes, which had become scarce, noting that "the rare copies which found their way to the market have been held at a high price." Indeed, copies had become so rare that Huey Long, pursuing his own populist campaign in Louisiana in the 1920s, offered to pay her $100 for a copy, equivalent today to at least $1,000.[33] Further restrictions on corporate power would follow during the New Deal, and later antitrust suits would challenge the dominance of new basic industries by such giant corporations as AT&T, IBM, and Microsoft. Tarbell's work would stand as a journalistic monument that transformed the American corporate economy.

In her later years, Tarbell also revealed some limitations. She never became reconciled to women's suffrage, the most significant social movement of her time. While she did write a good series on the deleterious effects of high tariffs, she lacked a deep understanding of basic economics, attributing social problems more to unethical men than to structural inequalities of power and wealth. Appointed by Woodrow Wilson to national economic commissions, she naively hoped for consensus between business and labor, dismissing the labor-union movement's demands for collective bargaining. Becoming, ironically, somewhat of an apologist for big business, she wrote admiring biographies of industrialists Elbert Gary of U.S. Steel and Owen Young of General Electric, and even found some admirable traits in Mussolini's Italian corporate state. As she might admit, she had proven to be a good journalist, but not a good theorist.

Tarbell as a Model Journalist

Tarbell's articles had an enormous influence. One reason for this impact was the character of her audience: "In 1902–4 the public had a background of knowledge which lent the articles a stirring interest. Men now forgotten were then vivid public figures; legal battles now dimmed by time were then excitingly real."[34] Yet the greater credit must be given to Tarbell herself and to the ways in which she personified the best qualities of a professional journalist.[35]

One basic criterion of good journalism is accurate and fair research. Tarbell conducted her investigation over four years, delving into a plethora of written materials: government hearings, court proceedings, trade publications, maps, contracts, hidden financial records, and even freight bills. She developed her own graphs and statistical tables to illustrate her argument. In the published volumes, the supportive documentation was half as long as the articles themselves.

Often, material was difficult to find, and important evidence was sometimes missing from court and legislative records. One instance involved the South Improvement Company, Rockefeller's first major effort to consolidate refineries and fix rail rates, an effort that Tarbell's father fought in vain. "Rockefeller always disavowed that he had anything to do with so predatory a scheme," but apparently contradictory evidence existed in a pamphlet that was now nowhere to be found. To Tarbell's considerable frustration, "all copies had mysteriously disappeared. Reportedly the Standard had purchased and destroyed them all." Finally, she found the last known copy in the New York Public Library; with it, she "could prove that Rockefeller was a linchpin of an illegal ring whose tactics he transferred to the Standard Oil Company."[36]

As the publication of the articles proceeded, she cultivated new sources and obtained more documents related to the South Improvement Company. Many persons, even former neighbors in Pennsylvania, feared to talk about Standard. However, some disgruntled persons within the giant oil corporation, including Rockefeller's own brother, gave her inside information in clandestine contacts that presaged the investigations of Nixon's Watergate activities seven decades later. A railroad clerk found shipping records that seemed suspicious and passed them on to his former teacher, an independent refiner (according to Tarbell, who may have invented a cover story to protect her sources). The refiner "had become convinced that I was trying to deal fairly with the matter; he had also convinced himself in some way that I was to be trusted. So one night he brought me the full set of incriminating documents. There was no doubt about their genuineness. The most interesting to me was the way they fitted in with the testimony scattered through the investigations and lawsuits." To publicize the wrongdoings while protecting the anonymity of their sources, "we worked out a plan by which the various forms and blanks could be reproduced with fictitious names of persons and places substituted for the originals."[37]

That article would terminate Tarbell's association with Henry Rogers, a Rockefeller partner, who had been a valuable source of information. Tarbell and Rogers had both grown up in the Oil Regions and liked each other, and Rogers had offered to review her findings before their publication. Tarbell took the opportunity to get an inside look at the corporation. She met with Rogers for two years, describing her visits to his office as "an adventure," on which the "alert, handsome, businesslike little chaps who received me at the entrance to the Rogers' suite piloted me unerringly by a route where nobody saw me and I saw nobody." Despite the intrigue, she kept her professional distance: "I made it quite clear to him, however, that while I should welcome anything in the way of information and explanation that he could give, it must be my judgment, not his, which prevailed." The interviews remained cordial and productive until she presented her proof of Standard's involvement with the South Improvement Company. When she refused to disclose her sources, the interviews ended. Journalistic standards had proven more important than friendship with Rogers or the prestige of his special treatment.[38]

Tarbell followed the expected forms of journalistic writing. As she instructed her research assistant: "The work we have in mind is a narrative history.... It is in no sense a piece of economic work, nor is it intended to be controversial, but a straightforward narrative, as picturesque and dramatic as I can make it, of the great monopoly." Tips from anonymous sources or allegations of Standard misconduct were checked against documentary records, and her written copy was reviewed separately by her assistant. She also submitted her material to independent lawyers and two of the nation's most prominent economists. In keeping with good newspaper practice, each installment was rewritten three times. The editors "pounded her and her stuff to make the best of it page by page, and of course never [did] a big person [take as] much merciless help as she did."[39]

As she pursued her story, Tarbell remained calm and focused on the work. Amid "a persistent fog of suspicion and doubt and fear," even her father warned her of the danger of investigating Standard. Others praised her and *McClure's* for their courage. Tarbell modestly, perhaps naively, disagreed: "Courage implies a suspicion of danger. Nobody thought of such a thing in our office.... We were neither apologists nor critics, only journalists intent on discovering what had gone into the making of this most perfect of all monopolies. What had we to be afraid of?"[40]

Tarbell's work can be used to illustrate four possible roles of the press, each involving different relationships to government. Most comfortably for government, the media can offer a forum for the exchange of information and ideas, a "public utility" to provide a "market place of ideas." Even without taking on causes or confronting the government, the press would serve democratic values by facilitating communication among scattered interests. As a forum, Tocqueville wrote, the press "causes political life to circulate through all parts of that vast territory." Newspapers foster both ideas and action, he wrote: "The effect of a newspaper is not only to suggest the same purpose to a great number of persons, but to furnish means for executing in common the designs which they have singly conceived."[41] Tarbell's articles provided information for Progressive reformers, who joined together to demand changes in national economic policy.

A second role is that of agenda setting: emphasizing certain problems or bringing new issues to the attention of the public and government. Bernard Cohen saw this as the greatest power of the media: "The press may not be successful much of the time in telling people what to think but it is stunningly successful in telling its readers what to think about." As one leading study concludes, "Television news shapes the American public's political priorities. . . . When television news focuses on a problem, the public's priorities are altered, and altered again as television news moves on to something new." "Priming" is a related way in which the media can affect public opinion, by suggesting the appropriate criteria by which to evaluate political events. When it comes to judging politicians, for example, the press may encourage the public to focus on their personal characteristics, such as honesty, or on their attitudes toward specific policy issues.[42]

Tarbell's articles served both to facilitate communication and to promote an agenda. Although there already was widespread concern about the power of monopolies, her stories made the conduct of Standard Oil a national priority. Her work also primed the public's consideration, focusing concern on the ethical conduct of the trust, rather than on its assumed economic efficiency. She and her muckraking colleagues recast politics as a morality play in which, as

Hofstadter put it, "evil-doing among the most respectable people is seen as the 'real' character of American life; corruption is found on every side." To solve these moral and economic problems, the Progressives "emphasized governance by legal rules. . . . If the laws are the right laws, and if they can be enforced by the right men, the Progressives believed, everything would be better."[43]

A related role of the press is advocacy. By urging action, the press challenges government. This role was central in earlier times, when newspapers were largely partisan organs, shaping their reports to reflect the views of their politically committed publishers. By the time Tarbell wrote, journalism had become a distinct profession, in which editorial opinion was generally separated from more objective reporting. Although she certainly had strong personal views, she held to her defined role: "My point of attack has always been that of a journalist after the fact, rarely that of a reformer, the advocate of a cause or a system."[44]

The fourth role of journalists in politics is investigation, which is typically critical of government, thus going beyond communication, agenda setting, and advocacy. "It is often said that journalism is the first rough draft of history; by contrast, investigative journalism provides the first rough draft of legislation. It does so by drawing attention to failures within society's systems of regulation and to the ways in which those systems can be circumvented by the rich, the powerful, and the corrupt." Although examples of news reporting can be found in ancient times (in such historians as Herodotus and Thucydides), journalism as a distinct profession dates only from the nineteenth century, and the first investigative reporting from accounts of the deplorable medical treatment of British troops during the Crimean War. The new form of journalism established new principles of objectivity—"independence of . . . the interests of the powerful"—and new techniques: direct observation, use of written sources, personal interviews, and dramatic serialization.[45]

Tarbell obviously adhered to the canons of investigative journalism. She took on the most powerful economic organization of her time, made expert use of the craft of an emerging profession, and stimulated public awareness as well as remedial action by the government. The quality of her work is undiminished a century later. Her investigation of Standard Oil placed fifth on a list recently compiled by journalists and historians of the one hundred most outstanding works of American journalism in the twentieth century.[46] Chronologically, it stands first among those honored reports, providing a model to this day for investigative reporters.

The Press as an Institution

Through the work of Tarbell and other journalists, the press had strongly affected a critical period of American economic development. But the institution also played an indispensable role in the events described in other chapters of this book. Investigative reporters uncovered the Watergate scandals leading to Nixon's impeachment. The media publicized both Senator Joseph McCarthy's attacks and his invasions of liberty. Truman's Marshall Plan gained public support because newspaper coverage emphasized communist threats abroad rather than domestic dissent.[47] Revelations in the media of the thalidomide tragedy spurred passage of new drug legislation. Thurlow Weed's enlistment of press support was critical in Lincoln's renomination in 1864. And, as we will see in the next chapter, the civil rights movement depended on media coverage for much of its success.

These events illuminate the character of the press—which now includes electronic media as well as the printed word—as a nongovernmental institution of American politics. Although reporters are not public officials, their work is vital to the democratic process. As Tocqueville wisely concluded: "The more I consider the independence of the press in its political consequences, the more am I convinced that in the modern world it is the chief and, so to speak, the constitutive element of liberty. A nation that is determined to remain free is therefore right in demanding, at any price, the exercise of this independence."[48] The authors of the Bill of Rights held the same view and wrote the guarantee of a free press into the First Amendment, along with the other central freedoms—speech, religion, assembly, and redress of grievances.

But freedom of the press differs in a fundamental respect from these other liberties. As Supreme Court Justice Potter Stewart argued: "The Free Press guarantee is, in essence, a structural provision of the Constitution." The other constitutional guarantees apply to individual rights, but the liberty of the press is far more than any specific right of reporters, editors, or publishers. "In contrast, the Free Press Clause extends protection to an institution. The publishing business is, in short, the only organized private business that is given explicit constitutional protection."[49]

Situated outside of government, the press is meant to be its critic and its adversary. Press freedom derives from British tradition, where it was seen as a "Fourth Estate more important by far" than the three official branches of government: King, Lords, and Commons. "The British Crown knew that a free press was not just a neutral vehicle for the balanced discussion of diverse ideas. Instead, the free press meant organized, expert scrutiny of government. The press was a conspiracy of the intellect, with the courage of numbers. This formidable check on official power was what the British Crown had feared—and what the American Founders decided to risk."[50]

The institutional importance of the press was underlined when the Nixon administration attempted to prevent publication of the "Pentagon Papers," a classified government account of the development of U.S. policy in Vietnam. In Justice Hugo Black's adamant opinion in favor of the case brought by the *New York Times:* "In the First Amendment the Founding Fathers gave the free press the protection it must have to fulfill its essential role in our democracy. The press was to serve the governed, not the governors. The Government's power to censor the press was abolished so that the press would remain forever free to censure the Government. The press was protected so that it could bare the secrets of government and inform the people."[51]

As an institution, the press illustrates the basic axiom of James Madison's explanation of the safeguards provided by the Constitution as "this policy of supplying, by opposite and rival interests, the defect of better motives."[52] Like the system of formal checks and balances, freedom of the press assumes, and fosters, rivalry among ambitious, even self-seeking, claimants to power. In the formal institutions, competition takes place among public officials, as can be seen in a president's skirmishes with Congress. An independent press brings "outsiders" into the contest, as potential adversaries of the "insiders." The press gets *into* government by being typecast as working *against* government.

American politics inescapably makes government and the press both mutually dependent and inherently prone to conflict. Government officials need the media—to distribute information, to gain citizen cooperation and approval, to win elections. The media, in turn, need officials to supply press releases, grant interviews, and provide access to the sites of newsworthy events. There is a symbiotic relationship between the large Washington press corps and the government's officials, press secretaries, and public information officers; they require each other to do their jobs. They seek favor from each other—a favorable news story for the official, an inside tip for the reporter.

Yet the character of these institutions inevitably makes them rivals. "Men in government, for good reasons as well as suspicious ones, are compelled to minimize or suppress information, to try to mold it by the amount they release and the timing of that release."

Elected officials and bureaucrats engage in extensive consultation and frequent compromise in the development of policy. They seek consensus, a united front, loyalty to superiors—all in the interest of better public policy, as they see it. In contrast, "men in the press, by practice and tradition, want to publish all they can learn as quickly as they can."[53]

Press routines clash with the habits of government. Newsmen must meet daily or weekly deadlines; they cannot hold their copy until it suits the schedules of government. The press defines news literally as what is new, but government policy is rarely innovative and therefore easily neglected. Reporters write narratives, linear "stories"; bureaucrats write studies, often circular analyses. Newsmen and newswomen are necessarily highly selective in choosing what to publish or broadcast, whereas their informants in government view press releases as always deserving priority attention. When policy issues are covered, officials would like to boast of their successes, while reporters are deliberately skeptical, even cynical. This conflict of interest was markedly evident in coverage of the Vietnam War: spokesmen for the military created triumphant "body counts"; reporters came to dispute even actual American successes.[54]

Similar conflicts arise from the conventions and techniques of newsgathering. Reporters, following accepted practices, rely on press handouts and statements by "authoritative sources," providing an opening for officials to advance their own interests and their particular interpretations of events. Journalists' reputations come from beating others to a scoop (while trying to avoid errors made in haste). This complex competition, exacerbated in recent years by the spread of all-news cable television and the Internet, encourages officials to manipulate events, or to arrange pseudo-events, to gain attention. Reporters employ leaks and confidential sources to get the inside information that government agencies want to withhold. The drama of the news is typically based on conflict between individuals or between government agencies, battles that officials would prefer to conceal. Scandal and corruption make headlines; elaborate descriptions of policy issues are killed or held for a slow day.[55]

Yet with all these differences, press and government have always been interdependent.[56] Their mutual reliance is founded on the constitutional separation of institutions. As Douglas Cater emphasized decades ago, the reporter "operates in a system in which power is divided. He as much as anyone, and more than a great many, helps to shape the course of government. He is the indispensable broker and middleman among the subgovernments of Washington." The constitutional separation of powers requires communication, if the checks and balances among the different branches of government are to be reconciled. Communication is the special competence of the press, making it the key intermediary institution of American politics.[57]

In a brilliant analysis, Timothy Cook has shown how the press operates as a political institution and has charted its effect upon the other, more formal institutions of government. This relationship is best described as a "negotiation of newsworthiness," where government decides what is "important" and the press decides what is "interesting." Following its routines, the press defines news as stories that are immediate, dramatic, personal, and derived from official sources. These preferences lead to a journalistic orientation toward "episodic outcroppings rather than continuing conditions, toward issues that fade quickly in public consciousness," and "toward simple if not simplistic renderings of problems, policies, and alternatives."[58]

In parallel fashion, officials, needing the press to gain attention from other power holders and the public, adopt the "production values" of journalism. From the president to the bureaucracy, Congress, and the Supreme Court, members of government increasingly engage in "government by publicity."[59] Policymakers give priority to issues that fit with these values; they stage events that will draw attention; they simplify their presentations. "Speeches that have no pithy, lively, and very short 'soundbites' (usually under ten seconds long) that can be extracted are disfavored over those that do; consequently speakers concerned about getting into the news have to craft their communications so as to be littered with soundbites." The result is that problems and solutions to the most serious political problems, those that are "static, pallid, and abstract," are avoided—and unresolved.[60]

In short, government and the press depend on each other, but their relationship is always uncertain. As they negotiate the checks and balances of American politics, they may become excessively antagonistic, resulting in government's zealous attempts to repress and manipulate information, and journalists' exaggerated emphasis on scandal and incompetence. They may also become too close, when government favors accommodating reporters, journalists tone down their stories to avoid embarrassing friendly officials, or members of the two groups rotate their jobs from one institution to the other. Their uncertain balance replicates the general tug-of-war of American political institutions.

The nature of the press has changed from Tarbell's time, not always for the better. Commercial pressures discourage competition, reduce news coverage, constrain crusades, and limit opportunities for able reporters. Readership and viewership have declined, as new sources of entertainment, such as movies and cable television, and new sources of information, such as the Internet, have challenged its significance. Some critics argue that media news and editorials unfairly favor conservative positions; others are convinced of their liberal bias. Yet others charge that "the stories journalists tell and the lenses that color their interpretation of events can sometimes dull their fact-finding and investigative instincts."[61] Critics further deplore the media's frequent substitution of punditry and armchair interpretation for direct reporting as well as its widespread focus on scandal, sex, and sensationalism.[62]

Perhaps the faults of contemporary journalism can be remedied. Perhaps, in keeping with Tocqueville, they must simply be accepted. "In order to enjoy the inestimable benefits that the liberty of the press ensures," he wrote, "it is necessary to submit to the inevitable evils that it creates."[63] Either way, however, effective democracy still requires the independent capacity of the press to disseminate information, revise the political agenda, advocate social improvements, and investigate the nation's faults. Those who do this vital work can still learn from the closing words of Ida Tarbell, a model journalist and democratic hero: "I see no more promising path than each person sticking to the work which comes his way. The nature of the work, its seeming size and importance matter far less than its right relation to the place where he finds himself. . . . It takes in all of us but puts it up hard to each of us to fit the day's work into the place where we stand."[64]

Chapter Ten
John Lewis

A Hero of Social Movements

Like our other figures, John Lewis lacks any special personal magnetism distinct from his life's deeds. By his own admission, "I'm not a handsome guy. I'm not flamboyant. I'm not what you would call elegant. I'm short and stocky. My skin is dark, not fair—a feature that was still considered a drawback by many black people in the early '60s. For some or all of these reasons, I simply have never been the kind of guy who draws attention."[1] Yet Lewis has drawn attention, both hostile and kind. In 1961, while still legally a minor, he was beaten almost to death when he dared to enter an Alabama bus station restricted to white persons. Two years later, he spoke passionately to a quarter of a million of his fellow Americans at the historic March on Washington. In 1965, he was savagely beaten again in Alabama as he walked across a bridge with other black citizens who wanted to vote. Today, John Lewis is the congressional representative from Atlanta, Georgia, and a Democratic leader in the U.S. House of Representatives.

This black American could easily be portrayed as a traditional hero, as a warrior in the African American struggle for equal rights. He might well be pictured much like a soldier, revealing immense personal courage as he bravely faced injury and possible death in the service of a noble cause. Yet John Lewis's story has an even broader significance, because his portrait places individual heroism within a larger frame, the social movement as a fundamental institution of American politics.

Lewis's childhood was grueling, as was inevitable for a boy both black and poor in the rigidly racist environment of Troy, Alabama, in the 1940s and 1950s. He became the first member of his family to finish high school, but civil rights leaders still found him "completely lacking in refinement," deprecating him as a "Negro whom no amount of education could polish."[2] Derided as "square," he was virtually puritanical in his personal life; until he was twenty-one he had never consumed so much as a beer. Even as a young adult, he spoke with a stammer, a particularly severe disability for a man who most wanted to be a preacher and took his inspiration from the nation's most gifted orator, Martin Luther King Jr.

Yet Lewis had one basic personal trait that would enable him to become a leader in twentieth-century America's transformative social movement. He was persistent, stubborn, determined, directed. Resolved to become a clergyman, he developed his speaking skills by delivering childhood sermons to the chickens scratching for food on his family's paltry farm. When older advisers cautioned student demonstrators in Nashville to back off, Lewis was undaunted, tersely insisting, "We're gonna march." When violence loomed in Alabama, he walked resolutely into the murderous blows. Later, facing defeat in his congressional campaign at the hands of Julian Bond, a far more glamorous black activist, he intensified his personal canvass for votes. Reflecting on his life, Lewis emphasizes this quality of persistence: "I had always believed much more in actions than in words. Keep on keeping on—that had always been my answer in a time of crisis."[3]

Persistence may be admirable, but it is not dramatic heroism. Indeed, Lewis downplays his own achievements:

> I don't think of myself as a hero. I think of myself as a participant, a participant in a movement who is more than lucky and blessed that I had an opportunity to be influenced by people like Martin Luther King Jr. and others. And sometimes I have said that I felt that I was what I called tracked down by the spirit of history to be used. . . . I just tried to do some good. I tried to make things a little bit better. And, in the process, got arrested a few times, got beaten a few times. But I don't think that is anything.
>
> To be a hero, you have to be very courageous. You have to be brave. And maybe I did stand up on the freedom rides and the march and all of that. . . . But there are things I am terrified of. I am terrified by lightning. Growing up as a child I saw what lightning could do. I don't like snakes. I can't deal with them. I never learned to swim.[4]

Lewis has been persistent in his pursuit of his overriding social goal, racial integration in "the beloved community"—his favorite phrase. His earliest politically relevant memory is of the humiliation of segregated seating in the local movie theater: "I hated it. I remember. I don't go to the movies too much even today. Because as a young child, we had to go upstairs, [to] what we referred to as the buzzard roost. And the white kids were all downstairs. So I just stopped going, just completely stopped going. I used to complain to my mother, my father, about why this and why that. And they would say, that is the way it is, that is the way it is."

But if Lewis gave up on the movies, he has devoted his life and risked his death to confront and defeat segregation. To the present day, he continues to urge the utopian vision of "a people united, driven by a moral purpose, guided by a goal of a just and decent community."[5] At any point in history, this goal might be an unrealizable dream; in contemporary America, it may even be a vision that

John Lewis

is disdained by both blacks and whites. But Lewis remains as stubborn as ever, even if he is perhaps, as Sean Wilenz named him, "the last integrationist" in the nation.[6]

John Lewis in the Civil Rights Movement

The question of race has, of course, been central to the history of the United States. The issue almost prevented adoption of the Declaration of Independence itself, when Southern states successfully demanded that Thomas Jefferson's condemnation of slavery be deleted from the text. At the Constitutional Convention, Madison admitted, "the institution of slavery formed the line of discrimination," and adoption of the Constitution depended on the "Great Compromise" guaranteeing all states an equal vote in the Senate. But as Lincoln correctly predicted, "government cannot endure permanently half slave and half free."[7] Thus the Civil War ensued. A century of interracial uncertainty followed, with episodes of reconstruction, repression, and segregation that have brought the United States, even today, to only uncompleted equality.

The critical years in the struggle for racial equality were 1960 to 1966—years that transformed the nation. The life of John Lewis in many ways parallels the course of the civil rights movement during these years and well illustrates the contribution of that movement to the institutions of American politics. Lewis lacked the charismatic appeal of Martin Luther King, but his persistence and his calm acceptance of physical danger made him a central figure in four major events during this period.

The first occurred in Nashville, Tennessee, in February 1960. Black students at local colleges deliberately violated local segregation laws by taking seats at lunch counters reserved for whites.[8] Trained in the philosophy of nonviolent resistance developed by Gandhi and King, 124 students sat calmly as they received not service but verbal and physical abuse, as the counters were closed, as they were arrested for violation of the segregation laws and—most importantly —as the mass media and political figures began to pay attention.

The sit-ins spread rapidly across the South and to other segregated facilities such as movie theatres and swimming pools. The immediate result of the protests was the desegregation, less than three months later, of the Nashville lunch counters and the formation of the Student Non-Violent Coordinating Committee (SNCC); the long-term result was the launching of a broad movement for full African American equality.⁹

Lewis was involved in the civil rights movement from the beginning. He came to Nashville to attend American Baptist College, a small school that had the great advantage of free tuition. When he joined the workshops in nonviolent resistance offered at the Negro institutions, his intelligence and steadiness were quickly recognized. Although he was not an especially prominent figure, his personality fit in well with the overall character of the demonstrators. "If individually they seemed less than heroic, being ordinary people of ordinary size and seemingly of ordinary human gifts, their dignity and their propriety were palpable." Lewis exemplified these qualities, as he sat with his friends before the first demonstration. "They were about to go up against the full power of the city of Nashville. Lewis had never thought of himself as being brave, and the others, he was sure, did not think of themselves that way either. What they were doing was not an act of courage, he decided; it was an act of faith. . . . He did not think of himself as being strong or brave, but he did believe that he had the requisite faith, and now he found in his faith the strength to go forward and do things which in another setting and under different conditions would have terrified him."[10]

The successes of the first sit-ins encouraged the civil rights advocates. They had also been heartened by the election of John F. Kennedy, which brought a possible ally to the White House, and by a Supreme Court ruling requiring the desegregation of buses on interstate routes. The next action of the movement was an effort to implement the Court decision and to extend it to desegregation of the facilities and restaurants at bus terminals. Small, integrated groups of riders set off in May 1961 on "freedom rides" from Washington to New Orleans. One of their two buses was set on by a mob in Anniston, Alabama. Expressing their racial hatred in a vicious combination that "was both a lynching and a picnic," the mob attacked the riders, set fire to the vehicle, and attempted to incinerate the passengers in the burning bus.[11] The second bus escaped to Birmingham, only to be greeted by members of the Ku Klux Klan, who beat the remaining passengers close to death.

SNCC members now assumed the major role, as the freedom ride resumed days later, under limited police protection, out of Birmingham en route to Montgomery. When they reached the state capital, Lewis was the first person off the bus, and he saw a frightening scene:

> And then, out of nowhere, from every direction, came people. White people. Men, women, and children. Dozens of them. Hundreds of them. Out of alleys, out of side streets, around the corners of office buildings, they emerged from everywhere, from all directions, all at once, as if they'd been let out of a gate. . . . They carried every makeshift weapon imaginable. Baseball bats, wooden boards, bricks, chains, tire irons, pipes, even garden tools—hoes and rakes. One group had women in front, their faces twisted in anger, screaming, *"Git them niggers. GIT them niggers!"*

Injured, in many cases unconscious, the passengers were eventually rescued. Fittingly, the rescue effort was the work of Floyd Mann, head of the Alabama state police, who put his commitment to public order above his personal support of segregation. In a familiar phrasing, Mann "did not think he was being a hero, he simply thought he was doing his job the way a good lawman ought to."[12]

The freedom riders spent the night barricaded in a local church against a threatening mob. Frantic calls to Attorney-General Robert Kennedy and his subsequent negotiations with the Alabama governor finally brought police protection as the freedom riders reboarded their buses and set off on a rapid dash to Mississippi. There, they were arrested, jailed, and held under harsh conditions for six weeks. They had come close to being killed, but they had also made important gains. They would soon see the desegregation of interstate travel facilities by administrative order from the U.S. Justice Department. The issue of civil rights had now moved to the head of the national agenda. "Freedom Rides were working, John Lewis realized, for they were beginning to ride into the nation's consciousness if not yet its conscience."[13]

The freedom rides had another significant consequence, which was a change in the generational composition of the movement. Through their bravery, or perhaps their foolhardy audacity, the young activists had become the catalyst of social change. After the violence in Montgomery, the established civil rights leaders joined the campaign, but they could not match the determination of the youth. Despite pleas from his supporters, King declined to board the bus when it resumed its journey, provoking complaints, even ridicule, from his otherwise admiring acolytes. Even Lewis, while he remains devoted to King's memory nearly four decades later, still regrets his absence.

Owing to his role as a leader during the freedom rides, Lewis had become a prominent figure, and he was now chosen chairman of SNCC. As such, he was one of only six black leaders who designed the next major event in the civil rights movement, the 1963 march on Washington. The march has become a mythical event in American history, remembered particularly for King's soaring oratory in his "I Have a Dream" speech. Few listeners were aware that the magnificent conclusion to King's speech was in fact an extemporaneous addition from his previous sermons. His peroration transformed a flagging speech—"politically sound but far from historic, nimble in some streaks while club-footed through others"—into a rhapsodic vision that "went beyond the limitations of language and culture to express something that was neither pure rage nor pure joy but a universal transport of the kind that makes the blues sweet."[14]

But politics, not oratory, was the true agenda of the march on Washington. The peaceful, integrated assembly of a quarter of a million people first alarmed, and then impressed, the power brokers in Washington as well as the national television audience. The chief purpose of the march was to gain support for civil rights legislation proposed by the Kennedy administration but now stalled in Congress. As the crowds left the capital, the president met with the leaders of the march and political lobbying intensified.

John Lewis's inclusion on the short list of speakers certified the rise of SNCC to national standing along with the venerable NAACP and the quieter Southern Christian Leadership Conference (SCLC). It also legitimized SNCC's tactics of confrontational protest. The young spokesman's prepared remarks were notably militant, even angry. He warned that "the black masses"—the first public substitution of "black" for "Negro"—were ready to "march through the South, through the heart of Dixie, the way Sherman did." Disdaining patience as "a dirty and nasty word," he rejected the Kennedy civil rights bill as "too little and too late." In its place, he urged his audience: "The revolution is at hand, and we must free ourselves of the chains of political and economic slavery."[15]

Lewis's prepared speech became the most critical moment in the march and taught him much about politics. He spoke the language of an absolute morality, of unambiguous distinctions between the wrongs of racial oppression and the rightness of racial equality. Prodded, Lewis believes, by the White House, Boston Archbishop Patrick O'Boyle insisted that he tone down the militancy of the speech, particularly the attack on "patience" and the advocacy of "revolution." In last-minute negotiations behind the statue of Abraham Lincoln, Lewis conceded, removing the objectionable phrases and the criticisms of the administration. The speech remained forceful, and Lewis treasures videotapes of the occasion. But now the students and their movement had begun to experience the ambiguities, compromises, and imperfect purity of real-world politics. Some would come to see the march not as a triumph for the cause of civil rights, but a "sellout" on the part of leaders who were "playing patsy with the Kennedy administration as part of liberal-labor politics."[16]

Over the next two years, resistance to desegregation became more desperate and violent, marked most tragically by the death of four schoolgirls in the bombing of a Birmingham church and the murder of three voting-rights workers in the summer of 1964 in Mississippi. Nevertheless, progress continued to be made. After the assassination of President John Kennedy, Lyndon Johnson took up the campaign for civil rights legislation, winning passage of the 1964 Civil Rights Act and the initial goal of the civil rights movement, the desegregation of public facilities.

The movement itself was changing. To dramatize political repression, black activists organized the Mississippi Freedom Democratic Party but were bitterly disappointed when its effort to gain representation was rejected at the Democratic national convention in 1964. SNCC itself was increasingly riven by ideological and personal conflicts. First evident in the march on Washington, these had grown both with failures, such as the Mississippi party, and with successes, such as the passage of civil rights bills in 1964 and 1965. These developments would lead to Lewis's ouster as chairman of SNCC and to a new emphasis on the winning of political power by blacks. The bridge from past to future stood at Selma, Alabama.

The Bridge at Selma

SNCC had begun a voting-rights campaign early on in Selma and had launched a serious effort in the fall of 1963, but these had largely failed. More blacks had been arrested than the three hundred who were finally allowed to register. Then, in 1965, Martin Luther King Jr. and the SCLC selected the area for a major push on voting rights. That effort faced not only opposition from the local authorities but also resentment from SNCC pioneers, including Lewis: "We dug in early, did the groundwork, laid the foundation. Then the SCLC came in again with their headline-grabbing, hit-and-run tactics ... then leaving after they'd gotten what they wanted out of it."[17]

For days, blacks marched to the courthouse in an attempt to register, only to be met with resistance from the local police, their peaceful protests often answered by violence. To win the struggle, the protestors needed to take it beyond the rural town of Selma, so as to gain the attention of the national government and the national news media. They consequently planned a march from Selma to Montgomery, the state capital. Increasingly critical of nonviolence, SNCC refused to participate in what it defiantly called "a classic example of trickery against the people"[18] — and King cautiously stayed away. Grasping the historic opportunity, Lewis led the Selma march, acting not on behalf of an organization but as an individual. "The local people wanted to march. I felt an obligation to be there with them, to get arrested and to go to jail. I felt I had to do it, and I felt very strongly about it. I made that decision and [as] I look back on it, it was the best decision, because the people wanted to do it. And I think it represented one of the turning points in the movement, and probably in American history."

As the marchers left town, they began to cross the Edmund Pettus Bridge, over the Alabama River, when state troopers on horseback blocked their way. The police rode into the rows of blacks, hurling tear gas, swinging whips, and pounding the marchers' heads with nightsticks as they knelt to pray. Lewis, at the head of the line, endured a fractured skull. He would remember "how strangely calm I felt as I thought: This is it. People are going to die here. *I'm* going to die here."[19]

But Lewis did not die, and the cause of voting rights took on new life. Media attention turned to the Selma confrontation. ABC interrupted its broadcast of the film *Judgment at Nuremberg* to show the violence, which fostered comparisons to Nazi war criminals. In Washington, President Johnson, reflecting widespread reaction, reported that when on "Sunday evening my wife and I watched TV and saw those ghastly scenes, our stomachs turned."[20]

The next day, the president went to Congress to ask for new legislation, the most radical intervention on behalf of civil rights since the Civil War. His concluding remarks about the plight of blacks marked at least the rhetorical victory of the civil rights movement. "Their cause must be our cause too," the president declared. "Because it is not just Negroes, but really all of us who must overcome the crippling legacy of bigotry and injustice. And we *shall* overcome." The president's invocation of the movement's credo brought King to tears, an emotional response that neither Lewis nor other civil rights workers had ever before witnessed. The movement now received an unprecedented "breadth of national support, and the strength of federal endorsement. . . . It was an emotional peak unmatched by anything that had come before," although it would also be unmatched "by anything that would come later."[21]

Back in Selma, the activists were divided. King, now returned, declared that they would again attempt to march to Montgomery, then hesitated, then decided to lead a symbolic march that halted and turned around once it had crossed the bridge out of Selma. After two weeks, with the sanction of a federal court order, a new march was organized, drawing thousands of supporters from all regions. Federal and state troops protected them as they moved down the highway for five days, and television carried images across the nation of their peaceful demands for the most basic democratic right. With broad public support, and with bipartisan legislative skill, the voting rights bill moved quickly, and largely unchanged, through

Congress. This second reconstruction of American race relations became law in August 1965.

But even as it triumphed, the movement began to deteriorate. Formally neutral at the time of the first attempted march across the Pettus Bridge, SNCC withdrew its support before the second attempt and moved its own campaign directly to Montgomery. Fundamental differences separated the younger activists from King: his nonviolent tactics, and even his genteel personality. "We don't believe in leadership," a SNCC spokesman said. "We think the people should lead."[22] Soon, even the modest leadership of John Lewis would be unacceptable. "By the end of 1968, SNCC scarcely existed anymore."[23]

In the end, even Lewis's heroism was unable to prevent the decay of the organization he had led. In the struggles that lay ahead, some of his virtues would become drawbacks. Trusting that his peers would always be friends, he would prove ill suited for the political maneuvering within SNCC. Committed to direct and physical action but limited in his education, he was not ready for the intense ideological debates that would soon preoccupy the group. Modeling himself as a preacher in the black oral tradition, he would rarely attempt the written tracts that circulated among the activists. Devoted to his Christian faith, he could not easily refute arguments based on the newer doctrines of Marxism, black nationalism, and redemptive violence.

In the moment, however, the movement had won, writing its claim for full voting rights into legislation. Selma became both the turning point and the conclusion of direct action in the civil rights effort. The great social movement would now become a political claimant, still facing resistance and difficulties, but now enfranchised, armed with the basic means to seek redress. By the turn of the century, the march to Montgomery would be commemorated by a plaque on the Pettus Bridge, by a voting-rights museum, and by a tribute paid by a new southern president to the time when "a single day in Selma became a seminal moment in the history of our country."[24] John Lewis, a plain but courageous man, had done his job.

Social Movements as Political Institutions

The civil rights movement has been a dramatic, even ennobling, experience for Americans. In a broader context, however, it also exemplifies the place of social protest movements as an institution within the overall politics of the United States.

We ordinarily think of an institution as a formal legal body, such as Congress, established by the Constitution and regulated by legal statutes. Typically, too, an institution is associated with a physical space, such as, in the case of Congress, the Capitol building. But social movements are neither established by law nor housed in monumental buildings. On the contrary, they often come into being to protest the actions of formal institutions, just as the civil rights movement opposed the laws of racial segregation and the legal authorities who enforced those laws.

But social scientists analyze institutions differently, defining them as regularized patterns of behavior that may exist independent of legal authorization or a particular physical location. In this analysis, political parties and the press, the focus of the previous two chapters, are American political institutions. To illustrate the distinction, compare marriage and courtship. Marriage is a formal institution, whose character and obligations are defined by law and which is formalized by designated officials in particular locations. Courtship is also an institution in any society, but it exists for the most part unregulated by law: no statute prescribes the rituals of mating. Courtship also is unrestricted by location. It occurs not only at formal dances but also in bars, workplaces, classrooms, and the back seats of automobiles.

In this broader definition, social movements are an institution within American politics, one that endures even as specific protests against political disadvantage come and go. Protest movements are in fact a recurrent pattern in American history, rather than rare exceptions to the calm workings of formal, legal authorities.[25] Major examples of these movements include the farmers who denounced their debts in Shay's Rebellion, before the Constitution was written, the abolitionists who scorned the Constitution's acceptance of slavery, the suffragettes who demanded inclusion in the nation's politics, and the labor union organizers who sought to expand workers' control of economic life. The civil rights movement of the 1960s had distinct members and activities, but it was by no means unprecedented in its character.

In an important sense, protest movements are actually legitimized by the formal institutions of American government. The nation's founding act, the Declaration of Independence, asserts not only a right of protest but, more broadly, that "it is the Right of the People to alter or to abolish" any form of government that threatens their "unalienable Rights," among them "Life, Liberty, and the pursuit of Happiness." Even after independence, Thomas Jefferson suggested that change in the government should be considered at twenty-year intervals, "so that it may be handed on, with periodical repairs, from generation to generation, to the end of time."[26]

The Constitution itself is the result of a sort of protest movement, although one conducted politely by eighteenth-century correspondence and conversation, rather than by twentieth-century street demonstrations. The Federal Constitutional Convention of 1787, which created the nation's basic formal institutions, was authorized only to propose changes in the rather weak central government laid out by the Articles of Confederation, while the power to make those changes remained with the existing Continental Congress and required the unanimous consent of the thirteen states. In reality, however, from its very first days the convention was determined to create an entirely new national government and to replace, not simply amend, the Articles of Confederation.[27] Disregarding established procedures, as well as the instructions it had been given, it bypassed the Continental Congress, providing for ratification by state conventions and by as few as nine states.

In justifying this genteel revolution, James Madison praised the good intentions of the framers of the Constitution. He defended the actions of a minority group pursuing changes with "no zeal for adhering to ordinary form," when it is "essential that such changes be instituted by some *informal and unauthorized propositions,* made by some patriotic and respectable citizen or number of citizens." The public good, he said, in terms that civil rights supporters could well endorse, was more important than legalistic procedures. If these citizens "had exceeded their powers, they were not only warranted, but required, as the confidential servants of their country, by the circumstances in which they were placed, to exercise the liberty which they assumed and . . . if they violated both their powers and their obligations, by proposing a Constitution, this ought nevertheless to be embraced, if it be calculated to accomplish the views and happiness of the people of America."[28]

Martin Luther King Jr. rarely cited Madison, but his justification of protest and civil disobedience similarly placed greater emphasis on the goals of a political movement than on its adherence to established practices. In his famous *Letter from the Birmingham Jail,* he insisted "that law and order exist for the purpose of establishing justice and that when they fail in this purpose they become the dangerously structured dams that block the flow of social progress." Protest is not a threat but a salutary supplement to established institutions. In fact, King argued: "We who engage in non-violent direct action are not the creators of tension. We merely bring to the surface the hidden tension that is already alive. We bring it out in the open, where it can be seen and dealt with."[29]

Social protest movements may be particularly evident, even

necessary, in the American political system. The Constitution established a system that intentionally makes change difficult. Action is purposely made complicated, what with the division of authority among the president, House, and Senate, the power of judicial review, the conflicts of federalism, and the influence of self-interested factions and ambitious politicians. Given these multiple checks and balances, Madison hoped, "a coalition of a majority of the whole society could seldom take place on any other principles than those of justice and the general good."[30]

These same barriers can, however, also prevent action that is just and good. The formal American institutions are slow-moving, characterized more by inertia than momentum. They resemble a "Tudor polity" of divided and often inefficient authority. New groups seeking political ends must endure not only resistance from their opponents but the structural handicaps cemented in the formal institutions. "The United States thus combines the world's most modern society with one of the world's more antique polities. The American political experience is distinguished by frequent acts of creation but few, if any, of innovation."[31]

One source of stability is the nation's democratic principles. But because we accept the doctrine of majority rule, it can be difficult for a minority to make its claims. As Tocqueville warned: "When an individual or a party is wronged in the United States, to whom can he apply for redress? If to public opinion, public opinion constitutes the majority; if to the legislature, it represents the majority and implicitly obeys it; if to the executive power, it is appointed by the majority and serves as passive tool in its hands. . . . However iniquitous or absurd the measure of which you complain, you must submit to it as well as you can."[32]

The very stability of the formal institutions thus stimulates regular disruptions, so that new groups and new demands may be heard. The force of majority opinion engenders protest by minority groups, who attempt to change the terms of political conflict and to create new majorities. Established institutional routines "are disturbed not by adaptive change within the party-policy system, but by the application of overwhelming external force."[33] In this way, the civil rights movement disrupted the static politics of the United States as it worked to fashion a new and supportive majority.

Civil Rights as a Social Movement

If social movements are in many ways unlike standard political institutions, they also show similarities. Movements, too, follow regular and distinctive patterns of behavior. Those patterns are less formal than parliamentary procedures or the rules of judicial practice, but they are still habitual and recurrent practices. Members of successful social movements must also master the practices of their institutions, although their learning comes through spontaneous inspiration and trial-and-error experimentation, not library research or traditional apprenticeships.[34]

John Lewis was a hero of the civil rights movement, but he differs from the other heroes of this book in the way he took action. The others acted largely within established organs of government or of formal organizations; Lewis and his colleagues sought to change those bodies through external action. The others followed established rules, even reasserting traditional procedures; Lewis and the civil rights movement developed new rules. But even in this different environment, Lewis exemplified democratic heroism. That heroism consisted of more than his personal bravery in the face of possible death. Like our other individuals, he succeeded because he persistently applied the principles of a vital political institution in a time of crisis.

The struggle for racial equality was not foreordained, nor was its success inevitable. That social conflict or social problems exist does not in itself explain the development of social protest. Black Americans faced discrimination long before the 1960s, in the form of slavery, legal segregation, economic subordination, and violent repression. These barriers would not fall from their own weight; progress required purposive human action. As a series of actions, the civil rights movement conformed to a familiar pattern. According to a leading theorist on the subject, Charles Tilly, the collective action of such movements follows a sequence of developments. These steps are elaborated by five concepts: interests, organization, mobilization, opportunity, and tactical methods.[35]

The *interests* involved in a social movement are founded in a group's objective conditions, but these interests are explained and articulated through personal interpretations.[36] Social movements develop when a group adopts new beliefs about its conditions and acts to change those conditions. The basis of authority changes, as a group no longer finds existing power relationships acceptable. The Declaration of Independence assured the nation's citizens that "when a long train of abuses and usurpations . . . evinces a design to reduce them under absolute Despotism, it is their right, it is their duty, to throw off such Government." Social movements promote the development of a new consciousness among their members. The civil rights movement eroded the traditional loyalties, or habits of submission, of "Negroes," as the authority wielded by whites and the laws of segregation lost their legitimacy.[37] If blacks were to maintain their allegiance to the American government, the political system would have to be changed, "laying its foundation on such principles, and organizing its powers in such form, as to them shall seem most likely to effect their Safety and Happiness."

Protests and demonstrations by SNCC and the other groups within the movement redefined the interests of African Americans. Changing the consciousness of blacks, these actions created new identities and new feelings of efficacy. John Lewis felt the change after his first arrest, during the Nashville sit-ins. As David Halberstam describes it: "The fear fell from him, and he felt as if a great burden had been lifted from his shoulders. He felt his own strength growing. . . . He felt empowered; part of something much larger than himself. It was as if he had crossed a great line, one that was both political and psychological; he had gone from being afraid of the white power structure to being emancipated." Or as Lewis himself said: "It was exhilarating—it was something I had earned, the sense of the independence that comes to a free person."[38]

Common interests lead to *organization* of persons who share a particular social identity and are bound together by interpersonal relationships. Southern blacks constituted a distinct social category, whose definition was established by both law and custom, as was the discrimination against them. Their identity was reinforced by dense interpersonal networks, partially created by segregation itself, particularly black churches. Lewis and SNCC built upon the traditions, and even the oral cadences, of these organizations.

Mobilization occurs when an organization is able to win control of potential resources and to stimulate loyalty to its purposes and actions. The fullest mobilization will occur "if the resources are free of competing claims, if the action clearly defends the interests of every member, and if the group is an all-embracing moral community."[39] SNCC exemplified such mobilization, and Lewis articulated its total commitment to its ideal. For two members who were married to each other, "the Movement became the only thing which was real. Their new families were composed of their closest friends in the Movement; their other families had become momentarily, at least, secondary and distant. . . . They did not judge each other on how good or complete the other person was on the normal scale of mating for young Americans; they judged each other on how good each was in the Movement."[40]

After mobilization, the outcome of collective action by social movements depends on the *opportunity* provided by the social context in which the movement operates. The social environment may provide better or worse conditions. The opportunities for success are greater when the protest is conducted by existing and respected groups, when these groups pursue goals already held to be legitimate, and when government support can be enlisted. Success may breed more success; as group members achieve some aims, they are emboldened to undertake further collective action, possibly leading to still more realization of their goals.[41]

The civil rights movement largely fit the requirements for success. It was visibly led by respected black clergy. Its goal was fulfillment of the American creed of equality, a principle that remained a national commitment in theory, even if it had been unfulfilled in practice.[42] In the 1960s, national government support was available, even if it came rather hesitantly and late. Nonviolent civil disobedience, in the original Nashville student sit-ins, brought initial success. These actions gave existing organizations "a much-needed shot in the arm by forcing them into active support for the students, into increasing and expanding their mobilization efforts, and into initiating protests on their own." As a result, "a loose alliance of black protest was created."[43]

Once protests had begun, the mass media turned the attention of the nation to the larger struggle, which led to further success. By the time of the Selma march, national news broadcasts, newly expanded to thirty minutes nightly, were eager for vivid reports. "Network television had dramatically affected not merely the pace but the very nature of social change in America. This was not, as it was beamed into millions of American homes, a mere political struggle; it was nothing less than a continuing morality play."[44] Lewis's insistence on continuing the Selma march took advantage of this dramatic opportunity.

Action follows from interests, organization, mobilization, and opportunity. Protest movements employ unconventional *tactical methods* because they cannot succeed through normal political channels, as was obvious in the case of Southern blacks, who could not vote. Movements change politics from a simple conflict between the protestors, such as blacks, and their opponents, such as Southern segregationists. The key element is the audience. Protestors understand a basic rule of combat: "If a fight starts, watch the crowd, because the crowd plays the decisive role. . . . The most important strategy of politics is concerned with the scope of conflict."[45] Protestors attempt to extend the scope of conflict by enlisting the audience—originally neutral or apathetic toward their cause—on their side.

Black civil disobedience enlarged conflict by deliberately disrupting established routines, beliefs, and alignments. The Selma protests marked a basic change in the civil rights movement from "a strategy of nonviolent persuasion which focused on changing the hearts and minds of one's opponents," as in the first lunch-counter sit-ins, to "coercive nonviolence." In the latter instance, "progress could be achieved if the movement, and its external allies, could force southern localities to implement progressive changes."[46] Civil disobedience thus provided the means to test the validity and morality of existing laws, and ultimately to change the political system.[47]

In the showdown at Selma, the movement's tactics were encapsulated in a culminating confrontation. The goal—the right to vote—was an unambiguous American value, so much so that supporters "often tended to suggest that equal voting rights was a more important and loftier aim than the other ends which the civil rights movement of the 1960s was seeking."[48] The behavior of the marchers was dignified and peaceful. In contrast, the brutal violence of the state troopers assured dramatic media coverage and aroused strong opposition to the segregationists in both the television and the political audiences. Gaining the support of external audiences was pivotal to the Selma campaign. The marchers, led by Lewis, extended the conflict from a confrontation between Alabama blacks and Alabama troopers to a national struggle over basic democratic rights. They successfully employed the one power available to the powerless, "activating third parties to participate in controversy in ways favorable to protest goals."[49] With these new allies—the media, religious groups, white citizens and congressional leaders of both parties—they won their goal, the passage of the Voting Rights Act.

For SNCC, this victory also demonstrated a less gratifying characteristic of social movements: their inevitable transformation and usual decline. Even as the movement achieved its greatest successes, SNCC found them empty and wrenchingly changed its ideology, its organization, and its membership. It turned increasingly radical, replacing its founding religious orientation with an emphasis on revolutionary struggle. In place of its original insistence on pacifism, it now held that "the emphasis on love and nonviolence was an anachronism which we could simply ignore." Led intellectually by executive secretary James Forman, the activists argued for a new emphasis on independent political action, rejecting alliances with liberals and Democrats, and promoted armed self-defense and retaliation in place of the earlier tactics of civil disobedience.[50]

Factionalism added to the movement's disintegration. "Hardliners" pressed for a hierarchical and professional organization in place of the open participatory community of the past, now deprecated as a "Freedom High." As Francesca Polletta put it, "the same deliberative practices that had been seen as practical, political, and 'black' came to be seen as ideological, impractical and 'white.'"[51] No longer trusting their colleagues as "a band of brothers" in "a circle of trust," rural Southern field organizers challenged the participation of college-educated whites or even of middle-class blacks. Winning control, they changed the racially integrated organization of the past into one dominated by African Americans, and then excluded whites completely. The new emphasis on racial objectives, summarized as "black power," brought renewed—but unfavorable—attention to the organization, accelerating its decline.

Much like past revolutionary groups, SNCC would soon also renounce its former leaders. Lewis had unintentionally laid the foundation for the new course when he accepted the separatist argument that "the civil rights movement must be black controlled, dominated, and led."[52] In an unanticipated coup, Lewis was deposed as chairman by Stokely Carmichael. In mid-1966, Lewis (and Julian Bond) resigned from SNCC, silently protesting its "repudiation of ourselves, of what we *were,* of what we stood for."[53] By the end of the decade, the protest group had ceased to exist, its members "scattered like seeds in the wind after their radicalism no longer found fertile ground in the southern struggle." They became, in the words of Clayborne Carson, "ordinary people who once did extraordinary things."[54]

Turning to Politics

The most clear-cut limitation of protest as a political technique is its transitory character, as is evident in the decay of SNCC. Protest is exhilarating; but passion fades, the shouts fade to whispers, the crowds disperse. As Michael Lipsky observes, "long-run success will depend upon the acquisition of stable political resources which do not rely for their use on third parties."[55] The Selma march sought and created those stable resources: a large bloc of black voters. Given these votes, over the next decades the number of African American public officials would increase by the thousands. Perhaps most notably, thirty-seven blacks were elected to the House of Representatives, a proportion of the 435 seats approaching the percentage of blacks in the nation's population. As the movement succeeded—indeed because it succeeded—it also changed its direction "from protest to politics."[56]

John Lewis took up this new direction. He continued his civil rights activities, working for various organizations, but he was "convinced that politics was the road we must now take to achieve the goals we had pursued until then through direct action."[57] After settling in Atlanta, he won election as a city councilman and then, in 1986, to Congress. As he gains in seniority and influence in the House, he exemplifies the new political emphasis of the movement. The turn toward the mainstream has brought its own problems, however. Ordinary politics is shot through with moral ambiguity. Even with their physical dangers, Lewis misses the clarity of the earlier causes:

> In the movement, things were more simple . . . more real. You could take strong moral positions, something was right, something was wrong . . . And there was something very pure, in my estimation, about the movement. It was almost holy, spiritual. The movement, in my estimation, had a cleansing effect on the very psyche of the American people . . .
>
> I think people shy away from these ideas and concepts in elected positions. Some people love humanity [but] they just don't like people. They think something is strange when you start talking about love and beloved community. I think there is a need—which some of us try to do in our own ways sometimes—there is a need to find a way to take some of the best qualities of the early days of the civil rights movement and inject it into the body politic. There is a need to what I call "humanize" American politics.

The differences are evident even in Lewis's congressional office, which is decorated with pictures taken during the civil rights struggles, side by side informational brochures on tourist attractions in Washington, and Georgia boosterism. On one wall is a SNCC photograph of a young Lewis and two friends, kneeling, with an inspiring caption, "Come let us build a new world together." On another wall, testimony to the diversity of Lewis's current activities, is an Atlanta street sign advertising Coca-Cola, which is headquartered in the city. A large cabinet holds awards, most of them from the days of the movement; but there is also one from the National Council of Jewish Women and another from the International Chiropractors Association, and a large Coke bottle encased in plastic. The only sculpture is a bust of a white man, Robert Kennedy. Lewis's schedule is crowded, but not only with issues of race; as a member of the Ways and Means committee, he must also spend time with tax lobbyists.

John Lewis proudly remembers the civil rights movement, and the nation will not soon forget the achievements of those years. The early sit-ins first brought the issue of race onto the national political agenda; the later protests, culminating in the Selma march, gave power to a large and formerly disenfranchised group; and black voting in turn transformed electoral politics and the American agenda.[58] Working within an informal but vital institution—the social movement—John Lewis thus helped to alter the formal political system.

A hero of that movement, Lewis is still persistent, still dedicated, still optimistic of progress, still bearing witness to his faith in the American creed of equality. Now he brings those virtues to bear within other institutions of American politics. Instead of leading protest marchers, he leads U.S. Representatives; instead of writing pamphlets, he writes legislation; instead of speaking to the powerless, he speaks their needs in the corridors of power. The last figure on our list of democratic heroes, he holds to his life-long maxim of duty, "Keep on keeping on."

CHAPTER ELEVEN
ORDINARY HEROES AND AMERICAN DEMOCRACY

We began our exploration of heroism by contrasting the actions of Achilles in *The Iliad* to those of emergency rescuers after the terrorist attacks of September 11, 2001. In concluding this study, let us recount two other stories, also drawn from ancient Greece and modern America.

Rather than a warrior such as Achilles, the hero of Sophocles' *Antigone* is an unarmed woman. Barred by her sex from public life, she has witnessed the death of her two brothers in civil war. The first, Eteocles, was loyal to the regime in power and is buried with full honors. The second, however—the rebel Polynices—is left to rot on the battlefield by a royal decree that openly defies Greek religious doctrine. In opposing the power of Creon, the king, Antigone invokes both her conscience and her family duty. She buries her vanquished brother, buries him a second time when the funeral dirt is removed by sentries, admits to her violation of the king's decree, and rejects all those who plead with her to renounce her transgression. When Creon insists on enforcing his edict banning her brother's burial, she proudly accepts her own death sentence.

On a late July afternoon in 1998, a crazed man armed with a revolver attempted to shoot his way into the U.S. Congress. In an ensuing gunfight, security guards Jacob Chestnut and John Gibson were killed, but they prevented any harm to the members of Congress. Five days later, their bodies lay in state in the Rotunda of the Capitol building. Paying tribute to the officers, President Bill Clinton declared: "What makes our democracy strong . . . is the countless individual citizens who live our ideals out every day, the innumerable acts of heroism that go unnoticed."[1]

These stories return us to the question posed at the beginning of this book. Who are the real heroes?

Most of us would probably agree with Senate majority leader Trent Lott, who, also speaking at the Capitol, stated that officers Chestnut and Gibson "should rightly be recognized in this hall of heroes [as] two men who did their job, who stood the ground and defended freedom." But why? These police officers were not extraordinary persons; in their everyday lives they evinced no unusual virtues. Their deaths were the tragic consequence of their daily work, which typically involved little more than shepherding docile tourists into waiting lines. And yet we are moved—properly moved—by their deaths.

Antigone's heroism is more debatable. Certainly she is courageous and principled. We cannot but be impressed by her emphasis on family duty and conscience, her resistance to a sacrilegious edict, and her defiance of an arbitrary ruler. As she tells Creon:

> That order did not come from God. Justice,
> That dwells with the gods below, knows no such law.
> I did not think your edicts strong enough
> To overcome the unwritten unalterable laws
> Of God and heaven, you being only a man.[2]

But admirable as her actions may appear, Antigone's conduct is troubling. She bases her claims to righteousness on individual, not social, grounds and often seems concerned as much with her own personal glorification as with communal morality. She rejects the help of her sister, she shows little concern for her promised husband, Creon's son, and she spurns the possibility of compromise—the king's silent acceptance of Polynices' first, unpublicized burial.

Antigone also argues, as does the play itself, that an inherent conflict exists between individual virtue and politics. To be a person of integrity and faithful to her family, Antigone must be a disobedient subject. Her absolutist ethic of individual conscience cannot be reconciled with the necessities of politics, which demand considerable loyalty of those governed. As Creon states in rebuttal:

> There is no more deadly peril than disobedience;
> States are devoured by it, homes laid in ruins,
> Armies defeated, victory turned to rout.
> While simple obedience saves the lives of hundreds
> Of honest folk.[3]

Finally, both Antigone and Creon disregard the importance of institutions in prescribing norms and behavior in politics. Both are convinced of their own thoroughgoing righteousness, which transforms their conflict into a personal battle of wills. Antigone disdains the institutions of law and monarchy, but Creon, too, subverts the institutional order of his polity when he disregards the advice of his counselors, the sentiment of the public, and the religious rituals that were an inseparable part of Greek political practice. His single-minded arrogance, his son warns, destroys his legitimacy, reducing him to "an excellent king—on a desert island."[4]

These stories raise three basic questions about heroism that will frame this chapter. First, to what extent is heroism equivalent to individual virtue? Second, what is the distinctive character of political heroism? And, third, how do institutions shape heroism? We will attempt to answer these questions in the light of the actions of the eight persons described in the preceding chapters.

Heroism as Individual Virtue

Inasmuch as heroism is highly valued, we tend to use the term to honor any virtuous action. As the survey of popular usage in chapter 2 showed, the title of hero has been bestowed on parents and soldiers, businessmen and radical protesters, faithful spouses and scientific geniuses. Indeed, heroism is very often equated with admirable individual character traits—and our eight heroes do possess such traits. One virtue common among them is modesty. Those in government did not actively seek the positions that made them heroes. Rodino and Watkins were reluctantly drafted to chair the impeachment and censure inquiries, Truman was a hesitant candidate for vice president, doubting his ability to succeed FDR as president, and Kelsey took on the thalidomide review as a routine introduction to her new job at the FDA. Our heroes were also modest about making claims to greatness. They rarely publicized, and in fact often minimized, their role in the specific events they influenced. Truman gave the title and credit for the Marshall Plan to his secretary of state; Justice wrote in the arcane language of court opinions, not for the general public; Weed made no public boasts about his contributions to saving the Union; Tarbell rejected the title of a crusader; Lewis submerged his ego in the work of SNCC.

In fact, these persons seemed in many ways modest in their innate abilities as well as in their behavior. None were credited with especially striking personal traits; all were quite taciturn, even somewhat retiring in the case of Justice. Aside from Rodino, they had no oratorical skills, Lewis had an early speech defect, and, aside from Tarbell, they were indifferent writers. They are illustrative of a distinction made by Henry Kissinger: The "political leaders with whom we are familiar generally aspire to be superstars rather than heroes," Kissinger wrote. "Superstars seek success in a technique for eliciting support; heroes pursue success as the outgrowth of inner values. . . . All people of great achievement are ambitious. But the key question is whether they are ambitious to be or ambitious to do."[5]

Our figures share another attribute, as impressive as it is prosaic: persistence. Rodino made a virtue of slowly building his case, just as Watkins patiently accumulated evidence against McCarthy. Kelsey persevered in her skeptical scrutiny of thalidomide; Tarbell steadily pursued her research in libraries and interviews. Moreover, Justice has stuck to the cause of equal rights for over thirty years, while Weed held to his partisan and patriotic positions through electoral defeat and the rebellion of the South. Lewis persisted in sit-ins and freedom rides despite the threat to his life. Truman even defined his work as persistence: "I've a job and it must be done—win, lose, or draw."[6]

Our individuals display yet another laudable characteristic, a courageous commitment to their values and perceived duties, even at the risk of personal loss. Courage is easily recognized in times of war. The military veterans of the invasion of Normandy personify democratic courage: "Most led ordinary lives before their supreme test on D-Day, and ordinary lives afterward as well. Most do not see themselves as heroes, and they talk hesitatingly, if at all, about the scenes of carnage that met them on that gray morning in 1944."[7] Their courage is the more remarkable when it is juxtaposed to their safer lives today. "A few wars later, they don't *look* that tough," wrote one commentator. "They wore bifocals, hearing aids and pacemakers. . . . But when the courage was desperately needed, they delivered it, and afterward, like the veterans who followed them into Korea and Vietnam, they got on with less remarkable lives."[8]

Courage is often identified with physical danger, such as a battle, but it has a broader meaning: "action in the face of danger that discounts the harmful effects of the action on the one who acts."[9] Among our heroes, Lewis faced the greatest hazard, immediate death, but the others also took risks—electoral defeat for Weed, Watkins, and Truman, ridicule for Rodino, job security for Kelsey, scorn for Tarbell, social isolation for Justice. They took risks that probably few others would accept because of their commitment to their own core values—fairness for Rodino and Watkins, generosity for Truman, scientific integrity for Kelsey, patriotism for Weed, truth for Tarbell, social equality for Justice and Lewis.

Modesty, persistence, courage, commitment to values. These are surely admirable characteristics, even if they may seem naively idealistic to some and are rarely manifested in our everyday lives. All the same, these qualities are evident in other putative heroes. For example, Paul Simon praised the baseball great Joe DiMaggio for virtues not unlike those found among our institutional heroes: his "excellence and fulfillment of duty (he often played in pain), combined with a grace that implied a purity of spirit, an off-the-field dignity and a jealously guarded private life."[10] Simon's sung lament in "Mrs. Robinson"—"Where have you gone, Joe DiMaggio? Our nation turns its lonely eyes to you"—testifies movingly to our collective need for such heroes.

But, as we have seen, political heroism is different from personal excellence. Even laudable individuals are far from ideal persons. They make tactical mistakes (Truman in Korea); they sometimes pursue goals that are objectionable (Watkins on Indian treaty termination) or petty (Rodino on private immigration bills) or fail to pursue goals that are worthwhile (Tarbell on women's suffrage); they may be limited in their vocational vision (Kelsey) or in their political sophistication (Lewis); they may be self-righteous (Justice) or occasionally corrupt (Weed). Heroes are human.

Moreover, admirable personal traits do not necessarily translate into admirable politics. For one thing, such traits may be as evident outside politics as within, as the example of DiMaggio suggests. We urge modesty on children and teenagers in our homes; we honor persistence among students in our schools; we cheer courage in athletics; we encourage commitment to values in our churches. That praise is earned through individual conduct, usually with no particular emphasis on the person's role in public life.

To some, in fact, virtue is not only a personal trait, but it is inherently antithetical to public involvement. For example, among Entrepreneurs and Nurturers—two of the heroic types identified by Amy Fried and elaborated in chapter 2—politics is viewed as irrelevant or even as corrupting. Both roles are heavily dependent on gendered stereotypes, emphasizing either a masculine "toughness" or a feminine "caring," but in both cases outside the sphere of politics.[11]

The distinction between personal goodness and public heroism is chillingly exemplified by the most fearsome event in Western history, the Holocaust. The "Righteous Gentiles" who rescued Jews from the Nazis certainly deserve our praise. We can draw still deeper inspiration from such communities as the French village of Le Chambon, whose entire population cooperated to hide Jews, thereby saving them from almost certain death. A community effort of this character implies "the banality of goodness,"[12] that almost all people are decent, and therefore fit for self-government. This optimistic conclusion fortifies our faith in the viability of democracy. At the same time, these heroic acts can also occasion regret, precisely because of their rarity. Those who undertook to rescue Jews were the exception, as Cynthia Ozick regretfully acknowledges. Most persons were bystanders—not vicious, but passive, in contrast to those few "astonishing souls who refused to stand by as their neighbors were being hauled away to the killing sites." Of these rare individuals Ozick comments: "It is typical of all of them to deny any heroism. 'It was only decent,' they say. But no: most people are decent; the bystanders were decent. The rescuers are somehow raised above the merely decent."[13]

A fundamental lesson of the Holocaust is that individual goodness is insufficient to maintain a just society. But political heroism is different from personal righteousness. Social decency rests on sound institutions that will foster good behavior on the part of citizens and leaders or, at the least, inhibit the abuse of power. The distinction between public and private virtue also helps to explain the honor paid to officers Chestnut and Gibson at the Capitol. Thousands of local residents and tourists waited hours in the brutal Washington heat to join in the tribute. The respect they felt went beyond the recognition of individual courage. It derived from the public character of the officers' bravery, their defense not of themselves or their families—commendable as those acts would be—but of a national public space. As one woman said in offering homage: "You don't have to be a President to deserve the respect the Rotunda offers. . . . They did their jobs and gave their lives for it."[14]

These mourners responded not simply as sympathizers but as members of a community. The same attitude would be evident in the respect paid to firemen and police officers for their valiant efforts on and after September 11 and in mass visits to the World Trade Center site, which became a virtual shrine to public service. The reaction of citizens in New York silently echoed Pericles' tribute to ancient Athens and its protectors: "This, then, is the kind of city for which these men, who could not bear the thought of losing her, nobly fought and nobly died."[15]

Political Heroism

There are many kinds of heroes; it would be presumptuous to claim the title, so highly valued in our language, for an exclusive class. But politics is a distinctive realm. It deals with the life of the community, beyond the lives of individuals and their circles of close friends and relatives. The actions of the heroes of this book demonstrate how government can promote an equitable and responsible society, as Justice did in expanding educational opportunities for Hispanic American children and as Kelsey did in safeguarding the health of newborns. They also show how government can protect liberty, as Rodino did in deposing an unethical president, and foster equality, as Lewis did in protesting the subjugation of African Americans.

The public role of an individual is distinct from, even sometimes in conflict with, the expectations of proper behavior that govern his or her private life. In ancient Greece, the essential nature of virtue (and its manifestation in heroes)—originally grounded in "family values"—evolved toward a definition based on political values, "a conception of justice which shifts the center of authority in moral questions from the family and the household to the *polis*."[16] In this larger environment, personal virtue acquires a degree of ambiguity. The individual virtue of modesty, for example, can benefit politicians who are able to subordinate their egos to their policy objectives. At the same time, such politicians may also be scorned for their "weak leadership," a charge leveled against Truman. Similarly, the virtue of persistence is central to democratic politics. In a democracy, consensus must be reached among a diverse group of people, and it takes steady effort over the long haul to achieve this consensus. But persistence may also be criticized as procrastination, as happened to Rodino.

A courageous commitment to principles is more difficult to discern in politics than in individual action. In the public realm, "a politically courageous individual acts for the public good or interest"[17]—but what constitutes the public good is even more difficult to discover than the rules of proper individual conduct. Politics also introduces special problems of ethics, as, for example, when politicians face a moral conflict between their personal beliefs and the ultimate sovereign in a democracy, majority opinion. More generally, politicians may have to choose between competing ethical principles. They may hold to an absolutist "ethic of ultimate ends," insisting that only morally correct means may be employed in pursuit of a goal, regardless of the circumstances. Alternatively, they may employ an "ethic of responsibility" that focuses instead on the eventual consequences of actions and accepts the moral ambiguity that "in numerous instances the attainment of 'good' ends is bound to the fact that one must be willing to pay the price of using morally dubious means." Contrary to an absolutist personal ethic, politicians may be justified in using such means as compromise, bargaining, lying, and even violence. "But to do that," Weber teaches us, "a man [or a woman] must be a leader, and not only a leader, but a hero as well."[18]

But what kind of hero? Most of the attention to political heroes is devoted to those outside of the mainstream—dissenters, "whistle-blowers," protesters. In *Marching to a Different Drummer,* Robin Berson praises the "unrecognized heroes of American history." Virtually defining heroism as antithetical to mainstream politics, she finds it among "dedicated deviants," people who "defied the social and moral conventions of their times." Heroism is further identified with praiseworthy individual characteristics: "devotion to conscience," loyalty to friends, "decency, an empathic capacity to embrace the entire human family."[19]

America's tradition of dissent has indeed produced its share of heroes. And yet no less a person than Henry David Thoreau illustrates the negative side of such "deviant" heroism. The famous individualist expressed his opposition to slavery and the Mexican War not by political activism but by refusing to pay his taxes and then virtuously withdrawing to a comfortable jail. Thoreau made no attempt to rally opposition to slavery, joined no abolitionist movement, and provided no practical lessons for the later civil rights revolution. In his classic essay on civil disobedience, he is smug and disengaged: "As for adapting the ways in which the State has provided for remedying the evil, I know of no such ways. They take too much time, and a man's life is gone. I have other affairs to attend to. I came into this world, not chiefly to make this a good place to live in, but to live in it, be it good or bad." Dismissing political action, Thoreau concludes, rather solipsistically, that "any man more right than his neighbors, constitutes a majority of one already."[20]

Political heroism requires more than individual goodness, since it is not self-evident how individual virtues should be applied to politics, as the story of Antigone demonstrates. Different principles may apply: "The salient social virtue of the private realm is particularistic benevolence for our intimate few, and the salient social virtue of the public realm of strangers is universal justice."[21] The meaning of accepted principles can also change. Even the individual value of "conscience," recently understood today as a quality "permitting people to make their own moral and political judgments," could earlier be understood as obligating obedience to established, even unjust, authorities.[22]

Moreover, democratic heroes do not merely illustrate virtue; they inspire it. Their political actions remind their fellow citizens of their collective experience, of the existence of a community beyond themselves. The self-government of democracy requires more than the promotion of self-regarding actions, even if laudable; heroes bring this larger vision into view. By their actions heroes may encourage others to increase their own participation in the community, to increase their day-to-day exercise of democratic responsibilities. As Emerson understood, a true hero can transform others into heroes. "With the great, our thoughts and manners easily become great. We are all wise in capacity, though so few in energy. There needs but one wise man in a company, and all are wise, so rapid is the contagion. . . . Thus we feed on genius, and refresh ourselves from too much conversation with our mates, and exult in the depth of nature in that direction in which he leads us."[23]

Great men and women become leaders when they inspire heroism in others. To be effective, they cannot act alone. In the words of Gary Wills: "The leader most needs followers. When those are lacking, the best ideas, the strongest will, the most wonderful smile have no effect. . . . It is not the noblest call that gets answered, but the *answerable* call. As Wills also points out: "The leader is one who mobilizes others toward a goal shared by leader and followers."[24] As leaders, Truman inspired American solidarity with Europe and American generosity, and Rodino made the nation more aware of the solemn heritage of its Constitution. Through the civil rights movement, leaders such as Lewis and Martin Luther King Jr., made blacks more conscious of their common needs and whites more conscious of the common humanity they shared with blacks. Fostering involvement and community, the movement advanced America's founding ideal, equality.

Political heroes must therefore be more than good men or women, however principled, conscientious, or morally right their convictions. In a democracy, they also must engage their compatriots and persuade them to adopt their convictions. In order to accomplish this goal, political heroes must understand and make skillful use of their nation's institutions. To be effective, they must also humbly acknowledge Weber's teaching: "Politics is a strong and slow boring of hard boards. . . . Only he has the calling for politics who is sure that he shall not crumble when the world from his point of view is too stupid or too base for what he wants to offer. Only he who in the face of all this can say 'In spite of all!' has the calling for politics."[25]

The Importance of Institutions

This book finds heroism in persons who employed the institutions of American government for the worthy purposes they represent. These men and women did not succeed because of their personal virtues. The explanation for their successes—for their fruitful heroism—is found in their institutional behavior, their fulfillment of their prescribed roles.

That our institutions produce such heroes is in keeping with Madison's warning, quoted earlier, that "enlightened statesmen will not always be at the helm" and in his skeptical insistence that "ambition must be made to counteract ambition. The interest of the man must be connected with the constitutional rights of the place."[26] It is consistent with the expectations of the framers of the Constitution, as Hofstadter emphasized:

> The men who drew up the Constitution in Philadelphia during the summer of 1787 had a vivid Calvinistic sense of human evil and damnation and believed with Hobbes that men are selfish and contentious. They were men of affairs, merchants, lawyers, planter-businessmen, speculators, investors. Having seen human nature in display in the market place, the courtroom, the legislative chamber, and in every secret path and alleyway where wealth and power are courted, they felt they knew it in all its frailty. To them a human being was an atom of self-interest. They did not believe in man, but they did believe in the power of a good political constitution to control him.[27]

The importance of political institutions has been given new emphasis in contemporary political science. The formal and informal institutions we have reviewed—Congress, the presidency, courts, bureaucracy, parties, the press, social movements—are recognized as "political actors in their own right." They function autonomously, transcending the play of external social forces, particular interests, and individual motivations. "Empirical observations seem to indicate that processes internal to political institutions, although possibly triggered by external events, affect the flow of history."[28]

A political decision is not a new experience, written on a blank slate, nor one decided on the basis of abstract, universal principles. It is influenced by the political institutions that make those decisions, by their norms, their resources, and their procedures, and by the interpretations of political life that those institutions promote. These effects are evident in our case studies. By adhering to the *norms* of the House, Rodino was able to be effective in pursuing the impeachment of Nixon. Similarly, Watkins found cause for McCarthy's censure in the latter's violations of the norms of the Senate. Justice relied on the norms of equal protection in requiring public education for the children of undocumented aliens, and Kelsey was justified in her cautious approach to the licensing of thalidomide by the norms of bureaucratic regulation. Our protagonists were successful because they could invoke institutional norms: their actions did not simply reflect personal preferences.

Institutions also provided *resources*. Truman was able to employ the central position of the presidency to set the national agenda and to bargain with foreign powers and with the Republicans in Congress. Weed secured Lincoln's renomination by enlisting placeholders who owed their positions to the patronage he dispensed. Tarbell had at her disposal the prestige and the financial backing of an independent press. As the leader of a social movement, Lewis could call on hundreds of unarmed protestors to gain the attention of the national news media.

Institutional *procedures* significantly shaped exploitation of these resources. The president is accorded national leadership in foreign policy, which assured congressional consideration of Truman's advocacy of the Marshall Plan. Justice's findings carried considerable weight in the appeals of *Plyler v. Doe* before the circuit court and Supreme Court because of the deference that appellate tribunals pay to a trial court's finding of facts. The approval of thalidomide could be delayed because FDA procedures called for a new period of evaluation with each round of drug reviews. The traditional autonomy of state parties enabled Weed to make deals in support of Lincoln's reelection.

Finally, institutions have an autonomous effect on the *interpretation* of political life. The institutions can in fact change reality, such that politics can be regarded "as education, as a place for discovering, elaborating, and expressing meanings, establishing shared (or opposing) conceptions of experience, values and the nature of existence."[29] Through their institutional behavior, our heroes fostered public understanding, even as they altered the political world itself. Rodino established new rules for presidential conduct, and Watkins brought new significance to Senate norms. Truman transformed the traditional foreign policy of the United States. Justice's orders extended the legal rights of aliens, and Kelsey's careful review led to more extensive safeguards on the nation's health. Weed built and sustained a party that would ultimately make the United States a greater and fairer nation, and Tarbell spurred the public and the government to rehabilitate American capitalism. Lewis pushed the public, the president, and Congress toward a fuller American commitment to racial equality.

These individuals were effective because they did their jobs within institutions that allowed them to do their good work, improving the established paths to beneficial goals. Without these institutions, they would still have been good people, but without much effect. Even within these institutions, however, the force of circumstances was needed to produce the heroic response. Rodino required

Nixon before he could assert the authority of the House of Representatives. Watkins required McCarthy before he could rise in defense of Senate traditions. Tarbell required John D. Rockefeller before she could rake the muck of Standard's oil. Lewis required Sheriff Jim Clark before he could mobilize a social movement on behalf of equal rights. Events provided the opportunity for ordinary heroes to do their institutionalized jobs.

It is also true, however, that these eight individuals could not have met the problems they confronted by relying on their respective institutions alone. Certain personal qualities were also necessary, even if not sufficient. Rodino handled Nixon's impeachment well, but Henry Hyde, his successor decades later, botched the Clinton impeachment. Watkins honored the norms of the Senate, but his colleague, McCarthy, debased the same norms. Truman was eventually acknowledged as a superior president, but historians consider Nixon severely flawed as an occupant of the same office. Justice used the powers of a judge to promote equality, but other jurists accepted and even encouraged segregation and discrimination. Kelsey virtuously insisted on administrative routine, but bureaucrats in other agencies have used their power to harass citizens. Weed was loyal to a great leader of his party, but many wardheelers followed corrupt chieftains. Tarbell wrote a landmark of investigative journalism, but some of her successors have used their craft to humiliate officials and demean public institutions. Lewis could be effective within the civil rights movement, but, in the hands of other leaders, SNCC's turn toward a radical view of black power eventually ended first its effectiveness and then its existence.

American institutions provide the framework for political heroism, but they do not guarantee that heroes will always be present when needed. These institutions do, however, increase the probability that such heroes will emerge. The common characteristic of American institutions, beginning with the Constitution, is a suspicion of power. In Madison's pithy summation: "It is of great importance in a republic not only to guard the society against the oppression of its rulers, but to guard one part of the society against the injustice of the other part." Institutions, if properly constructed, could help to realize the hope of the founders that "a coalition of a majority of the whole society could seldom take place on any other principles than those of justice and the general good."[30] In keeping with this suspicion of power, the Constitution provided its multitude of checks and balances and separations of powers. The same attitude informed later institutional developments, such as judicial review, complex administrative procedures, and the extension of suffrage. Further restraints on power have come through competitive political parties, a critical press, and social movements. American politics provides multiple points of access for multiple interests, stimulating wide participation even as it makes it difficult for any group to win a complete victory or for any issue to be finally settled.

Heroism in the Democratic Community

The institutional role of the democratic hero is not one of a bold or superhuman conqueror. An institutional hero is not a Caesar or Cromwell, or what Sidney Hook called the "event-making man" (or woman), someone who "finds a fork in the historical road, but also helps, so to speak, to create it." As Hook explains, such a person "increases the odds of success for the alternative he chooses by virtue of the extraordinary qualities he brings to bear to realize it. . . . It is the hero as event-making man who leaves the positive imprint that is still observable after he has disappeared from the scene."[31] Yet, as Hook would later warn, "a democratic community must be eternally on guard" against such persons. Quoting an old Chinese proverb, "the great man is a public misfortune," he cautions: "On the whole, heroes in history have carved out their paths of greatness by wars, conquests, revolutions and holy crusades." Such figures may be even more dangerous in democracies, because they resist the constraints of majority rule and are impatient with the slowness of its operations.[32] And a free society may be better off for their absence. As Judith Shklar warns, those who find the "noble hero irresistible might well reflect upon the cost to the rest of mankind, not excluding themselves, from among those who would have to pay for him."[33]

Democracy is more comfortable with "eventful" persons, those who participate in important events without changing the course of history in the manner of Caesar or Cromwell. Such persons are more readily available than "event-making" people. As an example of a person who is merely "eventful," Hook recalls the fabled Dutch boy who saved his town by putting his finger in the leaking dike: "Without meaning to strip the legend of its glamour, we can point out that almost anybody in the situation could have done it. All that was required was a boy, a finger, and the lucky chance of passing by. The event itself in the life of the community was of tremendous significance. . . . But the qualities required to cope with the situation were of a fairly common distribution."[34] Fortunately for the Dutch residents, Hook was not present to disparage this act. Even if it is only a legend, however, the tale informs us of democratic heroism. The boy acted not as an individual but as a citizen. He had absorbed the norms of his society that encouraged devotion to the public welfare rather than to personal safety—in this case, presumably flight to higher ground. Perhaps some other child or adult would have passed by later and saved the town; perhaps not. The fact remains that this particular individual did serve his community and surely merited his resulting renown.

Democratic heroes are like the Dutch boy, if we take dikes as a metaphor for the institutions of American politics. These institutions channel the often fierce competition among people and interests and work to keep ambition within well-worn paths. On occasion, though, leakages in the dikes threaten the safety of the nation's inhabitants. Then those who guard the levees are needed to put themselves forward and repair the damage. That is what the heroes of this book did, rebuilding in various ways the institutional constraints on power. Each played only a modest role, but it was a role particularly appropriate for democracy as well as one consonant with the original meaning of heroism. In epic poetry, heroes are regarded as "men of superhuman strength, courage or ability." In both the Greek and Latin origins of the term, however, a hero was a servant, a protector, a guardian.[35] To be heroes, akin to the eight figures examined in this book, our public servants need only to protect and to safeguard our institutions. That is heroism enough for a society of liberty and equality.

Democratic heroes work within democratic institutions in such a way as to produce successful results. The proudest boast of our eight heroes might well be a commonplace national adage: "Our Constitution works; our great Republic is a government of laws, and not of men."[36] They were not extraordinary characters, but they did significantly contribute to American life through their customary work. They personify the character of American democracy anticipated by Tocqueville: "If there are few instances of exalted heroism or of virtues of the highest, brightest, and purest temper, men's habits are regular. . . . Genius becomes more rare, information more diffused. The human mind is impelled by the small efforts of all mankind combined together, not by the strenuous activity of a few men."[37]

Over a century and a half ago, Abraham Lincoln warned of the dangers from people of "the family of the lion, or the tribe of the eagle. As he might still caution a modern audience: "Towering genius disdains a beaten path. . . . It *denies* that it is glory enough to serve under any chief. It *scorns* to tread in the footsteps of any predecessor, however illustrious." Rather than await such extraordinary men and women, Lincoln wisely advised that "for our future support and defence," we must rely on "general intelligence, sound morality and, in particular, a reverence for the constitution and laws." These qualities are clearly evident in the stories of our eight American heroes, doing their jobs. Through actions like theirs, rooted in the institutions of American politics, we may still redeem Lincoln's hope: "As a nation of free men, we must live through all time."[38]

Notes

1 We Call Them Heroes

1. A Lexis-Nexis search of major U.S. newspapers published on the first ten days after the attack found 438 articles on heroes at the World Trade Center alone.
2. The resisting passengers were Mark Bingham, Thomas Burnett, and Jeremy Glick, described by Jodi Wilgoren and Edward Wong, "On Doomed Flight, Passengers Vowed to Perish Fighting," *New York Times,* September 13, 2001, p. A1. See also "Facing the End," *Time,* September 24, 2001, p. 68.
3. Sally Jenkins, "Company of Heroes," *Washington Post,* September 20, 2001, p. C01.
4. Joan Walsh, "Giuliani's Moment," www.salon.com/news/feature/2001/09/12/giuliani (September 12, 2001).
5. Bertolt Brecht, *Galileo,* ed. and trans. Eric Bentley (New York: Grove Press, 1966), 13:22.
6. James Madison, *The Federalist,* no. 10 (1787) (New York: Modern Library, 1941), p. 57.
7. Ibid., no. 15 (1787), p. 92.
8. Homer, *The Iliad,* trans. Robert Fagles (New York: Penguin Books, 1990), p. 77.
9. One moving example is offered by James B. Stewart's *Heart of a Soldier* (New York: Simon and Schuster, 2002), a biography of Dan Hill, who rescued thousands at the World Trade Center.
10. Richard Morin, "United States of Mind," *Washington Post,* national edition, October 29, 2001, p. 35; Brian J. Gaines, "Where's the Rally? Approval and Trust of the President, Cabinet, Congress, and Government Since September 11," *PS* 35 (September 2002): 535.

11. See Jere Longman, *Among the Heroes* (New York: Farrar, Straus and Giroux, 2002).
12. The inspiring story of New York's Department of Design and Construction is told by William Langewiesche, *American Ground: Unbuilding the World Trade Center* (New York: Atlantic Monthly Press, 2002).
13. Mayor Giuliani, interviewed on *Larry King Live*, Cable News Network, September 18, 2001; transcript #091800CN.V22. Giuliani presents his own account of the response to the attacks in *Leadership* (New York: Hyperion, 2002), chap. 16.
14. Kevin Hannafin, the brother of one of the firefighters who died, quoted by Janny Scott, "In Neckties or Helmets, Victims Shared an Ethic," *New York Times*, November 14, 2001, p. B10.
15. Barbara E. Tuchman, "Biography as a Prism of History," in *Telling Lives: The Biographer's Art*, ed. Marc Pachter (Philadelphia: University of Pennsylvania Press, 1981), p. 133. See also Leon Edel, "The Figure under the Carpet," in ibid., pp. 16–34; and Lindsey Rogers, "Reflections on Writing Biography of Public Men," *Political Science Quarterly* 88 (December 1973): 725–27.

2 Models of American Heroism

1. Further information on the Heroism Project is available at www.heroism.org/about.html.
2. See Howard Chua-Eoan, "Heroes and Icons," *Time*, June 14, 1999, p. 69.
3. Walt Whitman, "I Hear America Singing," in *Leaves of Grass* (New York: Random House, 1950), p. 11.
4. Robin Kadison Berson emphasizes the contributions of dissenters in *Marching to a Different Drummer* (Westport, Conn.: Greenwood Press, 1994).
5. James D. Wilson, "Everyday Heroes," *Newsweek*, May 29, 1995, p. 26.
6. Stewart Lee Allen, et al., "Heroes & Heroines," *Mother Jones*, January–February 1992, pp. 43–50.
7. "Heroes Walk Among Us," Heinz Family Foundation, www.awards.heinz.org. The Amnesty International designation of heroes appeared in a solicitation for financial contributions.
8. Barry Schwartz, *George Washington: The Making of an American Symbol*

(1987), quoted in Amy Fried, "Is Political Action Heroic? Heroism and American Political Culture," *American Politics Quarterly* 21 (October 1993): 490–517 (the quotation is from pp. 494–95).
9. Dixon Wecter, *The Hero in America,* 2d ed. (Ann Arbor, Mich.: University of Michigan Press, 1996), p. 489.
10. Leo Lowenthal, "Biographies in Popular Magazines" (1956), quoted in Marshall W. Fishwick, *American Heroes: Myth and Reality* (Westport, Conn.: Greenwood Press, 1954), p. 183.
11. Fried, "Is Political Action Heroic?" p. 507. Of six possible correlations, only one—0.36 between "progressives" and "defenders"—is notably higher than would occur by chance. From liberal to conservative, the groups are aligned as progressives, nurturers, defenders, and entrepreneurs.
12. Ibid., pp. 495, 496.
13. Kenneth Clark, quoted in Don Wycliff, "Where Have All the Heroes Gone?" *New York Times,* July 31, 1985, p. C12.
14. See Marianne Means, "Power Plays in the Name Game," *Tampa Tribune,* December 3, 1997, Nation/World section, p. 16.
15. Arianna Huffington, "What Prompted the Transformation in My Political Thinking," *Los Angeles Times,* March 12, 2000, at: www.ariannaonline.com/latimes.html.
16. Lena Williams, "What It Takes to Make a Hero," *New York Times,* June 18, 1995, p. E5; Williams quotes Scott O'Grady in her article.
17. A search for "American heroes" via Google located almost three million references. A more restricted search via Nexis—limited to major newspapers and to the past ten years—located 1,389 references to "American heroes." We attempt only qualitative analysis of these large data sources.
18. For Helen Keller, see *The Story of My Life (*Garden City, N.Y.: Doubleday, 1954).
19. Stephen E. Ambrose, *Undaunted Courage* (New York: Simon and Schuster, 1996), provides a vivid account of the Lewis and Clark expedition.
20. Candace Allen and Dwight R. Lee, "The Entrepreneur as Hero," *Association of Private Enterprise Education Journal* 12 (Fall 1996), at: www.apee.org/journal/96fall.html#page1.
21. Peggy Noonan, *What I Saw at the Revolution* (New York: Random House, 1990), p. 253.

22. Wycliff, "Where Have All the Heroes Gone?" p. C12.
23. William McDonald, "Long-Delayed Lessons About Fathers and a War," *New York Times,* July 6, 1998, sec. 2, p. 16.
24. See the Roberto Clemente Walker website, biography page: www.robertoclemente21/biography.
25. James D. Wilson, "Everyday Heroes," *Newsweek,* May 29, 1995, p. 26.
26. Ralph Nader, "Foreword," in Anne Witte Garland, *Women Activists: Challenging the Abuse of Power* (New York: Feminist Press, 1988), p. 9.
27. See Duren Cheek, "Ragghianti Named to U.S. Parole Commission," *Tennessean,* June 29, 1999. The book based on Ragghianti's experiences is Peter Maas, *Marie: A True Story* (New York: Random House, 1983). The film based on the book, *Marie* (1985), was directed by Roger Donaldson and featured Sissy Spacek and U.S. Senator Fred Thompson in the lead roles.
28. Senator Biden, quoted in Dan Balz, "Young Democrats Reclaim Their Heritage—Letter from the Campaign: Atlantic City," *Washington Post,* September 15, 1983, p. A2.
29. Garland, *Women Activists,* p. xi. Garland writes of fourteen such individuals in her book, none widely known.
30. See www.pbs.org/wgbh/pages/frontline/shows/reaction/internet/silkwood.html. For an account, see Richard L. Rashke, *The Killing of Karen Silkwood* (New York: Penguin, 1982).
31. Fishwick, *American Heroes,* p. 231.
32. Thomas Carlyle, *On Heroes and Hero Worship* (1840) (London: J. M. Dent, 1964), p. 239.
33. Max Weber, "Politics as a Vocation," in *From Max Weber,* ed. Hans Gerth and C. Wright Mills (New York: Oxford University Press, 1958), p. 79.
34. Fishwick, *American Heroes,* p. 230.
35. G. W. F. Hegel, *The Philosophy of History* (1822), excerpted in *The Philosophy of Hegel,* ed. and trans. Carl J. Friedrich (New York: Modern Library, 1953), p. 35.
36. Karl Marx and Friedrich Engels, *The Communist Manifesto* (1848), in *Selected Works* (Moscow: Foreign Languages Publishing House, 1951), p. 43.
37. For the classic exposition, see Sidney Hook, *The Hero in History* (Boston: Beacon Press, 1943).

38. James Madison, *The Federalist*, no. 51 (1788) (New York: Modern Library, 1941), p. 337.
39. Among a multitude of sources for Lincoln's address, the most convenient may be this website: www.yale.edu/lawweb/avalon/presiden/inaug/lincoln1.htm.
40. Joseph Campbell, *The Hero with a Thousand Faces* (Princeton, N.J.: Princeton University Press, 1949), p. 391.
41. Hook, *The Hero in History*, p. 239.
42. "Courage of constancy" is from novelist Cormac McCarthy, *All the Pretty Horses* (New York: Vintage, 1992), p. 235.
43. Quoted in Caroline Paul, *Fighting Fire* (New York: St. Martin's Press, 1998), p. 217.
44. Elsewhere, I have attempted to develop more elaborate models of heroism. For a first effort, see my essay in Peter Dennis Bathory and Nancy L. Schwartz, eds., *Friends and Citizens: Essays in Honor of Wilson Carey McWilliams* (Lanham, Md.: Rowman & Littlefield, 2001), chap. 11. For a more recent version, visit my website: www.rci.rutgers.edu/~gpomper.

3 Peter Rodino: A Hero of the House

1. U.S. House of Representatives, Committee on the Judiciary, *Impeachment of Richard M. Nixon, President of the United States*, 93rd Cong., 2d sess., 1974, H. Rept. 93-1305, pp. 3-4.
2. All unattributed quotations are drawn from interviews with Congressman Rodino on April 15, 1983, and on April 5, 2000. I am also grateful to Professor William Berlin, author of a forthcoming biography of Congressman Rodino, for the many details and insights he provided me.
3. Jerry Zeifman, *Without Honor* (New York: Thunder's Mouth Press, 1995), p. 23. Although scornful toward the congressman, Zeifman was named chief counsel of the Judiciary Committee when Rodino became chair in 1973.
4. On the motivations and rewards of representatives, see the classic analysis of David R. Mayhew, *Congress: The Electoral Connection* (New Haven, Conn.: Yale University Press, 1974).
5. *Congressional Record*, 93d Cong., 1st sess., 1973, 119, pt. 31:39817. For an inside account, see Zeifman, *Without Honor*, pp. 59-71.

6. Carl Bernstein and Bob Woodward recount their historic work in *All the President's Men* (New York: Simon and Schuster, 1974). It may be that Nixon himself ordered the break-in at Watergate. Jeb Stuart Magruder, deputy director of the 1972 election campaign, recently claimed that he overheard Nixon giving the order in a call to John Mitchell, then attorney-general. See David Von Drehle, "30 Years Later, a Watergate Allegation," *Washington Post*, July 27, 2003, p. AO5.
7. Stanley I. Kutler, *The Wars of Watergate* (New York: Alfred A. Knopf, 1990), p. 406.
8. U.S. v. Nixon, 418 U.S. 683 (1974). Nixon's contemplated evasion, using edited transcripts of the tapes, is described by Stephen E. Ambrose, *Nixon: Ruin and Recovery, 1973–1990* (New York: Simon and Schuster, 1991), pp. 384, 395–96.
9. Kutler, *Wars of Watergate*, p. 243. Nixon's early and personal involvement in the cover-ups is detailed in chap. 9 of Kutler's book.
10. New evidence on Nixon's crimes has recently become available with release of extensive White House tapes. See Stanley I. Kutler, *Abuse of Power* (New York: Free Press, 1997).
11. Richard Reeves, "Assessing Watergate 30 Years Later," *New York Times*, June 23, 2002, sec. 4, p. 13.
12. Kutler, *Wars of Watergate*, pp. 254–56.
13. Committee on the Judiciary, *Impeachment of Richard M. Nixon*, pp. 320, 361.
14. Data are available through the Roper Center for Public Opinion Research, University of Connecticut, at www.ropercenter.uconn.edu. The principal sources are a Roper Poll of August 24–31, 1974, and a Gallup Poll of April 30–May 1, 1986.
15. Zeifman, *Without Honor*, p. 87.
16. Tip O'Neill, quoted in Jimmy Breslin, *How the Good Guys Finally Won* (New York: Viking Press, 1975), in the title of chap. 4 and p. 74.
17. See John Hibbing and Elizabeth Theiss-Morse, *Congress as Public Enemy* (Cambridge: Cambridge University Press, 1995), pp. 18, 19.
18. Neil MacNeil, *Forge of Democracy* (New York: David McKay, 1963), p. 7.
19. On political tactics at the Constitutional Convention, see John P. Roche, "The Founding Fathers: A Reform Caucus in Action," *American Political Science Review* 55 (December 1961): 799–816.

20. Gladys E. Lang and Kurt Lang, *The Battle for Public Opinion* (New York: Columbia University Press, 1983), p. 146.
21. George Mason, at the Constitutional Convention, quoted by James Madison, *Notes of Debates in the Federal Convention* [1787] (Athens: Ohio University Press, 1966), p. 39.
22. James Madison, *The Federalist,* no. 49 (1788) (New York: Modern Library, 1941), p. 330.
23. Theodore H. White, *Breach of Faith* (New York: Atheneum, 1975), p. 277.
24. On the electoral advantages of incumbents, see Mayhew, *Congress,* pp. 49–73.
25. Richard F. Fenno Jr., *Home Style* (Glenview, Ill.: Scott Foresman, 1978), pp. 241.
26. See Ross K. Baker, *House and Senate* (New York: W. W. Norton, 1989), chap. 2.
27. Herbert P. Asher, "The Learning of Legislative Norms," *American Political Science Review* 67 (June 1973): 500.
28. Woodrow Wilson, *Congressional Government* (1885) (New York: Meridian Books, 1956), p. 71.
29. See Lynette P. Perkins, "Member Recruitment to a Mixed Goal Committee: The House Judiciary Committee," *Journal of Politics* 43 (May 1981): 348–64.
30. See Tim Groseclose and Charles Stewart III, "The Value of Committee Seats in the House, 1947–91," *American Journal of Political Science* 42 (April 1998): 453–74; William L. Murrow, *Congressional Committees* (New York: Scribner's, 1969), pp. 42–43.
31. Charles Halleck, quoted in Tip O'Neill, *All Politics Is Local* (Holbrook, Mass.: Bob Adams, 1994), p. 153.
32. As quoted by Charles L. Clapp, *The Congressman: His Work as He Sees It* (Washington, D.C.: Brookings Institution, 1963), p. 23.
33. Breslin, *How the Good Guys Finally Won,* pp. 71–72.
34. See Lang and Lang, *Battle for Public Opinion,* p. 157.
35. The disguised reading was Michael Benedict's *The Impeachment and Trial of Andrew Johnson* (New York: Norton, 1973).
36. Zeifman, *Without Honor,* p. 85.
37. Rodino, concluding the debate on H. Res. 702, providing funds for the Judiciary Committee investigation: *Congressional Record,* 93d Cong., 1st sess., 1973, 119, pt. 28: 37145 (November 15, 1973).

38. Trends in public evaluations are presented in Lang and Lang, *Battle for Public Opinion,* p. 161.
39. Zeifman, *Without Honor,* p. 143.
40. White, *Breach of Faith,* p. 299.
41. Ambrose, *Nixon,* p. 416. But Nixon was still prepared, as late as a week before his resignation, to continue his fight. See Alexander M. Haig, *Inner Circles* (New York: Warner Books, 1992), p. 487. See also chap. 36, in which Haig provides a detailed account of Nixon's inconsistent reactions.
42. Kutler, *Wars of Watergate,* pp. 480–88, describes the creation of the bipartisan coalition.
43. Interview with William Berlin, February 15, 2000.
44. To add to the emotional strain, Bob Woodward and Carl Bernstein report, this incident occurred soon after Rodino had been informed that a kamikaze pilot was heading for the committee offices. See *The Final Days* (New York: Avon Books, 1976), p. 31.
45. Alexander Hamilton, *The Federalist,* no. 65 (1788), pp. 427–28.
46. Jeffrey Toobin, *A Vast Conspiracy* (New York: Random House, 1999), p. 304.
47. See David W. Rhode, *Parties and Leaders in the Postreform House* (Chicago: University of Chicago Press, 1991), chaps. 3 and 4.
48. Nicol C. Rae provides an excellent account of the 1994 Republican "revolution" in *Conservative Reformers* (Armonk, N.Y.: M. E. Sharpe, 1998). The selection of Henry Hyde to chair the Judiciary Committee is described on p. 69.
49. For a summary of these trends in party loyalty, continuing at this high level to 2002, see "Party Unity Background," *CQ Weekly* 60 (December 14, 2002), p. 3281.
50. Peter W. Rodino, "The Vote That Changed America," *New York Times,* July 27, 1999, p. A19.
51. Nixon's Republican defenders (except Trent Lott of Mississippi) fell 7 percent, on average, below their expected vote in 1974; Republicans voting to impeach gained an additional 5 percent. See Gerald C. Wright, "Constituency Response to Congressional Behavior," *Western Political Quarterly* 30 (September 1977): 401–10.
52. Bruce A. Ray, "Committee Attractiveness in the U.S. House, 1963–81," *American Journal of Political Science* 26 (August 1982): 612.

53. Perkins, "Member Recruitment to a Mixed Goal Committee," p. 363.
54. David J. Vogler, *The Politics of Congress*, 4th ed. (Boston: Allyn and Bacon, 1983), p. 158.
55. Edward V. Schneier and Bertram Gross, *Congress Today* (New York: St. Martin's Press, 1993), p. 102. For colorful details of the effects on the House Republicans, see Toobin, *Vast Conspiracy*, chaps. 18 and 19.
56. Schneier and Gross, *Congress Today*, pp. 237–38.
57. W. Carey McWilliams, *Beyond the Politics of Disappointment?* (New York: Chatham House, 2000), p. 113.
58. Thomas Gray, "Elegy Written in a County Churchyard," in *The Oxford Book of English Verse,* ed. Arthur Quiller-Couch (New York: Oxford University Press, 1955), pp. 533–34.

4 Arthur Watkins: A Hero of the Senate

1. Arthur Herman, *Joseph McCarthy* (New York: Free Press, 1999), p. 281.
2. William S. White, *Citadel* (Boston: Houghton Mifflin, 1956), p. 129.
3. See "Navaho Timeline," at www.lapahie.com/timeline. See also the 1998 Congressional testimony of the chairman of the Menominee Indian Tribe of Wisconsin concerning the adverse effects of the legislation, as well as his criticisms of Senator Watkins, at www.menominee.nsn.us/chairman.
4. William S. White, "Portrait of a 'Proper Washingtonian,'" *New York Times,* August 15, 1954, sec. 6, p. 12.
5. Arthur V. Watkins, *Enough Rope* (Englewood Cliffs, N.J.: Prentice-Hall, 1969), pp. ix, 10.
6. Democrat William Proxmire first won a special election in 1957, with 56 percent of the vote, then was reelected in the regular 1958 contest with 57 percent.
7. The development of the Wheeling speech and the original charges are thoroughly documented in the leading study of McCarthy, David M. Oshinksy, *A Conspiracy So Immense* (New York: Free Press, 1983), chap. 7. The specific "evidence" is listed on pp. 113–4. Also see, "Versions of the Wheeling Speech," in Albert Fried, *McCarthyism: A Documentary History* (New York: Oxford University Press, 1997), pp. 78–80.
8. Gallup Poll (June 4–9, 1950). All data from opinion polls were obtained

through the Roper Center for Public Opinion Research, University of Connecticut, at www.ropercenter.uconn.edu.
9. Oshinsky, *A Conspiracy So Immense*, pp. 108–9.
10. Richard M. Fried, *Nightmare in Red* (New York: Oxford University Press, 1990), pp. 4, 120.
11. David Halberstam, *The Fifties* (New York: Villard Books, 1993), p. 52.
12. Fried, *Nightmare in Red*, p. 9.
13. Robert Taft, quoted in Oshinsky, *A Conspiracy So Immense*, pp. 114, 133.
14. William F. Buckley Jr. and Brent Bozell, *McCarthy and His Enemies* (Chicago: Henry Regnery, 1954), p. 335.
15. George Reedy, quoted in Halberstam, *The Fifties*, p. 55.
16. Harold F. Gosnell summarizes these accusations in *Truman's Crises* (Westport, Conn.: Greenwood Press, 1980), pp. 505–6. Sources for the specific quotations are Dennis Merrill, ed., *The Documentary History of the Truman Presidency*, vol. 25, *President Truman's Confrontation with McCarthyism* (Bethesda, Md.: University Publications of America, 1995), p. 290. R. Fried, *Nightmare in Red*, p. 131; A. Fried, *McCarthyism*, p. 89; Merrill, *Documentary History*, p. 153.
17. Margaret Chase Smith, with William C. Lewis, Jr., *Declaration of Conscience* (Garden City, N.Y.: Doubleday, 1972), p. 9.
18. Richard H. Rovere, *Senator Joe McCarthy* (New York: Harper & Row, 1959), pp. 5–6.
19. Nelson Polsby, "Towards an Explanation of McCarthyism," *Political Studies* 8 (October 1960): 268.
20. Smith, *Declaration of Conscience*, pp. 16–17.
21. For analysis of the response to Smith's declaration, see Oshinsky, *A Conspiracy So Immense*, pp. 162–65, and Smith, *Declaration of Conscience*, pp. 21–61.
22. Janaan Sherman, *No Place for a Woman* (New Brunswick, N.J.: Rutgers University Press, 2000), p. 111. See chap. 8 for a detailed account of the contemporary environment.
23. Patricia L. Schmidt, *Margaret Chase Smith: Beyond Convention* (Orono: University of Maine Press, 1996), p. 213. See chaps. 3, 6, 7, and 10 for a full account of Smith's conflicts with the national Republican leadership.
24. For Eisenhower's diary entry, see Fred I. Greenstein, *The Hidden-Hand Presidency* (New York: Basic Books, 1982), p. 169.

25. Gallup Poll 54528.QK22 (March 19–24, 1954).
26. Greenstein, *The Hidden-Hand Presidency*, p. 182.
27. Fried, *Nightmare in Red*, p. 138.
28. Fried, *McCarthyism*, pp. 186–87.
29. Greenstein, *The Hidden-Hand Presidency*, chap. 5, expertly details and defends Eisenhower's intricate maneuvers; the quotation is on p. 198.
30. Ibid, pp. 225–26. Greenstein draws these conclusions from his insightful reanalysis of data in the classic study of contemporary attitudes, Samuel A. Stouffer, *Communism, Conformity and Civil Liberties* (Garden City, New York: Doubleday, 1955).
31. Watkins, *Enough Rope*, p. 35.
32. William S. White, "'Grand Jury' on McCarthy Has Senate's Full Support," *New York Times*, August 6, 1954, p. 6.
33. Watkins, *Enough Rope*, pp. 41–42.
34. U.S. Senate, *Report of the Select Committee to Study Censure Charges*, 83d Cong., 2d sess., 1954, S. Rept. 2508. The report is excerpted in the *New York Times*, September 28, 1954, pp. 20–25, and included in Watkins, *Enough Rope*, pp. 215–91.
35. Gallup Poll 54535.QK18 (August 5–10, 1954); Gallup Poll 110654.RK19D (October 15–20, 1954); Gallup Poll 54541.Q15 (December 31, 1954–January 5, 1995).
36. Watkins, *Enough Rope*, p. 114.
37. See Herman, *Joseph McCarthy*, pp. 291–92.
38. *Congressional Record*, 83d Cong., 2d sess., 1954, 101, pt. 12:16053.
39. Fried, *Nightmare in Red*, pp. 140–41.
40. Independent Wayne Morse, previously a Republican and later a Democrat, voted for censure. McCarthy voted "present." For a thorough discussion of the legislative maneuvering and voting, see Oshinsky, *A Conspiracy So Immense*, pp. 488–92.
41. Fried, *Nightmare in Red*, p. 141, also quoting Watkins's letter, written to M. E. Dalton on December 9, 1954.
42. Greenstein, *The Hidden-Hand Presidency*, p. 217.
43. Halberstam, *The Fifties*, p. 253.
44. Watkins, *Enough Rope*, p. 178.
45. Randall B. Ripley, *Power in the Senate* (New York: St. Martin's Press, 1969), p. 54. In the years since McCarthy, Ripley sees a shift in the character of the Senate "from decentralization to individualism."

46. Donald R. Matthews, "The Folkways of the United States Senate," *American Political Science Review* 53 (December 1959): 1065–73. My discussion of Senate norms is indebted to Matthews's article, which was later included as chap. 5 of his *U.S. Senators and Their World* (Chapel Hill: University of North Carolina Press, 1960).
47. See Ross K. Baker, *House and Senate* (New York: W. W. Norton, 1989), chap. 2.
48. Watkins, *Enough Rope,* pp. 139, 199–200.
49. Barbara Sinclair provides a good theoretical explanation of Senate norms in *The Transformation of the U.S. Senate* (Baltimore: Johns Hopkins University Press, 1989), chap. 2.
50. Matthews, "Folkways of the United States Senate," p. 1083.
51. See Ralph K. Huitt, "The Outsider in the Senate: An Alternative Role," *American Political Science Review* 55 (September 1961): 566–75.
52. Matthews, "Folkways of the United States Senate," pp. 1084–89. The quotation is on p. 1084.
53. Sinclair, *Transformation of the U.S. Senate,* p. 2; and see also chap. 11 for a general overview of these changes. Today, of course, senators can no longer be referred to by the male pronoun alone.
54. See Allen Weinstein and Alexander Vassiliev, *The Haunted Wood* (New York: Random House, 1999).
55. Herman, *Joseph McCarthy,* p. 320. Jacob Weisberg describes the contemporary controversy in "Cold War Without End," *New York Times Magazine,* November 28, 1999.
56. Oshinsky, *A Conspiracy So Immense,* p. 507.
57. Halberstam, *The Fifties,* 53.
58. *The Living Webster Encyclopedic Dictionary of the English Language* (Chicago: English Language Institute of America, 1975), p. 589.
59. *Service v. Dulles,* 354 U.S. 363 (1957). This decision restricted the authority of the secretary of state to discharge employees accused of security violations, reinstating a discharged Foreign Service officer.
60. See Jackie Koszczuk, "Lawmakers Struggle to Keep an Eye on Patriot Act," *CQ Weekly* 60 (September 7, 2002): 2284–88.

5 Harry Truman: A Hero as President

1. Woodrow Wilson, *Constitutional Government in the United States* (New York: Columbia University Press, 1908), p. 68.
2. Merle Miller, *Plain Speaking: An Oral Biography of Harry S. Truman* (New York: G. P. Putnam, 1973), p. 234.
3. See Alonzo M. Hamby, *Man of the People* (New York: Oxford University Press, 1995), pp. 274–84, for a detailed description of the nomination maneuverings.
4. David McCullough, *Truman* (New York: Simon and Schuster, 1992), p. 321.
5. Harry S. Truman, *Memoirs,* vol. 1, *Year of Decisions* (Garden City, N.Y.: Doubleday, 1955), p. 19. Truman continued to be modest even after two years in office. In 1947, according to notes in a recently discovered diary, he urged Dwight D. Eisenhower to run for president in 1948 as the Democratic nominee, and he offered to take the second position on the ticket, reverting to the office of vice-president. See "Truman Wrote of '48 Offer to Eisenhower," *New York Times,* July 11, 2003, p. A14.
6. *Dear Bess: The Letters from Harry to Bess Truman, 1910–1959,* ed. Robert H. Ferrell (New York: W. W. Norton, 1983), letter of September 22, 1947, p. 549.
7. Robert Shogan, *The Double-Edged Sword* (Boulder, Colo.: Westview Press, 1999), p. 93, quoting Drew Pearson and Truman.
8. Fred I. Greenstein, *The Presidential Difference* (New York: Free Press, 2000), p. 33.
9. Richard E. Neustadt, *Presidential Power* (New York: John Wiley, 1960), p. 3.
10. Stephen Skowronek, *The Politics Presidents Make* (Cambridge, Mass.: Harvard University Press, 1993), p. 41.
11. Marc Landy and Sidney M. Milkus, *Presidential Greatness* (Lawrence: University Press of Kansas, 2000), pp. 198–200.
12. Neustadt, *Presidential Power,* p. 47.
13. *Dear Bess,* ed. Ferrell, letter of September 30, 1947, p. 550.
14. See Gerald Pomper, "Labor and Congress: The Repeal of Taft-Hartley," *Labor History* 2 (Fall 1961): 323–44.
15. Richard Whelan, *Drawing the Line* (Boston: Little, Brown, 1990),

p. 222. For a detailed account of the Koean conflict, see chaps. 18–22; as well as William Stueck, *The Korean War: An International History* (Princeton, N.J.: Princeton University Press, 1995).
16. Neustadt, *Presidential Power,* p. 146.
17. Harry S. Truman, *Memoirs,* vol. 2, *Years of Trial and Hope* (Garden City, N.Y.: Doubleday, 1956), p. 431.
18. Joseph M. Jones, *The Fifteen Weeks* (New York: Harcourt, Brace & World, 1955), p. 259.
19. Thomas A. Bailey, *Presidential Greatness* (New York: Appleton-Century-Crofts, 1966), p. 325.
20. U.S. Bureau of the Census, *Statistical Abstract of the United States: 1995,* 115th ed. (Washington, 1995), Table 517, p. 333.
21. The full text of Acheson's speech, delivered in Cleveland, Mississippi, on May 8, 1947, can be found in Jones's authoritative account of the period, *Fifteen Weeks,* pp. 274–81.
22. Some historians see Truman's bellicose attitude toward the Soviet Union as a source of the cold war. The most noted critique is William A. Williams, *The Tragedy of American Diplomacy,* 2d rev. ed. (New York: Dell, 1972). The issue is debated well by Lloyd Gardner, Arthur Schlesinger, Jr., and Hans Morgenthau in *The Origins of the Cold War* (New York: Wiley, 1970).
23. Quoted in Jones, *Fifteen Weeks,* p. 272.
24. For discussion of different theoretical models of foreign policy, see Hans J. Morgenthau, *Politics Among Nations,* 2d ed. (New York: Alfred A. Knopf, 1954), chap. 1.
25. Roper/Fortune Survey, April 1–6, 1946. Data provided by the Roper Center for Public Opinion Research, University of Connecticut, at: www.ropercenter.uconn.edu.
26. Michael J. Hogan, *The Marshall Plan* (Cambridge: Cambridge University Press, 1987), pp. 26–27.
27. Dean Acheson, quoted in Jones, *Fifteen Weeks,* p. 281.
28. See Jones, *Fifteen Weeks,* pp. 254–56.
29. George C. Marshall, quoted in ibid., pp. 281–84.
30. See Hogan, *The Marshall Plan,* chap. 2.
31. Truman's informal comment is quoted by Richard E. Neustadt, "The Weakening White House," *British Journal of Political Science* 31 (January 2001): 5–6.

32. See Hamby, *Man of the People*, p. 403.
33. Although the quotation is commonly reported as Churchill's description of the Marshall Plan, he actually coined this language in praise of the Lend-Lease Act. See Warren F. Kimball, *The Most Unsordid Act: Lend-Lease, 1939–1941* (Baltimore: Johns Hopkins University Press, 1969). Professor Kimball, whose selfless research I gratefully acknowledge, finds no evidence that Churchill ever used the phrase in his later praise of the Marshall Plan. Apparently Jones, *Fifteen Weeks*, p. 256, used Churchill's words as a dramatic but unsubstantiated conclusion to his book, prompting decades of imitative error. For the general development of U.S. security policy in this period, see Benjamin O. Fordham, *Building the Cold War Consensus* (Ann Arbor: University of Michigan Press, 1998).
34. Neustadt, *Presidential Power*, pp. 9–10.
35. Bert A. Rockman, *The Leadership Question* (New York: Praeger, 1984), p. 223.
36. Wilson, *Constitutional Government*, p. 70.
37. James Lord Bryce, *The American Commonwealth*, 3d rev. ed. (New York: Macmillan, 1914), 1:80.
38. For illustrations of these three perspectives, see James MacGregor Burns, *Leadership* (New York: Harper and Row, 1978); Arthur M. Schlesinger, *The Imperial Presidency* (New York: Houghton Mifflin, 1974); and William Grover, *The President as Prisoner* (Albany: State University of New York Press, 1989).
39. See, for example, Edward S. Corwin, *The President: Office and Powers*, 5th rev. ed. (New York: New York University Press, 1984); Richard Pious, *The American Presidency* (New York: Basic Books, 1979); and Charles O. Jones, *The Presidency in a Separated System* (Washington, D.C.: Brookings Institution, 1994).
40. See James David Barber, *The Presidential Character* (Englewood Cliffs, N.J.: Prentice-Hall, 1972); Robert Gilbert, *The Mortal Presidency*, 2d ed. (New York: Fordham University Press, 1998); and Fred I. Greenstein, *The Presidential Difference* (New York: Free Press, 2000).
41. For a good overall review of the literature on the presidency, see John Hart, "Presidency (United States)," in *International Encyclopedia of the Social and Behavioral Sciences*, ed. Neil Smelser and Paul Baltes (Oxford: Elsevier, 2001).

42. Clinton Rossiter popularized the characterization of the president as chief in *The American Presidency* (New York: Harcourt Brace, 1956), chap. 1.
43. Neustadt, *Presidential Power*, p. 37; and see chap. 3 for his general discussion of the president's "power to persuade."
44. John F. Kennedy, concluding his first television debate with Richard Nixon, September 26, 1960. For a transcript of the debate, see http://www.jfklibrary.org/60-1st.htm.
45. Hamby, *Man of the People*, p. 399.
46. On the mobilization of interest groups during the development of the Marshall Plan, see James N. Rosenau, *National Leadership and Foreign Policy* (Princeton, N.J.: Princeton University Press, 1963).
47. Gallup Poll, July 23, 1947; Gallup Poll, June 1947; National Opinion Research Center Poll, March 1948.
48. Gallup Poll, December 7, 1947; Gallup Poll, November 28, 1948; Gallup Poll, March 1949.
49. On public support for the Marshall Plan, see Benjamin I. Page and Robert Y. Shapiro, *The Rational Public* (Chicago: University of Chicago Press, 1992), pp. 59, 199–202.
50. Quoted in Miller, *Plain Speaking*, p. 240.
51. Clark Clifford provides this account of Truman's conversation in Kenneth W. Thompson's *Portraits of American Presidents: The Truman Presidency* (Latham, Md.: University Press of America, 1984), 2:12.
52. Neustadt, *Presidential Power*, p. 53.
53. Quoted in Miller, *Plain Speaking*, p. 246.
54. *Dear Bess*, ed. Ferrell, letter of September 23, 1947, p. 549.
55. Hamby, *Man of the People*, p. 401.
56. On the development of Vandenberg's positions, see C. David Tomkins, *Senator Arthur H. Vandenberg: The Evolution of a Modern Republican* (Lansing: Michigan State University Press, 1970), pp. 212–33.
57. Dean Acheson, *Present at the Creation* (New York: W. W. Norton, 1969), p. 223.
58. The relationship of Vandenberg and Truman is developed by Francis Wilcox, dean of the Johns Hopkins School of Advanced International Studies, in Thompson, *Portraits of American Presidents*, pp. 132–33.
59. Neustadt, *Presidential Power*, pp. 52–53.
60. White House aide George Elsey, quoted in McCullough, *Truman*, p. 556.

61. For a discussion of "the plebiscitary presidency," see Theodore J. Lowi, *The Personal President* (Ithaca, N.Y.: Cornell University Press, 1984), pp. 161–73.
62. Truman's statement is from a speech written in April 1948, but never delivered, quoted in McCullough, *Truman*, p. 583.
63. Francis Heller, professor of law and political science at the University of Kansas, who assisted Truman in writing his memoirs, quoted in Thompson's *Portraits of American Presidents*, p. 186.

6 Wayne Justice: A Hero of the Judiciary

1. Alexander Hamilton, *The Federalist*, no. 78 (1788) (New York: Modern Library, 1941), p. 504.
2. All unattributed quotations are from an interview with Judge Justice on March 12, 1999.
3. I am indebted to the exhaustive study by Frank R. Kemerer, *William Wayne Justice: A Judicial Biography* (Austin: University of Texas Press, 1991) for details concerning Judge Justice's life and judicial opinions.
4. David Maraniss, "Justice, Texas Style," *Washington Post*, February 28, 1987, p. G1.
5. Ibid.
6. Denise Gamino, "High-Profile Justice Hitting Trail to Austin," *Austin American-Statesman*, May 25, 1998, p. A1.
7. Stuart Taylor, "U.S. Judge in Texas Draws Widespread Hostility with Liberal Rulings," *New York Times*, November 21, 1982, p. 26.
8. *San Antonio Independent School District v. Rodriguez,* 411 U.S. 1 (1973). For an overview of the case from the viewpoint of the Mexican-American family who brought suit against the school district, see Peter Irons, *The Courage of Their Convictions* (New York: Free Press, 1988), chap. 12.
9. I rely here on two excellent analyses by Elizabeth A. Hull: "Undocumented Aliens and the Equal Protection Clause: An Analysis of Doe v. Plyler," 48 *Brooklyn Law Review* 43 (1981), and "Undocumented Alien Children and Free Public Education: An Analysis of *Plyler v. Doe*," 44 *University of Pittsburgh Law Review* 409 (1983).
10. *McGowan v. Maryland,* 366 U.S. 420, 425–26 (1961).
11. *Muller v. Oregon,* 208 U.S. 412, 421–22 (1908).

12. *Craig v. Boren*, 429 U.S. 190, 210 n. 23 (1976), overruling *Gossett v. Cleary*, 335 U.S. 464 (1948).
13. *U.A.W. v. Johnson Controls*, 499 U.S. 187 (1991).
14. *Loving v. Virginia*, 388 U.S. 1 (1967).
15. These rights are elaborated in *Harper v. Virginia Board of Elections*, 383 U.S. 663 (1966); *Shapiro v. Thompson*, 394 U.S. 618 (1969); *Sherbert v. Verner*, 374 U.S. 398 (1963); and *Griffin v. Illinois*, 351 U.S. 12 (1956), respectively.
16. *U.S. v. Carolene Products Co.* 304 U.S. 144, 152 n. 4 (1938).
17. Hull, "Undocumented Aliens and the Equal Protection Clause," p. 420.
18. See Kemerer, *William Wayne Justice*, p. 239.
19. For a useful overview of legal strategy, see Walter F. Murphy, *Elements of Judicial Strategy* (Chicago: University of Chicago Press, 1964).
20. *San Antonio Independent School District v. Rodriguez*, 411 U.S. 1, 28 (1973).
21. Justice Lewis Powell, writing in support of establishing protections for illegitimate children, *Weber v. Aetna Casualty and Surety Company*, 406 U.S. 164, 175 (1972); opinion of Justice William Wayne Justice, *Doe v. Plyler*, 458 F. Supp. 569, 580–84 (1978).
22. *Doe v. Plyler*, at p. 589.
23. The circuit court appeals decision is found in 628 F. 2d 448, 459 (1980).
24. *Plyler v. Doe*, 457 U.S. 202, 215 (1982).
25. Ibid., at p. 223.
26. Ibid., at p. 230.
27. Hull, "Undocumented Aliens and the Equal Protection Clause," p. 73.
28. For example, the court upheld a North Dakota law imposing user fees on parents whose children ride on school buses: *Kadrmas v. Dickinson Public Schools*, 487 U.S. 450 (1988).
29. The decision remains controlling in its immediate area, according to Halle I. Butler, "Note: Educated in the Classroom or on the Streets: The Fate of Illegal Immigrant Children in the United States," 58 *Ohio State Law Journal* 1473 (1997). The holding, he argues, would bar legislation, introduced in Congress as a part of the 1996 spending bill, that would have allowed states to deny a free public education to the children of illegal immigrants.
30. See the *New York Times*, July 30, 1999, p. A1; and September 24, 2002, p. B5.

31. *Plyler v. Doe,* at p. 233.
32. Kemerer, *William Wayne Justice,* p. 124. The case is *U.S. v. Texas,* 321 F. Supp. 1043 (E.D. Tex. 1970).
33. Ibid., chap. 10, reports the bilingual education controversy. The case is *U.S. v. Texas* (Bilingual), 506 F. Supp. 405 (E.D. Tex. 1981).
34. Ibid., p. 178, and chap. 6, dealing with juvenile rights in reform schools. The case is *Morales v. Turman,* 326 F. Supp. 667 (E.D. Tex. 1971).
35. Ibid., p. 400 and chap. 15, on prison reform. The original decision is *Ruiz v. Estelle,* 503 F. Supp. 1265 (S.D. Tex. 1980). For a vivid description, see Maraniss, *Washington Post.*
36. Dissenting opinion of Justice Warren Burger, *Plyler v. Doe,* at pp. 242, 253.
37. Hamilton, *The Federalist,* no. 78, p. 505.
38. *Marbury v. Madison,* 1 Cranch 137 (1803).
39. Charles L. Black, *The People and the Constitution* (Westport, Conn.: Greenwood Press, 1960), p. 209.
40. Robert H. Jackson, *The Struggle for Judicial Supremacy* (New York: Alfred A. Knopf, 1941), p. 319. Jackson was later appointed a justice of the Supreme Court by Franklin Roosevelt.
41. Robert Dahl, *How Democratic Is the American Constitution?* (New Haven, Conn.: Yale University Press, 2002), pp. 152–53.
42. William Wayne Justice, "The New Awakening: Judicial Activism in a Conservative Age," 43 *Southwestern Law Journal* 657 (October 1989).
43. Ibid., p. 673. Justice's viewpoint receives scholarly support from H. Jefferson Powell, "The Original Understanding of Original Intent," 98 *Harvard Law Review* 885 (1985).
44. See Justice, "The New Awakening," p. 674. The quotation is from Judge J. Skelly Wright, "The Judicial Right and the Rhetoric of Restraint: A Defense of Judicial Activism in an Age of Conservative Judges," 14 *Hastings Constitutional Law Quarterly* 487, 522 (1987).
45. William Wayne Justice, "Two Faces of Judicial Activism," 61 *George Washington Law Review* 1, 7 (1992).
46. Gerald N. Rosenberg, *The Hollow Hope: Can Courts Bring About Social Change?* (Chicago: University of Chicago Press, 1991), p. 338; italics in the original. Rosenberg offers alternative explanations of desegregation and abortion rights in chaps. 5 and 9.

47. See Jack Bass, *Unlikely Heroes* (New York: Simon and Schuster, 1981), Tinsley E. Yarbrough, *Frank Johnson and Human Rights in Alabama* (University, Ala.: University of Alabama Press, 1981).
48. For the ruling on primary elections, see *Smith v. Allwright*, 321 U.S. 649 (1944); on legislative districts, see *Baker v. Carr*, 369 U.S. 186 (1962).
49. Dahl, *How Democratic Is the American Constitution?* p. 153.
50. Alexander M. Bickel, *The Least Dangerous Branch* (Indianapolis: Bobbs-Merrill, 1962), pp. 199, 26.
51. Jonathan D. Casper, "The Supreme Court and National Policy Making," *American Political Science Review* 70 (March 1976): 63.
52. See *Vacco v. Quill*, Docket No. 95-1858 (1997); *Washington v. Glucksberg*, Docket No. 96-110 (1997).
53. Peter H. Schuck, "Public Law Litigation and Social Reform," 102 *Yale Law Journal* 1763, 1774 (1993). See also "Book Note: Grand Illusion," 105 *Harvard Law Review* 1135 (1992).
54. David Schultz and Stephen E. Gottlieb, "Legal Functionalism and Social Change," 12 *Journal of Law and Policy*, 63 (1996).
55. Gamino, "High-Profile Justice," p. A1.

7 Frances Kelsey: A Hero of Bureaucracy

1. For Kelsey's summary of events, presented at a later conference, see Frances O. Kelsey, "Denial of Approval for Thalidomide in the U.S.," *Medicine and Health Since World War II: Four Federal Achievements* (Typescript, Bethesda, Md.: National Library of Medicine, December 9, 1993).
2. I interviewed Dr. Kelsey at the FDA headquarters in Rockville, Maryland, on February 3, 1998. All unattributed quotations are drawn from that interview.
3. A. M. A. Chemical Laboratory, "Deaths from Elixir of Sulfanilamide-Massengill," *Journal of the American Medical Association* 108 (April 17, 1937), pp. 1340, 1345; 109 (November 20, 1937), pp. 1724–1725, 1727.
4. Linda Bren, "Frances Oldham Kelsey: FDA Medical Reviewer Leaves Her Mark on History," in *FDA Consumer Magazine,* March–April 2001, available at www.fda.gov/fdac/features/2001/201_kelsey.html.
5. Margaret Truman, "The Doctor Who Said No," in Truman, *Women of Courage* (New York: Morrow, 1978), p. 220.

6. Kelsey, "Denial," p. 7.
7. Truman, "The Doctor Who Said No," pp. 221–22.
8. See Mancur Olson's discussion of collective goods in *The Logic of Collective Action* (Cambridge, Mass.: Harvard University Press, 1971).
9. Peter Woll, *American Bureaucracy*, 2d ed. (New York: Norton, 1977), pp. 65–67.
10. Frederick C. Mosher, *Democracy and the Public Service* (New York: Oxford University Press, 1968), p. 11.
11. Terry M. Moe, "The Politics of Bureaucratic Structure," in *Can the Government Govern?* ed. John E. Chubb and Paul E. Peterson (Washington, D.C.: Brookings Institution, 1989), p. 286. The classic analysis of business-government relations is Marver H. Bernstein, *Regulating Business by Independent Commission* (Princeton, N.J.: Princeton University Press, 1955). Moe provides a different perspective in "Regulatory Performance and Presidential Administration," *American Journal of Political Science* 26 (May 1982): 197–224.
12. Hugh Heclo, "Issue Networks and the Executive Establishment," in *The New American Political System*, ed. Anthony King (Washington, D.C.: American Enterprise Institute, 1978), p. 102.
13. Moe, "Politics of Bureaucratic Structure," p. 291.
14. See International Society for Pharmaceutical Engineering, "Food and Drug Legislation—The Story Behind the Law," at www.gmpist.com/histlaw.htm. For a detailed chronology of drug legislation and FDA activity, see U.S. Food and Drug Administration, "Milestones in U.S. Food and Drug Law History," at www.fda.gov/opacom/backgrounders/miles.html.
15. Insight Team of the Sunday Times of London, *Suffer the Children: The Story of Thalidomide* (New York: Viking Press, 1978), pp. 3–4.
16. Anthony Downs, *Inside Bureaucracy* (Boston: Little, Brown, 1967), pp. 32, 33, 34.
17. *Suffer the Children*, pp. 32–41.
18. Ibid., p. 68. The battle over thalidomide approval in the United States is detailed in chap. 5.
19. "Thalidomide: Potential Benefits and Risk," transcript of an open public scientific workshop, sponsored by FDA, the National Institutes of Health and the Centers for Disease Control and Prevention (Bethesda, Md., September 9, 1997), p. 2.

20. Truman, quoting Merrell's instructions to its sales force, in "The Doctor Who Said No," p. 225.
21. Ibid., p. 231.
22. Ibid., p. 228.
23. The political environment permitted delay, however. The agency is better able to withhold its approval of a particular drug when media attention is limited and when there is no public consituency clamoring for access to that drug. Both of those conditions applied to thalidomide at that time. See Daniel P. Carpenter, "Groups, the Media, Agency Costs, and FDA Drug Approval," *American Journal of Political Science* 46 (July 2002): 490–505.
24. *Suffer the Children*, p. 79.
25. "Frances Oldham Kelsey: FDA Medical Reviewer Leaves Her Mark on History," p. 2.
26. *Suffer the Children*, p. 113.
27. Ibid., p. 80.
28. Steven Harris, "The Right Lesson to Learn from Thalidomide" (1992) at w3.aces.uiuc.edu:8001/Liberty/Tales/Thalidomide.html. It stands as testimony to Dr. Kelsey's commitment to scientific objectivity that I learned of this critique only because she herself gave it to me, despite its criticism of her greatest life achievement.
29. "Problems Raised for the FDA by the Occurrence of Thalidomide Embryopathy in Germany, 1960–1961," *South Dakota Journal of Medicine and Pharmacy* (January 1964); "Clinical Testing of Drugs," *Journal of New Drugs* 3 (January–February 1963).
30. See Joseph B. Gorman, *Kefauver: A Political Biography* (New York: Oxford University Press, 1971), pp. 351–56; the quotation is from p. 355.
31. On the effects of the thalidomide controversy on later FDA procedures, see "Frances Oldham Kelsey: FDA Medical Reviewer Leaves Her Mark on History," p. 5; on the procedures used in the later review of the drug, see "Thalidomide: Potential Benefits and Risk."
32. *Suffer the Children*, p. 245. See also the concluding chapter, on contemporary issues of drug regulation.
33. On the new uses of thalidomide for treatment of leprosy, AIDS, and other diseases, see Sheryl Gay Stolberg, "Their Devil's Advocates," *New York Times Magazine,* January 25, 1998, p. 20.

34. Jim Dwyer, "Ferraro Is Battling Blood Cancer with a Potent Ally: Thalidomide," *New York Times,* June 19, 2001, B1.
35. Randolph Warren, "Living in a World with Thalidomide" in *FDA Consumer Magazine,* March–April 2001, at www.fda.gov/fdac/departs/2001/201.word_html.
36. Bren, "Frances Oldham Kelsey," p. 6.
37. Theodore J. Lowi, *The End of Liberalism* (New York: W. W. Norton, 1969), p. 40.
38. Hugh Heclo, *A Government of Strangers* (Washington, D.C.: Brookings Institution, 1977), p. 11.
39. Downs, *Inside Bureaucracy,* pp. 59, 60.
40. Charles E. Jacob, *Policy and Bureaucracy* (Princeton, N.J.: Van Nostrand, 1966), p. 47.
41. Max Weber, *Science and Society,* excerpted in *From Max Weber,* ed. Hans Gerth and C. Wright Mills (New York: Oxford University Press, 1958), p. 215. An alternative, but not contradictory, formulation is developed from rational-choice theory by Downs, *Inside Bureaucracy,* chap. 3.
42. Weber, *Science and Society,* pp. 198, 199, 216.
43. Woll, *American Bureaucracy,* p. 251.
44. Emmette S. Redford, *Democracy in the Administrative State* (New York: Oxford University Press, 1969), pp. 80–81.
45. Jonathan Daniels, *Frontier on the Potomac,* quoted in Richard E. Neustadt, *Presidential Power* (New York: Wiley, 1960), p. 41.
46. Morris Fiorina, *Congress: Keystone of the Washington Establishment* (New Haven, Conn.: Yale University Press, 1977), p. 66.
47. See Arthur Maass, *Muddy Waters: The Army Engineers and the Nation's Rivers* (Cambridge, Mass.: Harvard University Press, 1951).
48. Woll, *American Bureaucracy,* p. 80.
49. See Moe, "Politics of Bureaucratic Structure," pp. 273–77.
50. Heclo, "Issue Networks and the Executive Establishment," pp. 87–124. The quotations are from pp. 96, 99. Heclo offers an insightful examination of top-level bureaucrats in *A Government of Strangers.*
51. Norma M. Riccucci, *Unsung Heroes* (Washington, D.C.: Georgetown University Press, 1995), p. 3. In chap. 6, Riccucci provides a useful parallel study of another health professional in the national bureaucracy,

Dr. Vince Hutchins, who developed the government's maternal and child health programs.

52. Theodore J. Lowi developed these important distinctions in "American Business, Public Policy, Case Studies, and Political Theory," *World Politics* 16 (July 1964): 677–715. The quoted material is from pp. 692, 695.
53. Redford, *Democracy in the Administrative State*, p. 84.
54. Ibid., pp. 85, 86, 87, 88.
55. Downs, *Inside Bureaucracy*, p. 259.
56. *Washington Post*, January 23, 1997, p. M01.

8   Thurlow Weed: A Hero in Party Politics

1. Ambrose Bierce, *The Devil's Dictionary* (1906) (New York: Dover Publications, 1958), p. 101.
2. E. E. Schattschneider, *Party Government* (New York: Holt, Rinehart and Winston, 1942), p. 1.
3. Joseph Schumpeter, *Capitalism, Socialism, and Democracy* (New York: Harper, 1950), p. 285.
4. Wilson Carey McWilliams, "Parties as Civic Associations," in *Party Renewal in America*, ed. Gerald M. Pomper (New York: Praeger, 1980), p. 51.
5. George H. Mayer, *The Republican Party, 1854–1966*, 2d ed. (London: Oxford University Press, 1967), p. 33.
6. The phrase is from the only noteworthy biography of Weed: Glendon G. Van Deusen, *Thurlow Weed: Wizard of the Lobby* (Boston: Little, Brown, 1947).
7. See the helpful biographical sketch by Helen C. Boatfield in the *Dictionary of American Biography* (New York: Scribner's, 1936), 10:598–600.
8. David M. Potter, *Lincoln and His Party in the Secession Crisis* (New Haven, Conn.: Yale University Press, 1962), p. 69.
9. Van Deusen, *Thurlow Weed*, pp. 51, 78.
10. For an excellent analysis of Lincoln's own formidable political skill, see Avram Fechter, "Lincoln: The Master Politician," Henry Rutgers Honors Thesis, Rutgers University, 2001.
11. See Murat Halstead, *Caucuses of 1860*, reprinted as *Three Against Lincoln*, ed. William Hesseltine (Baton Rouge: Louisiana State University Press,

1960), pp. 40–42. The vice-presidential offer to Lincoln is reported by Van Deusen, *Thurlow Weed*, p. 251.

12. Weed related the fascinating story of these critical discussions in his later memoir. See Harriet A. Weed, ed., *Life of Thurlow Weed*, vol. 1, *Autobiography of Thurlow Weed* (Boston: Houghton Mifflin, 1883), pp. 602–14. It was also published as "Mr. Lincoln and Three Friends in Council," in *Galaxy* 11 (February 1871), pp. 247–56, which is available through the Cornell University digital library collection, "The Making of America," cdl.library.cornell.edu/cgi.
13. Weed later wrote that "nothing was then said in regard to the future of the 'Herald'" and denied that there was "one word spoken, suggested, or intimated in our conversation conveying the idea of personal interest or advancement." However, he also noted that "Mr. Lincoln frequently expressed to me his desire in some way to acknowledge his sense of obligation to Mr. Bennett," who, during the 1864 campaign, was in fact offered the post of ambassador to France. Bennett's son also received a military commission, perhaps another reward. See *Autobiography of Thurlow Weed*, vol. 1 of *Life of Thurlow Weed*, ed. H. Weed, pp. 618–19.
14. For analysis of the political maneuvers during the secession crisis, see Potter, *Lincoln and His Party*, pp. 71–176.
15. Thurlow Weed Barnes, "Memoir of Thurlow Weed" (1884), in *Life of Thurlow Weed*, ed. H. Weed, 2:330.
16. David H. Donald, *Lincoln* (New York: Simon and Schuster, 1995), p. 322.
17. See Henry Adams, *The Education of Henry Adams* (1918) (Boston: Houghton Mifflin, 1962), chap. 10. See also *Autobiography of Thurlow Weed*, vol. 1 of *Life of Thurlow Weed*, ed. H. Weed, chaps. 66, 67; and "Memoir of Thurlow Weed," also in *Life of Thurlow Weed*, vol. 2, chaps. 27–29.
18. John C. Waugh, *Reelecting Lincoln* (New York: Crown Publishers, 1997), p. ix.
19. Harold M. Hyman, "Election of 1864," in *The Coming to Power: Critical Presidential Elections in American History*, ed. Arthur M. Schlesinger Jr. (New York: Chelsea House, 1972), p. 144.
20. *The Collected Works of Abraham Lincoln*, ed. Roy P. Basler (New Brunswick, N.J.: Rutgers University Press, 1953), 6:514.

21. James M. McPherson, *Battle Cry of Freedom* (New York: Oxford University Press, 1988), p. 760.
22. See ibid., pp. 761–71.
23. Hyman, "Election of 1864," p. 156.
24. *Life of Thurlow Weed,* ed. H. Weed, 2:444. See also the investigation of an amateur historian, Jack Burden, "Abraham Lincoln and the Use of Money," at www.jackburden.com/cfr/case2.htm.
25. Lincoln to Weed, February 19, 1863, in *Collected Works of Abraham Lincoln,* ed. Basler, 6:112–13; Weed to Lincoln, February 1, 1863, in ibid., 6:83–84.
26. In a letter to John Nicolay, September 11, 1863, in *Lincoln and the Civil War in the Diaries and Letters of John Hay,* ed. Tyler Dennett (New York: Dodd, Mead, 1939), p. 91.
27. Donald, *Lincoln,* p. 478.
28. Mayer, *The Republican Party,* p. 115.
29. Donald, *Lincoln,* p. 503. The quotation is I Samuel 22.2.
30. Harry J. Carman and Reinhard M. Luthin, *Lincoln and the Patronage* (New York: Columbia University Press, 1943), p. 236.
31. Ibid., pp. 245, 246.
32. Waugh, *Reelecting Lincoln,* p. 185.
33. See Donald, *Lincoln,* pp. 502–7; Van Deusen, *Thurlow Weed,* pp. 307–8; and Waugh, *Reelecting Lincoln,* pp. 199–200.
34. For an especially clear account of the conflict between Lincoln and congressional Republicans, see Waugh, *Reelecting Lincoln,* pp. 223–29.
35. Carman and Luthin, *Lincoln and the Patronage,* p. 271.
36. Letter of John Hay to John Nicolay, September 29, 1864, in *Lincoln and the Civil War,* ed. Dennett, p. 221.
37. In a letter to William Seward, September 10, 1864, quoted by Donald, *Lincoln,* p. 533.
38. In a letter of August 22, 1864, to Seward, quoted in J. G. Randall and Richard N. Current, *Lincoln the President: Last Full Measure* (New York: Dodd, Mead, 1955), pp. 213.
39. Waugh, *Reelecting Lincoln,* p. 328. For an account of the campaign events, see pp. 304–39.
40. See James A. Rawley, *The Politics of Union: Northern Politics During the Civil War* (Lincoln: University of Nebraska Press, 1974), pp. 160–61; Carman and Luthin, *Lincoln and the Patronage,* pp. 286–98.

41. Rawley, *Politics of Union*, p. 163.
42. David H. Donald, "A. Lincoln, Politician," in *Lincoln Reconsidered* (New York: Vintage Books, 1956), p. 81.
43. Quoted in Donald, *Lincoln*, p. 539.
44. Hyman, "Election of 1864," p. 163.
45. Anthony Downs, *An Economic Theory of Democracy* (New York: Harper and Row, 1957), p. 28. The theory of political parties is further developed in the masterful work of John H. Aldrich, *Why Parties?* (Chicago: University of Chicago Press, 1995).
46. Even in the allegedly "nonideological" period of the 1950s, there were considerable attitudinal differences between Democratic and Republican party activists. See the classic article, Herbert McClosky et al., "Issue Conflict and Consensus Among Party Leaders and Followers," *American Political Science Review* 54 (June 1960), pp. 406–27.
47. Van Deusen, *Thurlow Weed*, pp. 73, 138.
48. Clinton Rossiter, *Parties and Politics in America* (Ithaca, N.Y.: Cornell University Press, 1960), p. 37.
49. Waugh, *Reelecting Lincoln*, p. 305 and, quoting James Bennett, p. 307.
50. Weed to Lincoln, October 18, 1863, in *Collected Works of Abraham Lincoln*, ed. Basler, 6:514.
51. On these major events in the history of the Whigs, see Michael F. Holt, *The Rise and Fall of the American Whig Party* (New York: Oxford University Press, 1999) pp. 830–33, 945–49.
52. Boatfield, *Dictionary of American Biography*, p. 599.
53. On the election of 1848, see Holt, *Rise and Fall of the American Whig Party*, pp. 320–30.
54. Ibid., p. 553.
55. Aldrich, *Why Parties?* p. 155.
56. Mayer, *The Republican Party*, p. 34.
57. *Autobiography of Thurlow Weed*, vol. 1 of *Life of Thurlow Weed*, ed. H. Weed, p. 604.
58. *Life of Thurlow Weed*, ed. H. Weed, 2:304, 306.
59. Ibid., 2:328.
60. Stanley Kelley, Jr., "Politics as a Vocation: Variations on Weber," in *Politicians and Party Politics*, ed. John G. Geer (Baltimore: Johns Hopkins University Press, 1998), p. 345.
61. Adams, *Education of Henry Adams*, pp. 147–48.

62. *Autobiography of Thurlow Weed*, vol. 1 of *Life of Thurlow Weed*, ed. H. Weed, p. 605.
63. In a letter to Lincoln, October 18, 1863, in *Collected Works of Abraham Lincoln*, ed. Basler, 6:514.
64. Nicolay reports this conversation of March 30, 1864, in ibid., 7:268–69.
65. Quoted in William L. Riordon, *Plunkitt of Tammany Hall* (New York: E. P. Dutton, 1963), p. 13.
66. Dissenting opinion of Powell in *Branti v. Finkel*, 445 U.S. 507, 527–28 (1980).
67. Dissenting opinion of Antonin Scalia in *Rutan v. Republican Party of Illinois*, 497 U.S. 62, 104–10 (1990).
68. McWilliams, "Parties as Civic Associations," p. 60.
69. "Two Journalists," *Atlantic Monthly*, September 1883, p. 418, available through the Cornell University digital library collection, "The Making of America," cdl.library.cornell.edu/cgi.

9 Ida Tarbell: A Hero of the Press

1. Richard Hofstadter, *The Age of Reform* (New York: Alfred A. Knopf, 1955), p. 136, citing Census Bureau studies of the time. The estimate for the top one percent, admittedly based on imprecise data, is made by Kevin Phillips, *Wealth and Democracy* (New York: Broadway Books, 2002), p. 122.
2. Alexis de Tocqueville, *Democracy in America* (1835), ed. Phillips Bradley (New York: Vintage Press, 1954), 2:171.
3. The term was coined by President Theodore Roosevelt. See his speech, "The Man with the Muckrake," in *The Muckrakers*, ed. Arthur Weinberg and Lila Weinberg (New York: Simon and Schuster, 1961), p. 60. This book offers a valuable collection of the most prominent muckraking articles.
4. Ida M. Tarbell, *All in the Day's Work* (1939) (Boston: G. K. Hall, 1985), p. 36.
5. Kathleen Brady, *Ida Tarbell: Portrait of a Muckraker* (New York: Putnam, 1984), p. 206.
6. Ida Tarbell, *The Business of Being a Woman* (New York: Macmillan, 1912), pp. 5, 54.
7. Hofstadter, *Age of Reform*, p. 185.

8. Ibid., pp. 188, 189, 191.
9. Members of the group later bought another periodical, the American. Among those who might meet in the two magazines' newsrooms were Tarbell, Lincoln Steffens, Ray Stannard Baker, Willa Cather, Upton Sinclair, John Reed, William Allen White, Finley Peter Dunne (Mr. Dooley), and a magnificent editor, John S. Phillips.
10. Lincoln Steffens, *Autobiography* (New York: Harcourt Brace, 1931), pp. 392–93.
11. Weinberg and Weinberg, *Muckrakers*, p. xviii. "The publicity men of reform" is from Eric Goldman, *Rendezvous with Destiny* (New York: Alfred A. Knopf, 1952), p. 176.
12. Steffens, *Autobiography*, p. 393.
13. In a 1933 letter to Alice Rice, quoted in Brady, *Ida Tarbell*, p. 139.
14. Tarbell, *All in the Day's Work*, pp. 242, 399.
15. Allan Nevins, *John D. Rockefeller*, ed. William Greenleaf (New York: Scribner's, 1959), pp. 317–18.
16. Tarbell, *All in the Day's Work*, pp. 203, 204, 205.
17. Nevins, *John D. Rockefeller*, pp. 155, 209.
18. Ida M. Tarbell, *The History of the Standard Oil Company* (1904) (Gloucester, Mass.: Peter Smith, 1963), 1:3–4.
19. Nevins, *John D. Rockefeller*, p. 48.
20. Daniel Yergin, *The Prize: The Epic Struggle for Oil, Money, and Power* (New York: Simon and Schuster, 1991), p. 42.
21. Brady, *Ida Tarbell*, p. 144 and, quoting Tarbell, p. 145.
22. Tarbell, *History of the Standard Oil Company*, 2:192–230; the quotation is from p. 196, the price of oil in New York is cited on p. 227.
23. Ibid., 2:225, 227, 229–30.
24. Tarbell, *All in the Day's Work*, pp. 239, 241.
25. Yergin, *The Prize*, p. 105.
26. Edmund Morris, *Theodore Rex* (New York: Random House, 2001), p. 418.
27. Quoted in Henry F. Pringle, *Theodore Roosevelt* (Norwalk: Easton Press, 1931), p. 360.
28. See Nevins, *John D. Rockefeller*, pp. 319–23; the quotation is from p. 323.
29. Yergin, *The Prize*, p. 110.
30. *Standard Oil Co. of New Jersey v. U.S.*, 221 U.S. 1 (1911). The quotation is from Justice Harlan's concurring opinion, at p. 82.

31. Brady, *Ida Tarbell*, p. 160.
32. Tarbell, *All in the Day's Work*, p. 364.
33. Tarbell, *History of the Standard Oil Company*, 1:vii. See also Yergin, *The Prize*, p. 520.
34. Nevins, *John D. Rockefeller*, p. 318.
35. These "best qualities" concern both the ethics and the craft of journalism. The ethical principles of the profession are laid out in the Code of Ethics of the Society of Professional Journalists, available at www.spj.org/ethics_code.asp. Although Tarbell wrote before these principles were formally adopted, in 1926, they still provide sound criteria for evaluation. The standards governing the practice of the craft are less specific but are suggested in journalism textbooks, such as Bruce Porter and Timothy Ferris, *The Practice of Journalism* (Englewood Cliffs, N.J.: Prentice-Hall, 1988).
36. Brady, *Ida Tarbell*, p. 124.
37. Tarbell, *All in the Day's Work*, pp. 226–27.
38. Ibid., pp. 212–28; the quotations are from pp. 215–16.
39. Brady, *Ida Tarbell*, pp. 125, 132, here quotes letters from Tarbell to her research assistant, John M. Siddall, on September 11, 1901, and from Viola Roseboro, the *McClure's* editor, to another writer, Ada Pierce McCormick, on March 2, 1930.
40. Tarbell, *All in the Day's Work*, p. 206.
41. Tocqueville, *Democracy in America*, 1:195, and 2:119.
42. Bernard Cohen, *The Press and Foreign Policy* (Princeton, N.J.: Princeton University Press, 1963), p. 13. Shanto Iyengar and Donald R. Kinder, *News That Matters* (Chicago: University of Chicago Press, 1987), p. 33; see also chap. 3, on agenda-setting, and chap. 7, on framing. An earlier important study of the role of the press in agenda-setting is Donald Shaw and Maxwell McCombs, *The Emergence of American Political Issues: The Agenda-Setting Function of the Press* (St. Paul, Minn.: West, 1977).
43. Hofstadter, *Age of Reform*, p. 202.
44. Tarbell, *All in the Day's Work*, p. 399. The evolution of the press in America is ably traced by Darrel M. West, *The Rise and Fall of the Media Establishment* (Boston: Bedford/St. Martin's Press, 2001).
45. Hugo de Burgh, *Investigative Journalism* (London: Routledge, 2000), provides these characterizations on pp. 3 and 34–38. On the role of war

correspondents, see Phillip Knightley, *The First Casualty* (New York: Harcourt, Brace, Jovanovich, 1975).
46. The list, which was developed by leading journalists and historians under the auspices of New York University's Faculty of Journalism, is available at www.nyu.edu/gsas/dept/journal/dept_news/news_stories/990301_topjourn.htm.
47. See Douglass Cater, *The Fourth Branch of Government* (Boston: Houghton Mifflin, 1959), p. 15.
48. Tocqueville, *Democracy in America*, 1:200.
49. Potter Stewart, "Or of the Press," 50 *Hastings Law Journal* 705, 707 (1999), a reprint of the original article, which appeared in 26 *Hastings Law Journal* 631 (1975).
50. Stewart, "Or of the Press," p. 708.
51. *New York Times Co. v. U.S.*, 403 U.S. 713, 717 (1971).
52. James Madison, *The Federalist*, no. 51 (1788) (New York: Modern Library, 1941), p. 337.
53. William J. Small, *Political Power and the Press* (New York: Norton, 1972), p. 10.
54. See Peter Braestrup's account of press distortions in the coverage of Vietnam: *Big Story* (Boulder, Colo.: Westview Press, 1977); and David Halberstam's account of the distortions of government press officers during the war: *The Best and the Brightest* (New York: Random House, 1992).
55. The classic analysis of relations between press and government is Leon V. Sigal, *Reporters and Officials* (Lexington: D. C. Heath, 1973). See also Herbert Gans, *Deciding What's News* (New York: Vintage, 1979).
56. Six useful case studies of the relationship between government and the press are found in Martin Linsky et al., *How the Press Affects Federal Policymaking* (New York: W. W. Norton, 1986).
57. Cater, *Fourth Branch of Government*, pp. 7–11; the quotation is from p. 7.
58. Timothy E. Cook, *Governing with the News: The News Media as a Political Institution* (Chicago: University of Chicago Press, 1998), p. 167.
59. Cook, *Governing with the News*, p. 113. On the president in particular, see Samuel Kernell, *Going Public: New Strategies of Presidential Leadership*, 2d ed. (Washington, D.C.: CQ Press, 1993).
60. Cook, *Governing with the News*, p. 113.

61. Kathleen Hall Jamieson and Paul Waldman, *The Press Effect* (New York: Oxford University Press, 2003), p. 1. This volume offers an incisive analysis of press coverage of the presidential election of 2000 and the events of September 11, 2001.
62. See West, *Rise and Fall of the Media Establishment*, chaps. 5, 7; James Fallows, *Breaking the News* (New York: Pantheon, 1996); Thomas Patterson, *Out of Order* (New York: Vintage, 1993); and Larry J. Sabato, *Feeding Frenzy* (Baltimore: Lanahan, 1991).
63. Tocqueville, *Democracy in America*, 1:192.
64. Tarbell, *All in the Day's Work*, pp. 404–5.

10   John Lewis: A Hero of Social Movements

1. John Lewis, *Walking with the Wind: A Memoir of the Movement* (New York: Simon and Schuster, 1998), p. 209.
2. Taylor Branch, *Parting the Waters: America in the King Years, 1954–63* (New York: Simon and Schuster, 1988), p. 261.
3. Lewis, *Walking with the Wind*, p. 301.
4. All unattributed quotations are from interviews with Congressman Lewis conducted on February 18, 1999 and March 16, 2000.
5. Lewis, *Walking with the Wind*, p. 473.
6. Sean Wilenz, "The Last Integrationist," *New Republic*, July 1, 1996.
7. James Madison expressed this interpretation in his journal of the Convention: *The Records of the Federal Convention of 1787*, ed. Max Farrand (New Haven, Conn.: Yale University Press, 1911), 2:10. The Lincoln quotation is from his 1858 "House Divided" speech, available in many sources, including www.pbs.org/wgbh/aia/part4/4h2934t.html.
8. The history of the student movement and the civil rights campaign more generally is skillfully told from the students' perspective in David Halberstam, *The Children* (New York: Random House, 1998). The first sit-ins had in fact occurred two weeks earlier, in Greensboro, North Carolina.
9. The leading study of SNCC is Clayborne Carson, *In Struggle: SNCC and the Black Awakening of the 1960s* (Cambridge, Mass.: Harvard University Press, 1995).
10. Halberstam, *The Children*, pp. 103–6.
11. Ibid., p. 262.

12. Ibid., p. 313.
13. Ibid., p. 301.
14. Branch, *Parting the Waters*, pp. 875–76, 882.
15. Lewis, *Walking with the Wind*, pp. 216–18.
16. James Forman, *The Making of Black Revolutionaries* (New York: Macmillan, 1972), p. 335. See also Carson, *In Struggle*, chap. 7.
17. Lewis, *Walking with the Wind*, p. 303.
18. Forman, *Making of Black Revolutionaries*, p. 441.
19. Lewis, *Walking with the Wind*, p. 328.
20. Quoted in David J. Garrow, *Bearing the Cross* (New York: Random House, 1986), p. 409.
21. Ibid., p. 166.
22. SNCC spokesman quoted in ibid., p. 423.
23. Anthony Oberschall, *Social Movements* (New Brunswick, N.J.: Transaction Publishers, 1993), p. 268. In chap. 10, Oberschall furnishes an excellent theoretical analysis of the decline of the social movements of the 1960s.
24. President Clinton, marking the anniversary of the march on Washington, *New York Times*, March 6, 2000, p. A12.
25. For an overview of the role of social movements in American history, see William A. Gamson, *The Strategy of Social Protest*, 2d ed. (Belmont, Calif.: Wadsworth, 1990).
26. In a letter to Samuel Kercheaval, July 12, 1816, quoted in Alpheus T. Mason, *Free Government in the Making*, 2d ed. (New York: Oxford University Press, 1956), p. 374.
27. On the political intentions of the framers, see John P. Roche, "The Founding Fathers: A Reform Caucus in Action," *American Political Science Review* 55 (December 1960): 799–816.
28. James Madison, *The Federalist*, no. 40 (1788) (New York: Modern Library, 1941), pp. 257–59. The italics are Madison's.
29. Martin Luther King, Jr., *Why We Can't Wait* (New York: New American Library, 1963), p. 68.
30. James Madison, *The Federalist*, no. 51, p. 341.
31. Samuel P. Huntington, *Political Order in Changing Societies* (New Haven, Conn.: Yale University Press, 1968), p. 129.
32. Alexis de Tocqueville, *Democracy in America* (1835), ed. Phillips Bradley (New York: Vintage, 1954), 1:271.

33. Walter Dean Burnham, *Critical Elections and the Mainsprings of American Politics* (New York: W. W. Norton, 1970), p. 183.
34. Francesca Polletta provides a keen theoretical analysis of social movements in *Freedom Is an Endless Meeting* (Chicago: University of Chicago Press, 2002), chap. 1.
35. See Charles Tilly, *From Mobilization to Revolution* (New York: McGraw-Hill, 1978), pp. 5–7.
36. Ibid., p. 61.
37. See Max Weber, "Politics as a Vocation," in *From Max Weber*, ed. H. H. Gerth and C. Wright Mills (New York: Oxford University Press, 1958), pp. 78–80.
38. Halberstam, *The Children*, pp. 139–40.
39. Tilly, *From Mobilization to Revolution*, p. 71.
40. Halberstam, *The Children*, pp. 396–97, speaking of Diane Nash and James Bevel.
41. See Tilly, *From Mobilization to Revolution*, chap. 4.
42. This conflict between the Creed and empirical reality was the basic premise of the pioneering work on American race relations by Gunnar Myrdal, *An American Dilemma* (New York: Harper, 1948).
43. Oberschall, *Social Movements*, p. 234.
44. Halberstam, *The Children*, p. 485.
45. E. E. Schattschneider, *The Semi-Sovereign People* (New York: Holt, Rinehart and Winston, 1960), p. 3. Walter Lippmann developed a similar theory earlier in *The Phantom Public* (New York: Macmillan, 1937).
46. Garrow, *Bearing the Cross*, p. 221.
47. On civil disobedience, see Ronald Dworkin, *Taking Rights Seriously* (London: Duckworth, 1977), chap. 8.
48. David J. Garrow, *Protest at Selma* (New Haven, Conn.: Yale University Press, 1978), p. 147.
49. Michael Lipsky, "Protest as a Political Resource," *American Political Science Review* 62 (December 1968): 1153.
50. Forman, *Making of Black Revolutionaries*, p. 448. Forman details his and SNCC's changing view throughout the book.
51. Polletta, *Freedom Is an Endless Meeting*, p. 23.
52. Lewis, *Walking with the Wind*, p. 350.
53. Ibid., p. 368. For parallel accounts of the leadership contest, see Car-

son, *In Struggle,* pp. 199–204; Polletta, *Freedom Is an Endless Meeting,* chap. 4; and Forman, *Making of Black Revolutionaries,* pp. 433–56.
54. Carson, *In Struggle,* p. 306.
55. Lipsky, "Protest as a Political Resource," p. 1158.
56. The phrase is taken from a notable article by Bayard Rustin, "From Protest to Politics," *Commentary* 39 (February 1965): 25–31.
57. Lewis, *Walking with the Wind,* p. 408.
58. On the effects of the race issue on party alignments, see Edward G. Carmines and James A. Stimson, *Issue Evolution* (Princeton, N.J.: Princeton University Press, 1989).

11 Ordinary Heroes and American Democracy

1. James Bennet, "Somber Washington Pauses to Honor Two Slain Guards," *New York Times,* July 29, 1998, p. A13.
2. Antigone, ll. 452–56, in Sophocles, *The Theban Plays,* trans. E. P. Watling (New York: Penguin Books, 1947), p. 138.
3. Ibid., ll. 672–76, p. 144.
4. Ibid., l. 741, p. 146.
5. Henry Kissinger, "With Faint Praise," review of Norman Rose, *Churchill: The Unruly Giant,* in *New York Times Book Review,* July 16, 1995, p. 7.
6. *Dear Bess: The Letters from Harry to Bess Truman, 1910–1959,* ed. Robert H. Ferrell (New York: W. W. Norton, 1983), letter of September 30, 1947, p. 550.
7. R. W. Apple, "Looking Back," *New York Times,* June 7, 1994, p. A1.
8. Christopher S. Wren, "Midlife Macho," *New York Times Magazine,* May 4, 1986, p. 86.
9. Fred Frohock and Roger Sharp, "Courage and the Public Service" (Syracuse, N.Y.: Courage Foundation, 1989), p. 5.
10. "The Silent Superstar," *New York Times,* March 9, 1999, p. A23.
11. See Amy Fried, "Gendered Heroism, Limited Politics," *Women and Politics* 17, No. 2 (1997): 43–75. On heroic types, see Amy Fried, "Is Political Action Heroic? Heroism and American Political Culture," *American Politics Quarterly* 21 (October 1993): 490–517.
12. See Robert McAffee Brown, "They Could Do No Better," in *The*

Courage to Care: Rescuers of Jews During the Holocaust, ed. Carol Rittner and Sondra Myers (New York: New York University Press, 1986), pp. 143–47; the quotation is from Pierre Sauvage, "Ten Questions," in *Courage to Care,* p. 141.
13. Cynthia Ozick, "Of Christian Heroism," *Partisan Review* 59 (Winter 1992), pp. 46, 48.
14. Bennet, "Two Slain Guards," p. A13.
15. Pericles' funeral oration, in Thucydides, *History of the Peloponnesian War,* trans. Rex Warner (London: Penguin Classics, 1954), p. 148.
16. Alasdair MacIntyre, *After Virtue: A Study in Moral Theory,* 2d ed. (Notre Dame, Ind.: University of Notre Dame Press, 1984), pp. 132–35; the quotation is on p. 133.
17. Frohock and Sharp, "Courage and the Public Service," p. 5.
18. Max Weber, "Politics as a Vocation," in *From Max Weber,* ed. H. H. Gerth and C. Wright Mills (New York: Oxford University Press, 1958), pp. 121, 128.
19. Robin Kadison Berson, *Marching to a Different Drummer* (Westport, Conn.: Greenwood Press, 1994), p. xi.
20. Henry David Thoreau, "On the Duty of Civil Disobedience," in *Social and Political Philosophy,* ed. John Somerville and Ronald E. Santoni (Garden City, N.Y.: Doubleday, 1963), pp. 289–90.
21. Brad Lowell Stone, "Liberalism and the Science of Human Nature," *Society* 38 (September–October 2001), p. 77.
22. See Gordon Schochet, "Persuading the Heart: Appeals to 'Conscience' in the English Revolution," in *Historians and Ideologues: Essays in Early-Modern Historiography and Political Thought in Honor of Donald R. Kelley,* ed. Anthony Grafton and J. H. M. Salmon (Rochester, N.Y.: University of Rochester Press, 2001), pp. 154–80; the quotation is from p. 162.
23. Ralph Waldo Emerson, "Representative Men" (1850), in *Essays and Lectures* (New York: Literary Classics of the United States, 1983), pp. 626–27.
24. Garry Wills, *Certain Trumpets* (New York: Simon and Schuster, 1994), pp. 13, 17.
25. Weber, "Politics as a Vocation," p. 128.
26. James Madison, *The Federalist,* no. 10 (1787) (New York: Modern Library, 1941), p. 57; *The Federalist,* no. 51 (1788), p. 337.

27. Richard Hofstadter, *The American Political Tradition* (New York: Alfred A. Knopf, 1955), p. 3.
28. James G. March and John P. Olsen, "The New Institutionalism: Organizational Factors in Political Life," *American Political Science Review* 78 (September 1984): 738, 739. Two outstanding works of the new institutionalism are Theda Skocpol, *Protecting Soldiers and Mothers: The Political Origins of Social Policy in the United States* (Cambridge, Mass.: Harvard University Press, 1992); and John Aldrich, *Why Parties?* (Chicago: University of Chicago Press, 1995).
29. March and Olsen, "New Institutionalism," p. 741.
30. James Madison, *The Federalist,* no. 51, pp. 339, 341.
31. Sidney Hook, *The Hero in History: A Study in Limitation and Possibility* (Boston: Beacon Press, 1943), pp. 156–57.
32. Sidney Hook, "The Hero and Democracy," *Kettering Review,* Summer 1993, p. 78.
33. Judith Shklar, *Ordinary Vices* (Cambridge, Mass.: Harvard University Press, 1984), p. 236.
34. Hook, *Hero in History,* pp. 154–55.
35. On the original meaning of "hero," see Eric Partridge, *Origins: A Short Etymological Dictionary of Modern English,* 2d ed. (New York: Macmillan, 1959), p. 287. The definition of the hero of epic poetry is from the *Compact Edition of the Oxford English Dictionary* (New York: Oxford University Press, 1971), p. 1296.
36. This was President Gerald Ford's first comment after he took the inaugural oath to succeed Richard Nixon. Ford's speech is available at: www.ford.utexas.edu/library/speeches/740001.htm
37. Alexis de Tocqueville, *Democracy in America,* ed. Phillips Bradley (New York: Vintage, 1954), 2:350.
38. "Address to the Young Men's Lyceum of Springfield Illinois" (1838), in *The Portable Abraham Lincoln,* ed. Andrew Del Blanco (New York: Viking Press, 1992). The quotations are from pp. 24, 26. Lincoln's original emphasis in the first sentence is omitted.

Index

Abortion, 53, 130, 150
Acheson, Dean, 93, 103, 105–6
Achilles, 1, 4–6, 28, 236
Activists, Protesters, and Reformers archetype, 24, 29
Adams, Henry, 178
Amnesty International, 15
Anti-communism: in domestic politics, 63, 66–67, 69, 81; in foreign policy, 93–94, 107. *See also* McCarthyism; Marshall Plan
Antigone, 236–38, 246

Bennett, James Gordon, 163, 174
Berlin, William, 261, 264
Berson, Robin, 245
Bickel, Alexander, 131
Biden, Joseph, 25
Black, Hugo, 204
Blackmun, Harry, 124
Bond, Julian, 211, 233
Bozell, Brent, 64
Brecht, Bertolt, 5
Brennan, William, 109, 123
Brown v. Board of Education, 112, 132
Bryce, James Lord, 99
Buckley, William F., 64
Bureaucracy: as institution, 134, 141, 151, 153–54, 157; norms of, 140, 152–53, 156–57, 249; routines of, 138, 151–52, 155–56
Burger, Warren, 127
Bush, George H. W., 48, 85
Bush, George W., 19

Caesar, Julius, 252–53
Cameron, Simon, 163
Campbell, Joseph, 28
Carlyle, Thomas, 26
Carmichael, Stokely, 233
Carson, Clayborne, 233
Champions of Adversity archetype, 20
Chase, Salmon, 166–68, 170, 181
Chestnut, Jacob, 236–37, 243
Civil rights movement, 214–19, 221–22, 230–32
Civil War, 2, 16, 85, 160, 162, 164, 170, 173, 181, 214
Clark, Kenneth, 17–18
Clark, Jim, 251
Clark, William, 20
Clay, Henry, 161, 176
Clemente, Roberto, 23, 29
Clinton, William J., 18, 54, 82, 85, 237; impeachment of, 50–53, 55–56, 251

Cohen, Bernard, 201
Constitution of the U.S.: as check on power, 27, 205, 226, 252, 254; framing of, 214, 224–25, 248; provisions of, 85, 116, 120, 126, 134, 204. *See also* Judicial review, and democratic theory; *Plyler v. Doe.*
Cook, Timothy, 207
Cromwell, Oliver, 252–53

Dahl, Robert, 128
Davis, Angela, 18
Davis, Jefferson, 18, 170, 174
Declaration of Independence, 213, 224, 228
Democratic heroes. *See* Heroism, in "ordinary heroes"

Election of 1860, 162, 175, 177
Election of 1864, 163–69, 171–75
Election of 1946, 89, 93
Election of 1948, 64, 269
Election of 1972, 35
Eliot, T. S., 13
Emancipation Proclamation, 163–64
Equal Protection clause, 116–18, 120, 122, 132
"Ethic of responsibility," 245

Fechter, Avram, 280
Federalist papers. *See* Hamilton, Alexander; Madison, James
Ferraro, Geraldine, 150
Finkbein, Sherry, 150
Food and Drug Administration: history of, 135, 139, 140, 148–49; procedures, 137–39, 147, 150, 153, 250
Forman, James, 232
Freedom rides. *See* Civil rights movement
Fremont, John C., 166–67, 170, 174
Fried, Amy, 17, 259
Fried, Richard, 70

Gandhi, Mohandas, 214
Gary, Elbert, 197
Geismar, Lee, 157
Gender and politics. *See* Sexual discrimination
Gibson, John, 236–37, 243
Giuliani, Rudolph, 3–4, 7–8
Greeley, Horace, 165, 167, 169, 171, 181
Greenstein, Fred, 267
Guardians at the Gates archetype, 24, 29

Halberstam, David, 58, 63, 229
Hamilton, Alexander, 6, 51
Hamlin, Hannibal, 168
Harris, Steven, 147
Harrison, William Henry, 161
Hay, John, 169
Hegel, G. W. F., 26
Heroes: "event-making" and "eventful," 252–54; personal characteristics, 26, 28, 239–43, 251; personal characteristics and politics, 244–47, 251–53. *See also* Institutions, and heroism

Heroism: in ancient Greece, 1, 236–38, 244; archetypes of, 19, 25; in film, 18, 22–23; in "ordinary heroes," 5, 7–9, 29, 56, 107, 133–34, 172, 250–51, 254; popular meanings of, 12–13, 15–16, 19, 28. *See also* Institutions, and heroism

Hofstadter, Richard, 187, 202, 248

Holocaust, 8, 242, 243

Hook, Sidney, 28, 252–53

Hoover, Herbert, 75, 85, 94, 104, 155

Hoover, J. Edgar, 75, 155

House Judiciary Committee, 43–44, 53; in Clinton impeachment, 50, 52–53, 55; in Nixon impeachment, 31, 36, 39, 45, 47, 49

House of Representatives: norms of, 43–45, 52, 54, 249; political characteristics, 42–43, 54

Huffington, Arianna, 18

Hull, Elizabeth A., 273

Hyde, Henry, 52, 55, 251

Impeachment. *See* Clinton, William J., impeachment of; Nixon, Richard M., impeachment of

Institutions, and heroism, 6, 9–10, 27–28, 238, 248–51, 293

Investigative journalism, 202–3, 251

Iron curtain, 62, 93

Issue networks, 139, 155. *See also* Bureaucracy, routines of

Jackson, Andrew, 128

Jefferson, Thomas, 128, 214

Johnson, Andrew, 168

Johnson, Lyndon Baines, 82, 91, 112, 219, 221

Journalism: and democratic theory, 200–205, 209; development in U.S., 187–88, 208; as institution, 188, 203, 205–8, 249. *See also* Television, and civil rights movement

Judicial review, and democratic theory, 127–31

Judiciary, as institution, 115, 249

Justice, William Wayne, *chapter 6;* 10, 239–41, 245, 249–51; career of, 110, 112; character of, 108–10, 112–13, 132–33; judicial philosophy of, 113–15, 119, 121, 125–26, 128–130; photograph, 111. See also *Plyler v. Doe*

Kafka, Joseph, 134

Kefauver, Estes, 148–49

Keller, Helen, 20, 186

Kelley, Stanley, 178

Kelsey, Frances Oldham, *chapter 7;* 10, 149, 239–41, 245, 249–51, 278; as bureaucrat, 153, 156–57; career of, 134–138, 140, 148; character as scientist, 136, 144, 146–47, 151, 158; photograph, 137; review of thalidomide, 142–46, 150–51. *See also* Food and Drug Administration; Thalidomide

Kelsey, Fremont, 136

Kennedy, John F., 18, 24, 74, 101, 215, 219
Kennedy, Robert F., 216, 235
Kevadon. *See* Thalidomide
Kimball, Warren F., 271
King, Martin Luther, Jr., 12, 19, 24, 211–12, 214, 217, 225, 247; at Selma, Alabama, 220–22
Korean War, 62, 65, 90–91, 241

Latinos and politics, 125
Lewis, John, *chapter 10;* 11, 239–41, 245, 248–51; career of, 210–13, 233–35; character of, 210–11, 218, 222, 227, 234–35; and development of civil rights movement, 214–19; photograph, 213; at Selma, Alabama, 220–23; and social movements, 227–31. *See also* Civil rights movement; March on Washington; Student Non-Violent Coordinating Committee
Lewis, Meriwether, 20
Lincoln, Abraham, 28, 214, 254–55; in Civil War, 85, 163–64, 167, 169; as hero, 12, 16, 84; as presidential candidate, 165–66, 168, 170–72, 179–80
Lipsky, Michael, 233
Lowenthal, Leo, 16–17
Lowi, Theodore, 106

MacArthur, Douglas, 90
Madison, James, 5–6, 27, 42, 85, 205, 226, 252; at Constitutional convention, 214, 225

Mann, Floyd, 216
March on Washington, 210, 217–19
Marshall, George C., 65, 69, 96–97, 101–3, 106. *See also* Marshall Plan
Marshall, John, 128
Marshall Plan, 86, 88–89, 91, 99; development of, 95–98; political strategies, 101–7, 203, 239, 250
Martyrs archetype, 23
Marx, Groucho, 56, 64
Marx, Karl, 26, 64
Mass media. *See* Journalism
Matthews, Donald, 76–77
McCarthy, Joseph, 90, 203, 240, 251; career of, 58, 62–63, 65, 67, 75; effect on Senate elections, 60, 64, 66, 72; Senate censure of, 66, 69–74; Senate norms and, 76–83. *See also* Anti-Communism, in domestic politics; McCarthyism
McCarthyism, 61, 63–65, 73–75, 81–83
McClellan, George, 170–71, 174
McClure's magazine, 185, 188–89, 196–97, 200, 285
Merrell drug company, 142–148, 152, 156
Moulton, Barbara, 138
Muckrakers, 184, 187–189, 195, 284
Mussolini, Benito, 197

Nader, Ralph, 24
Neustadt, Richard, 100
Nevins, Allen, 189–90, 192
New institutionalism, 248–49, 293

Nicolay, John, 179
Nixon, Richard M., 18, 70, 75, 204, 251; impeachment of, 31, 36–37, 40, 45, 47–55, 203, 249; role in Watergate scandal, 38–39
Nurturers archetype, 21, 242

O'Boyle, Archbishop Patrick, 218
Oklahoma City attacks, 19, 23
"Ordinary heroes." *See* Heroism, in "ordinary heroes"
Oshinsky, David, 81
Ozick, Cynthia, 242

Parties: as institutions, 159–60, 172–76, 178–81, 249; theories of, 159, 173, 180
Pasteur, Louis, 185
Pendergast, Tom, 86
Pericles, 243
Peripheral neuritis. *See* Thalidomide
Phillips, John S., 189
Plunkitt, George Washington, 180
Plyler, James, 114
Plyler v. Doe, 119–21, 123–25, 127, 132–33, 250
Polletta, Francesca, 232
Powell, Lewis, 119, 121, 180
Presidency: concepts of, 89, 99–100, 106; as institution, 84–85, 90–91, 99, 101–3, 106, 250
Press. *See* Journalism
Progressive movement, 184, 186–188
Proxmire, William, 80
Public opinion polls: on Clinton impeachment, 52; on Marshall Plan, 95, 101–2; on McCarthy, 62, 69, 72; on Nixon impeachment, 39

Ragghianti, Maria, 24
Rayburn, Sam, 103
Raymond, Henry, 169–70
Reagan, Ronald, 12, 18, 20
Redford, Emmette, 153, 157
Rescuers archetype, 22–23, 29
Richardson-Merrell corporation. *See* Merrell drug company
Rockefeller, John D., 190–93, 195, 198–99, 251
Rodino, Peter, *chapter 3;* 10, 31, 90, 135, 239–41, 244, 247, 249–51; career of, 32–34, 49; character of, 35, 40–41, 46, 48–49; conduct of impeachment inquiry, 41, 44–48, 51–53, 56; on Constitution of the U.S., 48, 55, 247; photograph, 33. *See also* Nixon, Richard M., impeachment of; Watergate
Rogers, Henry, 199
Roland, Manon, 185
Roosevelt, Franklin Delano, 12, 20, 84, 87–88, 128, 184
Roosevelt, Theodore, 184, 188–89, 195–96
Rosenberg, Gerald, 130, 132
Rosenberg, Julius and Ethel, 63

Scalia, Antonin, 180
Schumpeter, Joseph, 159
Schwartz, Barry, 15

Selma, Alabama, voting rights campaign, 219–23, 230–31, 233, 235
Senate, norms of, 56, 67–68, 76–80, 82, 249
September 11 terrorist attacks, 1, 3–4, 6–7, 23, 83, 236, 243
Seward, William, 162–63, 169, 176–77
Sexual discrimination, 68, 117
Shklar, Judith, 253
Silkwood, Karen, 25
Simon, Paul, 241
Skowronek, Stephen, 89
Slavery issue in Civil War, 162, 164–65, 169–70, 175–78, 224
Smith, Margaret Chase, 65, 67–68, 76
Social movements: as institution, 223–26, 249; patterns of, 227–31
Standard Oil Company, 184, 189–90, 196, 198, 201, 203; as monopoly, 191–94, 196, 199
Starr, Kenneth, 50, 54
Steffens, Lincoln, 24, 188, 284
Stewart, Potter, 204
Student Non-Violent Coordinating Committee (SNCC), 214, 216–20, 228–29, 233–34, 239; decline of, 222, 232–33, 251

Taft, Robert, 32, 64, 90, 95
Taft-Hartley Act, 32, 90
Tarbell, Ida M., *chapter 9;* 11, 183, 239–40, 249–51; career of, 184–85, 196–97; and feminism, 186, 197, 241; as journalist, 187–90, 198, 200–203, 209; photograph, 185; in Standard Oil investigation, 189–91, 193–95, 198–99
Taylor, Zachary, 161, 176
Television, and civil rights movement, 203, 221, 230, 249
Thalidomide, 156–57, 203, 239–40, 249–50; medical effects of, 134–35, 140–41; political effects of, 148–51; testing of, 142–47, 150, 152
Thoreau, Henry David, 245–46
Tilly, Charles, 228
Tocqueville, Alexis de, 183–84, 201, 203, 209, 226, 254
Trailblazers archetype, 20–21
Truman, Harry S., *chapter 5;* 10, 18, 65, 82, 84, 239–41, 244, 249–51; career of, 86–87; character of, 87–88, 107; domestic policies of, 89–90; foreign policies of, 90, 94, 98, 203; photograph, 87; and presidency as institution, 88–89, 91, 99, 101–6, 249; as presidential candidate, 89, 103, 269. *See also* Korean War, Marshall Plan
Truman, Margaret, 144
Tuchman, Barbara, 9
Tydings, Millard, 66

Undocumented aliens, 118, 122. See also *Plyer v. Doe*
Union party of 1864. *See* Election of 1864
U.S. Congress. *See* House Judiciary Committee; House of Representatives; Senate

Vandenberg, Arthur, 104–6

Washington, George, 15–16, 18, 28, 84
Watergate, 18, 24, 35–39, 50–51, 53, 199, 203
Watkins, Arthur, *chapter 4;* 10, 83, 239–41, 249–51; career of, 59–60, 75; and censure of McCarthy, 71–78; character of, 58–60, 69; photograph, 61. *See also* McCarthy, Joseph; Senate, norms of
Weber, Max, 26, 152–53, 245, 247
Wecter, Dixon, 16
Weed, Thurlow, *chapter 8;* 11, 159, 180, 182, 187, 239–41, 249–51; career of, 160–61; character of, 162, 173, 176–78, 181; in Civil War, 162–163, 165, 170, 178; in election of 1864, 164–68, 171–72, 174–75, 203; and patronage, 167, 169, 179, 249; photograph, 161
Whig party, 160–61, 174–76
Whitman, Walt, 13
Wilenz, Sean, 213
Wiley, Alexander, 74
Wills, Gary, 247
Wilson, Woodrow, 99, 184, 196–97
World Trade Center attacks, 1–2, 8, 23, 243
World War II, 16, 23, 48, 69, 86, 91–94, 110, 240

Yarborough, Senator Ralph, 112
Yergin, Daniel, 193

Zola, Emile, 185
Zwicker, General Ralph, 69, 72, 74

About the Author

Gerald M. Pomper is Board of Governors Professor Emeritus of Political Science at the Eagleton Institute of Politics of Rutgers University. A specialist in U.S. elections and politics, he is the author or editor of twenty books, including *Passions and Interests, Elections in America,* and *Voters' Choice*. In 2001, he published *The Election of 2000,* the seventh and last volume in a twenty-four-year series on U.S. national elections. His analysis of the 2004 election is a chapter in Michael Nelson, ed., *The Elections of 2004* (Congressional Quarterly Press).

After his formal retirement in 2001, Pomper was interim director of the Walt Whitman Center at Rutgers, where he conducted a year-long symposium on "The Future of American Democratic Politics" among distinguished scholars from major universities in the United States. Papers from that symposium were published in 2003 by Rutgers University Press. He has participated in an Eagleton project to improve campaign discourse, and, with Richard Lau, in research on U.S. Senate elections, resulting in *Negative Campaigning* (Rowman and Littlefield, 2004).

On Ordinary Heroes and American Democracy was first published in 2004 by Yale University Press, and nominated for a Pulitzer Prize. One early reviewer commented: "Pomper's inspiring book provokes us to think about how American democracy and American political institutions foster the heroism of ordinary people."

Educated at Columbia and Princeton, Pomper also has been a Fulbright or visiting professor at Tel-Aviv University, Oxford, and Australian National University, and held the first Tip O'Neill Chair in Public Life at Northeastern University. He has been honored for career achievement by the American Political Science Association and has served as an expert witness on campaign finance, reapportionment, and political party regulation. At Rutgers for forty years, he was chair of the University and Livingston College political science departments for nine years, and chaired a select committee that in 1996 proposed major changes, since adopted, in undergraduate education on the New Brunswick campus.

His civic activities include eight years on his local board of education, including two years as president, membership on his local zoning board, current membership on the borough's Redevelopment Authority, summer institutes for high school teachers, evaluations for New Jersey's former department of higher education, and service as chair of the Free Speech Committee of the American Civil Liberties Union. He continues to teach regularly at Rutgers and other institutions and writes scholarly articles and regular columns for the *Newark Star-Ledger*.

Paradigm Publishers is committed to preserving ancient forests and natural resources. We elected to print *On Ordinary Heroes and American Democracy* on 30% post consumer recycled paper, processed chlorine free. As a result, for this printing, we have saved:

5 Trees (40' tall and 6-8" diameter)
2,097 Gallons of Wastewater
843 Kilowatt Hours of Electricity
231 Pounds of Solid Waste
454 Pounds of Greenhouse Gases

Paradigm Publishers made this paper choice because our printer, Thomson-Shore, Inc., is a member of Green Press Initiative, a nonprofit program dedicated to supporting authors, publishers, and suppliers in their efforts to reduce their use of fiber obtained from endangered forests.

For more information, visit www.greenpressinitiative.org